A REASON FOR FAITH

**NAVIGATING LDS DOCTRINE
& CHURCH HISTORY**

LAURA HARRIS HALES, EDITOR

Published by the Religious Studies Center, Brigham Young University, Provo, Utah, in cooperation with Deseret Book Company, Salt Lake City.

Visit us at rsc.byu.edu.

© 2016 by Brigham Young University. All rights reserved.

Printed in the United States of America by Sheridan Books, Inc.
DESERET BOOK is a registered trademark of Deseret Book Company.

Visit us at DeseretBook.com.

Any uses of this material beyond those allowed by the exemptions in US copyright law, such as section 107, "Fair Use," and section 108, "Library Copying," require the written permission of the publisher, Religious Studies Center, 185 HGB, Brigham Young University, Provo, Utah 84602. The views expressed herein are the responsibility of the authors and do not necessarily represent the position of Brigham Young University or the Religious Studies Center.

Cover design by Hales Creative, LLC, and interior layout by Alex Masterson.

ISBN: 978-1-9443-9401-1

US Retail: $24.99

Library of Congress Cataloging-in-Publication Data

Names: Hales, Laura H. (Laura Harris), editor.
Title: A reason for faith : navigating LDS doctrine and Church history / Laura Harris Hales, editor.
Description: Provo, Utah : Religious Studies Center, Brigham Young University ; Salt Lake City, Utah : Deseret Book, [2016] | ?2016
Identifiers: LCCN 2015049529 | ISBN 9781944394011
Subjects: LCSH: Church of Jesus Christ of Latter-day Saints--Apologetic works. | Church of Jesus Christ of Latter-day Saints--Doctrines. | Mormon Church--Doctrines. | Church of Jesus Christ of Latter-day Saints--History. | Mormon Church--History.
Classification: LCC BX8635.5 .R43 2016 | DDC 289.3--dc23 LC record available at http://lccn.loc.gov/2015049529

To Greg Dursteler

—for giving me a reason to ask questions.

My dear young friends, we are a question-asking people because we know that inquiry leads to truth. That is the way the Church got its start—from a young man who had questions. In fact, I'm not sure how one can discover truth without asking questions.

—President Dieter F. Uchtdorf, CES fireside for young adults at Brigham Young University on November 1, 2009.

Contents

Acknowledgments	ix
Prologue *Laura Harris Hales*	xi

---

1. Joseph Smith and Money Digging *Richard Lyman Bushman*	1
2. Remembering the First Vision *Steven C. Harper*	7
3. Translating the Book of Mormon *Brant A. Gardner*	21
4. Anachronisms in the Book of Mormon *Brant A. Gardner*	33
5. The Testimonies of the Book of Mormon Witnesses *Alexander L. Baugh*	45
6. The Restoration of the Priesthood *Ronald O. Barney*	59
7. Isaiah in the Book of Mormon *Kent P. Jackson*	69
8. The Explanation-Defying Book of Abraham *Kerry Muhlestein*	79
9. Joseph Smith and the Kinderhook Plates *Don Bradley and Mark Ashurst-McGee*	93

10. The Practice of Polygamy 117
    Brian C. Hales and Laura Harris Hales

11. Joseph Smith's Practice of Plural Marriage 129
    Brian C. Hales

12. Freemasonry and the Latter-day Saint
    Temple Endowment Ceremony 143
    Steven C. Harper

13. Race, the Priesthood, and Temples 159
    W. Paul Reeve

14. Finding Lehi in America through DNA Analysis 179
    Ugo A. Perego

15. Latter-day Saint Women in the Twenty-First Century 193
    Neylan McBaine

16. Homosexuality and the Gospel 203
    Ty Mansfield

17. Science and Religion: Friends or Foes? 221
    David H. Bailey

Index 241

Acknowledgments

I want to thank the authors who graciously gave of their time and scholarship to make this anthology happen. Many of the scholars didn't know me before I contacted them, but they quickly conveyed a willingness to participate in this project. Their abundant graciousness, humility, and patience with a relative novice was more than I could have expected. The families who supported the authors and allowed them to work long hours to meet publishing deadlines are also worthy of mention. Your sacrifice did not go unnoticed. Helpful comments from Jed L. Woodworth, Matthew J. Grow, Reid L. Neilson, and Richard E. Turley Jr. as well as BYU Religious Studies Center readers and editors on early drafts were invaluable. Thomas Wayment, my editor, was always available to answer my questions and offer advice. Sincere thanks to the Religious Studies Center staff for their help, including Devan Jensen, Brent Nordgren, Joany Pinegar, Madison Swapp, Alison Brimley, Shanna D'Avila, Hadley Griggs, Allyson Jones, Alex Masterson, Leah Welker, and Lauren Whitby. My husband, who saw this project as more than I ever envisioned, gave me the bravery to embark on such an ambitious endeavor. He is my greatest source of encouragement and support. But most of all, I am grateful for this gospel and the love of a Savior who mends broken things and opens doors once closed.

Prologue

I have a friend who loves boating. He learned to water-ski before he learned his alphabet, and the years he spent gliding across the lake were obvious to anyone who witnessed his expert form, whether on choppy or smooth water. One of his first purchases as an adult was a ski boat. Through the years he would save his money and gradually upgrade until he ended up with the one he owned when we started dating. It was well used when he purchased it, but he had meticulously repaired the engine, reupholstered the seats, and spent hours cleaning, buffing, and waxing the exterior, preparing it for many fun-filled Saturday afternoons.

As a city girl who had had little experience with boats and water-skiing, I was anxious to share his hobby. When summer came, we made our inaugural trip to Lake Powell with his children and extended family, who also owned well-loved boats. I was the amateur in the crowd, prepared for my initial voyage with sunglasses, a wide-brimmed hat, and plenty of sunscreen. My friend backed the boat down the ramp, tied the boat to the dock, and asked me to watch the children while he parked the truck—it would be just a few minutes. So the kids and I jumped into the boat, put on our life jackets, and waited.

After about ten minutes, his young daughter started tugging at my arm. When I turned to her, she pointed and uttered a single word: "Look." About three inches of water had filled the stern of the boat, and that amount was rapidly increasing. I panicked. First, I hastily lifted the children out of the boat; then I looked for something to scoop the water out. After failing to find a bucket, in desperation I grabbed a Frisbee and started frantically removing the water at a much slower rate than it was being replenished. As I watched the stern sink and the bow rise, I thought about abandoning ship, even though the boat remained securely anchored to the dock, but I held my ground after glancing up with relief at the sight of my friend.

To my surprise, instead of assisting me in removing the water he dove into the lake and started fiddling with the bottom of the boat. His head popped up a minute later, and he was smiling and laughing. Catching my befuddled look, he explained that he had forgotten to put the plug in the bilge drain. Some water always gets into the bilge from people getting in and out of the boat, so he would remove the plug after each boating trip, allowing the water to drain out and preventing any damage to the motor during storage. With the plug securely fastened and the water removed, the engine finally started, and we resumed our boating adventure. My friend was lucky: hours of maintenance before the boat was submerged could not make up for a forgotten plug once the boat was in the water. His engine could easily have been damaged beyond repair that day.

An anchor is an object that holds something firmly in place. The rope securely tied to the dock anchor kept the boat from drifting from the dock, but it did nothing to protect the motor from water unexpectedly engulfing its casing. Our testimonies can be compared to the boat. They need a firm anchor, the safest of which is a belief in the Atonement of Christ, but that alone sometimes is not enough to keep them secure in unexpected circumstances. The boat itself needs to be watertight.

Like many members of the Church, I have children who were blindsided by things that contradicted prior perceptions about gospel topics. Having come across *new* information outside of nurturing channels such as family study and Church-sponsored instruction, they felt betrayed. As their mother, I was ill equipped to answer their questions. Like my experience on the boat, the situation emerged unexpectedly, and I did not know how to address the problem. Instead of stopping the gush of water, I ineffectively tried to remove it with a poor tool. My children needed information that I didn't have.

It became apparent that I needed to not only teach my children about Christ but also some of the other issues that they would come into contact with as they left my home and set sail on their own. I decided to integrate additional material into our existing family gospel dialogue, providing a supportive environment to explore sensitive topics. Educating my teenagers on lesser-known aspects of Church history and doctrine became a priority rather than an afterthought.

Finding resources to teach the more sensitive concepts proved difficult. I didn't have the time to process lengthy scholarly articles on each topic and condense the material into a cohesive presentation for my family. What I needed was a basic primer on each of the topics, and for that I would need help. So I approached respected LDS scholars and asked if they would summarize their research not only for me and my children but also for my neighbors and fellow members of the Church. I'm not sure if it was a bold or a desperate move, but it worked. They readily agreed that the type of book I was suggesting could be a great resource.

We are taught that the mission of the Church is to proclaim the gospel to the world, to perfect the Saints so they can receive the ordinances of the gospel, to redeem the dead, and to care for the poor and needy. With limited teaching time, the Church generally designs curriculum centered on saving principles. In addition to these basic study materials, the Church has released essays on many gospel topics and continually adds to the catalog of resources on Church websites.

In teaching the gospel to a worldwide membership, the Church cannot possibly hope to touch on every topic of interest in the level of detail that would satisfy every member. It falls upon individuals to study out for themselves and teach their families about subjects that are outside this scope. Thus prepared, members may be less inclined to let something they don't understand unravel their convictions.

This anthology enlarges the traditional LDS dialogue; it addresses criticisms of the Church and its doctrines from a faithful perspective. Within these pages, readers will explore subjects commonly referred to in Church curriculum, but with expanded material and additional context. Instead of only recounting Joseph Smith's struggle to determine which church was true and his decision to pray in a grove of trees, it describes the various accounts of the First Vision, when they were written, and why differences in wording reflect the Prophet's growing understanding of the experience. And rather than discussing the meaning of the teachings found in the Book of Abraham, readers will be presented with prevailing theories on its origin.

The tone of these chapters is straightforward. No controversies have been deliberately avoided or glossed over, but neither is there space for them to be fully explored. This is not meant as a defensive book but rather as an introduction to many topics worthy of study from an informed perspective. Most of these issues have been researched extensively by LDS scholars for decades, and readers can be comforted in knowing there are resources to turn to for direction. Discovery can be an enjoyable, enlightening, and faith-promoting experience.

This book seeks to provide the most recent research by top LDS scholars and to create a safe environment for exploration within a faithful framework. Even so, these discussions may generate thoughts and questions that might be surprising or even bothersome as existing beliefs are stretched. In fact, readers may grieve at the loss of perceptions held dear. Yet they can be consoled by the realization that their expanded understanding is based upon accurate teachings. The information in these essays can begin an exciting process of discovery for readers. As scholars provide perspective and context to both the Church's history and present policies, they also share valuable tools for lifelong learning and study. When gospel questions arise, the antidote for uncertainty is more knowledge and more contemplation, which takes time—"even by study and also by faith."[1] It is the continual search for truth, both secular and spiritual, that will give us a reason for faith.

About the Editor

Laura Harris Hales is a freelance copy editor, author, and mother of five avid truth seekers. She received a bachelor's degree in international relations from Brigham Young University and a master's degree in professional writing from New England College. She has also worked as both a paralegal and as an adjunct professor of English. With her husband, Brian C. Hales, she coauthored *Joseph Smith's Polygamy: Toward a Better Understanding* and maintains the website JosephSmithsPolygamy.org.

Note

1. D&C 88:118.

1

Joseph Smith and Money Digging

Richard Lyman Bushman

In the mid-1970s, as I began work on the manuscript that was to become Joseph Smith and the Beginnings of Mormonism, *I anticipated that Joseph Smith's money digging would be the toughest issue to tackle. The stories of the Smith family performing magic rituals in the woods while hunting for buried gold or boxes of watches were the single element of the Prophet's history that most differentiated Mormon accounts of his early life from the accounts of non-Mormons. Fawn Brodie, whose* No Man Knows My History *was the standard scholarly biography at the time, devoted much of a chapter to the Smiths' nocturnal expeditions and their attempts to elude the guardian spirits who protected the treasure.*[1] *At a trial in 1826, a witness told of Joseph directing money diggers to pursue a trunk that kept sinking deeper into the earth whenever their spades struck it.*[2] *None of this appeared in Mormon accounts. Joseph admitted to employment by Josiah Stowell (also Stoal) in 1825 to dig for Spanish coins, but he claimed he had little faith in the venture and eventually persuaded Stowell to give it up. Later he implied that the stories about his treasure seeking were unfounded exaggerations of this one incident.*

The treasure-seeking stories of Joseph Smith's youth have done more than cast a shadow on his character. They supply a secular explanation for his extraordinary religious claims. As early as 1831, the Palmyra newspaper editor Abner Cole speculated that the guardian spirits of Joseph's treasure seeking had transmuted in his imagination into the angel Moroni and that the buried treasure was transformed into the gold plates.[3] Joseph changed his treasure quest into a religious mission for a single purpose; both pursuits were forms of his effort to gain financial security for his impoverished family. When treasure seeking failed him, he tried religion.[4]

Joseph's Treasure Seeking

The response of Mormon historians in the 1970s was to deny almost everything. Beyond the Josiah Stowell incident, they argued, all the money-digging stories were fabrications of Joseph Smith's enemies. They claimed that the sources for the stories were corrupted and therefore not to be trusted. Most of the accounts came from a set of affidavits collected by Philastus Hurlbut, an embittered former Mormon who was hired by Smith's sectarian enemies in the Kirtland area to dig up dirt on the Smiths back in New York. Hurlbut set out in the summer of 1833 to see what he could find that might support a theory about the origins of the Book of Mormon, and while he was in Palmrya, he interviewed neighbors of the Smiths. They came up with one story after another of the family's low character and of their involvement in treasure seeking. Unwilling to work for a living, they said the Smiths went in for money digging.[5]

Church historians thought Hurlbut's motives were too suspect to trust his findings. What reason was there to believe him? He could easily have written the affidavits himself or distorted what people said to make the Smiths look bad. He found exactly what his employers wanted him to find. Could that be taken as sound historical evidence? Once the money-digging stories got into circulation through a book entitled *Mormonism Unvailed*, published in 1834, then similar stories proliferated—so argued the Church historians.

Another fabrication, in their view, involved a purported trial in 1826 in which Joseph Smith was accused of "glass looking"—looking into a peep stone to find lost objects and buried treasure. The details of this trial came to light in 1873 based on court minutes that were supposedly brought to Utah by a niece of the justice at the trial, later a missionary with Daniel S. Tuttle, the Episcopal bishop of Utah.[6] All this seemed too contrived to be taken seriously, and Church historians dismissed it all as the work of overzealous critics who sought to discredit the Prophet.[7] Mormon historians thus not only told a different story from secular historians, they also differed in their judgment of what constituted legitimate sources of the historical facts.

This was the state of affairs when I began work on Joseph Smith's early life in the mid-1970s. By that time I was a professor of early American history at Boston University and an active member of the historical guild, where I had many professional friends and colleagues. When I wrote, I had to answer to professional standards as well as satisfy Church members. What was I to do about money digging, with all of its implications for Joseph Smith's story? The first thing I decided was that I could not dismiss all of Hurlbut's affidavits with the wave of a hand. Academic historians had taken them seriously, and so should I. The sources may indeed have been corrupted by Hurlbut's animosity against Joseph Smith, but many documents are written for contentious purposes and still figure into the reconstruction of events; every source is biased in one way or another. The art of the historian is to extract historical truth from the maze of human memories, however distorted. Hurlbut's affidavits had to be read and evaluated like any other source.

Developments in scholarship about this time had a deep effect on my work. A zealous evangelical scholar named Wesley P. Walters produced an article that changed the minds of many Mormon historians about Smith's 1826 glass-looking trial. Digging through courthouse documents one summer, Walters found a receipt demonstrating that the 1826 trial had actually been held. The receipt did not verify every detail of the hearings, but it did associate the recovered minutes with the 1826 sources from the archives, tying it pretty securely to that time and place.[8] The other piece of scholarship to impact my analysis was Keith Thomas's massive *Religion and the Decline of Magic*, published in 1971.[9] Thomas collected a huge amount of material to demonstrate the pervasive influence of magic at virtually all levels of society in the seventeenth century. This influence is also sometimes referred to as folk magic or popular religion. Members of Parliament and village seers alike used peep stones to discover objects and see visions. The miracles of magic intermingled with the miracles of Christianity in a single system of belief. Some clergy condemned and ridiculed these practices as false and potentially evil supernatural power, but others absorbed magical elements into their religious beliefs. A highly orthodox Puritan was known to press a pin into his doorjamb to ward off evil spirits. This fascination with magic began to fade among the educated classes in the late seventeenth century, but it did not disappear among ordinary people. According to Yale historian Jon Butler, folk magic was prevalent among Yankees well into the nineteenth century.[10]

This research enabled me to see the magic in Joseph Smith's life in a new light. As I read the Hurlbut affidavits, I picked up clues that not only the Smiths but also many of their neighbors were looking for treasure in Palmyra in the 1820s.[11] They were ashamed enough to try to cover it up, and the enlightened elements in the village scoffed at these folk traditions, but there was substantial evidence that in the farmhouses people were wondering how to invoke magical forces to lead them to treasure. The Smiths may have been subscribing to folk religion, but in this they were part of a culture found virtually everywhere among Yankees of their generation.[12] It may not have been the most uplifting activity, and some scoffed, but it was something like reading astrological charts today—a little goofy but harmless.

The only harm came when someone tried to deceive others to get gain. That was why Joseph Smith was put on trial. Was he trying to hoodwink the Stowells? When Josiah Stowell said he believed in Joseph, the sting was removed.¹³ Scholars still argue whether Joseph Smith was convicted of glass looking in 1826, but the point is moot.¹⁴ Church scholars now acknowledge that he had a seer stone and did look for lost objects as a young man. The difference is that since Thomas and Butler published their research, folk magic is no longer toxic. It was too commonplace to be scandalous. Magic and Christianity did not seem at odds with one another. The combination was altogether too common in the nineteenth century for it to invalidate Joseph Smith's more conventional religious claims. In Mormonism and for many Christians, folk traditions and religion blend. To call the two incongruous seems more like a matter of religious taste than a necessary conclusion.

At present, a question remains about how involved Joseph Smith was in folk magic. Was he enthusiastically pursuing treasure seeking as a business in the 1820s, or was he a somewhat reluctant participant, egged on by his father?¹⁵ Was his worldview fundamentally shaped by folk traditions? I think there is substantial evidence of his reluctance, and, in my opinion, the evidence for extensive involvement is tenuous. But this is a matter of degree. No one denies that magic was there, especially in the mid-1820s. Smith never repudiated folk traditions; he continued to use the seer stone until late in life and used it in the translation process.¹⁶ It certainly had an influence on his outlook, but it was peripheral—not central. Biblical Christianity was the overwhelming influence in the Book of Mormon and the Doctrine and Covenants. Folk magic was in the mix but was not the basic ingredient.¹⁷

I occasionally hear of people who are still offended by a prophet who dealt in treasure seeking, but very few. The most important issue when I began to write in the 1970s has faded in importance. Even highly orthodox Latter-day Saints are not offended by treasure seeking and seer stones, and to my knowledge, the seasoned critics rarely foreground the question. I wonder if this is not the fate of many charges against Joseph Smith. Will they lose their virulence as the years go by?

We need to keep in mind that the wheels of history grind slowly, but they grind exceeding fine. What seems central at one moment in time will lose force as the years go by. Magic moved to the sidelines over the years; will other issues be next? We should be careful about putting too much weight on the criticisms of the moment when it is uncertain how enduring they will be.

About the Author

Richard Lyman Bushman is an early American historian who has taught at Brigham Young University, Boston University, and Columbia University, where he was Gouverneur Morris Professor of History. Among his books are *From Puritan to Yankee: Character and the Social Order in Connecticut, 1690–1765*, which received the Bancroft Prize for 1967, and *The Refinement of America: Persons, Houses, Cities*. He is best known to Latter-day Saints for *Joseph Smith: Rough Stone Rolling*. In *Believing History: Latter-day Saint Essays*, Dr. Bushman shares reflections on his faith and his own struggle to find a basis for belief in a skeptical world. He has served in the Church as bishop, stake president, and patriarch. He and his wife, Claudia, are the parents of six children and have twenty grandchildren.

NOTES

1. Fawn M. Brodie, *No Man Knows My History: The Life of Joseph Smith the Mormon Prophet* (New York: Alfred A. Knopf, 1946), 16–33.

2. Brodie, *No Man Knows My History*, 407.

3. Dan Vogel, ed., *Early Mormon Documents*, 5 vols. (Salt Lake City: Signature Books, 1996–2003), 2:243–45. For Cole, see Andrew H. Hedges, "The Refractory Abner Cole," in *Reason, Revelation, and Faith: Essays in Honor of Truman G. Madsen* (Provo, UT: FARMS, 2002).

4. For a modern statement of this hypothesis, see Wesley P. Walters, "From Occult to Cult with Joseph Smith, Jr.," *Journal of Pastoral Practice* 1 (1977): 121–31.

5. Dale W. Adams, "Doctor Philastus Hurlbut: Originator of Derogatory Statements about Joseph Smith, Jr.," *John Whitmer Historical Association Journal* 20 (2000): 76–93.

6. Daniel S. Tuttle, "Mormons," in *A Religious Encyclopaedia: Or, Dictionary of Biblical, Historical, Doctrinal, and Practical Theology*, ed. Philip Schaff, 3 vols. (New York: Funk and Wagnals, 1882–83), 2:1575–81.

7. Richard Lloyd Anderson, "Joseph Smith's New York Reputation Reappraised," *BYU Studies* 10, no. 3 (Spring 1970): 283–314.

8. Wesley P. Walters, "Joseph Smith's Bainbridge, N.Y. Court Trials," *Westminster Theological Journal* 36, no. 2 (Winter 1974): 123–55.

9. Keith Thomas, *Religion and the Decline of Magic* (New York: Scribner's, 1971).

10. Jon Butler, "Magic, Astrology, and the Early American Religious Heritage, 1600–1700," *American Historical Review* 84, no. 2 (April 1979): 317–46.

11. Richard Lyman Bushman, *Joseph Smith: Rough Stone Rolling* (New York: Alfred A. Knopf, 2005), 48–50.

12. Alan Taylor, "Rediscovering the Context of Joseph Smith's Treasure Seeking," *Dialogue* 19, no. 4 (Winter 1986): 18–28.

13. Josiah Stowell, as dictated to J Stowell Jr., letter to Mr J S Fullmer, in *Early Mormon Documents*, ed. Dan Vosel (Salt Lake City: Signature Books, 1996–2003), 4:80–81.

14. Gordon S. Madsen, "Joseph Smith's 1826 Trial: The Legal Setting," *BYU Studies* 30, no. 2 (Spring 1990): 91–108.

15. Dan Vogel, "The Locations of Joseph Smith's Early Treasure Quests," *Dialogue* 27, no. 3 (Fall 1994): 197–231.

16. Susan Staker, "Secret Things, Hidden Things: The Seer Story in the Imaginative Economy of Joseph Smith," in *American Apocrypha: Essays on the Book of Mormon*, ed. Dan Vogel and Brent Lee Metcalfe (Salt Lake City: Signature Books, 2002), 235–74.

17. Mark Ashurst-McGee, "Moroni: Angel or Treasure Guardian?," *Mormon Historical Studies* 2, no. 2 (Fall 2001): 39–75.

2

Remembering the First Vision

Steven C. Harper

*J*OSEPH SMITH REMEMBERED THAT HIS FIRST SPOKEN PRAYER, UTTERED in the woods near his parents' home in western New York State when he was about fourteen years old, evoked a vision of heavenly beings who forgave him and taught him that Christianity had gone astray. The historical record includes four accounts of this vision that were dictated or written by Joseph and several secondary accounts written by contemporaries who heard him relate the event. These records have been extensively studied, with critics highlighting their inconsistencies and believers explaining the differences in terms of the Prophet's varied audiences and intentions. But there seems to be more going on in the accounts than an effort to put into words Joseph's first encounter with deity. Closely examining both the historical record and the science of memory formation lends insight into the reasons for the discrepancies and Joseph's growing understanding of his experience.

Joseph Smith's recorded memories of the First Vision reveal more than his encounter with deity or his theophany. They reflect his growing awareness of its meaning as he transformed sensory impressions into subjective meanings. He consciously experienced the vision as it occurred, but he also reexperienced and interpreted it over time. Reading the historical record closely in light of what is now known about forces that influence memory reveals insights into Joseph's subjective experience of the original event as well as the ongoing effects of it as manifest in subsequent memories. This approach suggests that Joseph's first telling of his experience to a Methodist minister shaped the ways in which he told the vision shortly after the event and also over time.

8 Steven C. Harper

Primary Accounts of the First Vision

Between 1832 and 1842, Joseph wrote or caused scribes to write four known documents describing his vision. Some of these were copied and\or revised into other documents. Besides Joseph and his scribes, five other known writers recorded versions of the event during Joseph's lifetime.[1]

1832 Account

The first written account of Joseph's First Vision is found in Joseph's earliest autobiography: a rough, six-page statement filled with grand themes expressed by a man of limited education.[2] This document is not dated, but it was apparently written in response to a revelation that commanded the Saints to keep history that documented their faith, life, and deeds.[3] This account describes a highly personalized experience. Using the language of religious revivals, Joseph described his consciousness of his sins and of his frustrating inability to find forgiveness in a church that he thought should match the New Testament model that emphasizes the Atonement of Christ and the personal redemption it offered Joseph.[4]

1835 Accounts

In the fall of 1835, Joseph Smith told an eccentric visitor about his first vision. Joseph's scribe captured some of the dialogue in a journal entry, including Joseph's description of the events that led to the translation and publication of the Book of Mormon. In this account, Joseph described the vision as the first in a series of events that led to the translation of the Book of Mormon. He emphasized the opposition he felt in the grove and that he attempted to pray but initially couldn't. It describes one divine personage appearing in a pillar of fire, followed shortly by another, and mentions that Joseph saw many angels as well. Joseph added, perhaps as an afterthought, that he was about fourteen at the time of his vision. A week later, on November 14, Joseph told another inquirer about the vision. Unfortunately, his scribe recorded only that Joseph told an account of his "first visitation of Angels," but not a description of the vision itself.[5]

1838–39 Account

Joseph published two accounts of the vision during his lifetime. The first and best known of these two accounts is found in Joseph's manuscript history, begun April 27, 1838, and continued in 1839. Joseph enlisted the help of George Robinson and Sidney Rigdon to help write this account, and later James Mulholland and Howard Coray also helped him record and refine it. A version of this account can be found in Joseph Smith—History 1:1–20 in the Pearl of Great Price.[6]

1842 ACCOUNT
The second account Joseph Smith published during his lifetime was written in response to *Chicago Democrat* editor John Wentworth's request for a "sketch of the rise, progress, persecution and faith of the Latter-day Saints" as source material for a friend, George Barstow, who was writing a history of New Hampshire. There is no known evidence that Barstow used Joseph's account, but Joseph had it printed in the March 1, 1842, issue of the *Times and Seasons* newspaper, making it the first account published in the United States. In July 1843, a historian named Israel Daniel Rupp wrote to Joseph asking for a chapter on the history of Mormonism for inclusion in his book *An Original History of the Religious Denominations at Present Existing in the United States.* Joseph met Rupp's refreshing invitation to tell his own story by supplying essentially the same account as the one in the letter to Wentworth, which Rupp subsequently included in his book.[7] This account is concise but revealing. It says that the two divine beings Joseph saw looked exactly alike, and they told him that the existing churches believed in incorrect doctrines.[8]

Though each account describes Joseph's encounter with Deity, there are differences in the retellings. These differences could initially seem concerning to readers, but historians would be skeptical if they were identical, considering the passage of time and the different purposes for which they were written. But beyond those observances, there seems to be more at work here.

THE SCIENCE OF MAKING MEMORIES

Neuroscience has shown that "memory is not fixed at the time of learning but takes time to develop its permanent form." So some leading psychologists consider it "a mistake to assume that interpretation of recalled knowledge happens only at the preloading, perceptual stage—to assume that once knowledge 'enters memory' (through the front door), it is happily stored away, to be 'retrieved' intact at later times of 'recollection.'"[9] Joseph Smith's earliest memories of his theophany were based on factual, sensory, and emotional elements. Those facts accumulated more and more meaning in light of subsequent experience. For example, just as World War I was the Great War until after World War II, the vision became interpreted as Joseph's first vision only after subsequent ones, as shown by his 1835 journal entry describing the vision as the first event in the process that resulted in the Book of Mormon. The part of memory that becomes possible with the passage of time and new experiences is sometimes called interpretive memory. The passage of reflective time in light of subsequent experience helps explain why Joseph recorded his most significant interpretive memory of his vision in his 1838–39 narration.

Historians often assume that an experience recorded at or shortly after the event will be accurate and that later memories are less accurate in proportion to the historical distance between them and the event. But these assumptions are usually too simplistic. While it is true that time is an enemy to memory, it is also true that memory strengthens over time, counterintuitive as that may seem.[10]

Both distortion and accuracy in remembered events have been proven by experiments and observations and are to be expected. One way distortion occurs is when semantic memories blend with autobiographical ones. Joseph probably unconsciously conflated semantic memories with autobiographical ones, meaning that he mixed cultural knowledge—information he simply knew from frequent exposure in his youth in an evangelical and visionary culture—with what he knew from his own experience. To put it simply, memories are both accurate and inaccurate. They are both distorted reconstructions of the past and true perceptions of the past as seen from the present. It is not safe to take for granted that Joseph's memory was perfectly accurate at the time of his experience and that it grew increasingly inaccurate in proportion to the passage of time. Suspending this assumption while analyzing the historical record in light of how memories form or consolidate can lead to new analysis and yield valuable insight.

Consolidating Memories

As Joseph processed new experiences, in part by recuperating and reforming stored information, fragments of old memories combined with current experiences to produce memories that could be vivid or vague. The degree of clarity depended mainly on how deeply he consciously processed any given detail of the experience at the time and how frequently and consciously he later recalled it. Each time he did this, he reoriented himself relative to his original experience.

This process is called memory consolidation. Some leading theorists compare it to pouring water from a leaky bucket into a much less leaky bucket. The memory that consolidates, like the water that makes it into the less leaky bucket, is remarkably stable over time.[11] No one knows exactly why, but repeatedly rehearsed personal narratives resist erosion over time, and some actually strengthen. It may be that frequent rehearsal of an event over time forges long-term links between related perceptions and previous knowledge, which could explain why some autobiographical memories actually become more precise and complete over time.[12]

Joseph Smith remembered or forgot elements of his experience based on what he knew at the time and how often and how deeply he rehearsed them. In 1835 he vividly described the parts of the experience that he processed deeply and then added as an afterthought his approximate age as best his vague memory of it could recover. Likewise, in 1839 he remembered that an unusual religious excitement occurred in his region only "sometime in the second year after our removal to Manchester," but he felt sure that it began with the Methodists. He remembered that the vision occurred in the "morning of a beautiful clear day early in the spring of eighteen hundred and twenty," but apparently he could not recall precisely which day. He noted that after the vision he was "between fourteen and fifteen years of age," which his scribe later qualified further by inserting "or thereabouts."[13]

The ideas that Joseph Smith consolidated best, and thus remembered most vividly, were the ones he associated most meaningfully with the resolution to his terrible problem of finding the right way to be saved. These were points at which emotion and cognition combined, as in his 1832 autobiography's description, "my mind became exceedingly distressed," or his 1839 history's marriage of "serious reflection and great uneasiness" and "laboring under the extreme difficulties caused" by competing preachers and doctrines. The 1835 account in Joseph's journal says that he was "wrought up in [his] mind" and "perplexed in mind" and describes his increasing consciousness of the possibility of a divine answer and his "fixed determination to obtain" one.[14] His 1832 account says that his mind became "seriously imprest with regard to the all important concerns for the welfare of [his] immortal soul," that denominational strife made him grieve and "marvel exceedingly," that as he "pondered" he became "exceedingly distressed," "felt to mourn," and finally "cried unto the Lord for mercy" and experienced a theophany that filled his soul with love for days and led him to "rejoice with great Joy."[15] Intense emotion and repeated reflection combined to create the Prophet's most vivid and enduring memories. By remembering these parts of his experience and allowing for the natural process of forgetting others, he became aware of what was meaningful about it.

Rejection of the 1832 Account

Since Joseph Smith's ability to form memories depended largely on what he already knew, his culture conditioned the ways he remembered his original experience, and subsequent experiences expanded his ability to rehearse meaningful reflections of what he had experienced.[16] His 1832 autobiography is "a traditional form of spiritual autobiography familiar to him and those around him."[17] Joseph remembered his vision in terms of acceptable spiritual discourse, mimicking a generic style and tone that emphasized personal sinfulness and redemption by Christ.

There are reasons to question whether Joseph's 1832 autobiography was satisfying to him and to surmise that he felt conflicted about its contents. He probably intended this document to serve as source material for the Church's historians, Oliver Cowdery and John Whitmer, who began their histories where this one ends.[18] Neither of them, however, seemed to know it existed. Joseph Smith never published it and probably did not circulate it. He appears to have regarded it as an unusable draft. Perhaps he thought it too marred by his being "deprived of the bennifit of an education," but it seems most likely that the perspective that came with the passage of time and subsequent experiences made this memory sound increasingly unsatisfying to his ears.

It is the memory of a teen aspiring to convince an evangelical clergyman of his legitimate conversion experience. Yet, even as he dictated this memory in 1832, Joseph's revelations had tended away from evangelical Protestantism toward nearly universal salvation in degrees of heavenly glory and temple ordinances mediated by priesthoods, moving the gospel Joseph was in the process of restoring well beyond what is reflected in the autobiography he wrote that year.[19] Then why would he record a memory that was not fully satisfying to him?

One answer is that Joseph Smith's 1832 autobiography can be read as a conflicted consolidation of his memory. Some literary scholars theorized why. The puzzle, they noted, is not that Joseph's story squared with acceptable ways of writing evangelical autobiography, but that the story was so poorly received.[20] They hypothesize, presumably based on Joseph's later report that his first oral telling of his experience was flatly rejected by a Methodist preacher, that he originally told a story so unorthodox that he was rejected, so he recast the story safely in 1832 "as if it were primarily a vision granted to assure him of his personal redemption and the need for men to repent, and not to assure him of the apostasy of all churches and the need for a Restoration," as his 1839 account would emphasize.[21]

In the 1838–39 process of reforming his story for allies and against enemies, Joseph described his first telling of the vision, in which he unexpectedly received reproach rather than validation:

> Some few days after I had this vision I happened to be in company with one of the Methodist Preachers who was very active in the before mentioned religious excitement and conversing with him on the subject of religion I took occasion to give him an account of the vision which I had had. I was greatly surprised at his behaviour, he treated my communication not only lightly but with great contempt, saying it was all of the Devil, that there was no such thing as visions or revelations in these days, that all such things had ceased with the [p. 3] apostles and that there never would be any more of them. I soon found however that my telling the story had excited a great deal of prejudice against me among professors of religion and was the cause of great persecution which continued to increase.[22]

It was a jarring experience for Joseph to have his crisis resolved one day and then have that resolution rejected by an authority days later. That experience upset his memory of it and, as one can see by the emphasis he placed on it in 1839, he continued to form and reform the ways he remembered it over time.

In telling his experience to the preacher, Joseph sought assurance that the resolution to his crisis was real. Instead, the preacher's flat rejection likely created cognitive dissonance in the young man, resulting in an internal conflict Joseph sought to reduce by remembering differently. In such circumstances, people regularly recast their past so that it conforms to their culture. But making a memory public, Joseph learned, also makes the memory contestable.[23] This interpretation of Joseph's memories suggests that the minister's rejection retarded, to a degree and for a time, Joseph's willingness and perhaps even his ability to tell his story.

Joseph's original, unrecorded telling led to rejection by the minister and the world he represented. When Joseph worked up the will to tell it again in his 1832 autobiography, he recast the story as an evangelical script, conforming to his culture and seeking validation. There is no evidence that he did so conspiratorially or even consciously, but rather as part of the ongoing process of consolidation. Joseph was apparently reticent to tell his story at all after it was initially rejected, which explains both why the 1832 story says what it does and why Joseph seems not to have favored or shared it. The past Joseph Smith recorded in 1832 may have been more pleasing to the minister than Smith's original telling, but it did not resonate with Joseph's present. Whatever the reasons, the 1832 consolidation of Joseph Smith's memory was not the memory that would develop. But by the time he collaborated on his earliest autobiography, Joseph Smith's memory had become fixed on one point: his ministry began with the vision in the woods.[24]

Associative Retrieval and the 1835 Account

Joseph's autobiographical act of composing the 1832 narrative required a different type of memory retrieval than the November 1835 journal entry that captures his unplanned telling of the story. He composed the 1832 document in an act of intentional, explicit remembering, which required a systematic search of memory known as strategic retrieval. But when telling the story of his vision to a visitor in the autumn of 1835, Joseph relied on associative retrieval, resulting in a memory formed automatically by an unsolicited cue rather than by a systematic search. The 1832 and 1835 records are thus two unique memories of the same event, each formed when different kinds of cues activated different pieces of the past stored in different parts of Joseph's brain. Because the memories are of the same event, they are quite similar, but because their retrieval cues enabled Joseph to recover varied pieces of the past, they are also quite distinct. The 1835 record of spontaneous memory shows that, given the right cues and context, Joseph could produce a memory of the event that did not depend on or respond to the Methodist minister, either attempting to please him, as in 1832, or lashing back at him, as in 1838–39.

Retrieval and the 1835 and 1838–39 Accounts

Like the 1832 and unlike the 1835 story, the 1838–39 consolidation of Joseph Smith's memory was strategic, cued by the intentional, explicit act of composing history. Indeed, the awful year, much of it spent in jail in Liberty, Missouri, bookended by Joseph's 1838 and 1839 history drafts, provided the present that cued this memory of the past. Defensive from the outset, the extant 1839 draft of this document declared that it was written to "disabuse the publick mind" by counteracting "the many reports which have been put in circulation by evil disposed and designing persons" who were militating against Joseph's character and his church, and it continues at times as a protest against the Protestant clergy.

Joseph's crisis in this account is caused by clergymen who created a contest for souls and turned the Bible into a battleground. Richard L. Bushman observed how Joseph Smith's earliest recorded memory of the vision and this one share the story "of a lonely adolescent, occupied with spiritual agonies, trying to account for his fabulous experiences." He notes how the later document "has a more confident public tone" and asserts that "Joseph, still the perplexed youth, is also the prophet about to usher in the last dispensation."[25] The perspective is enlarged and institutional. The revelation is not simply another manifestation of Christ to a born-again soul, but an indictment of Christian churches and creeds. It is not simply the marvelous experiences of Joseph Smith but the story of "the rise and progress of the Church of Jesus Christ of Latter-day Saints."[26]

The 1839 narrative begins with the facts of Joseph's life in the same straightforward style that characterizes earlier accounts, but then it begins to muse about the events, identifying and assigning meaning in the process. In other words, Joseph Smith's factual memory of the preacher's rejection catalyzed an important interpretive memory that is manifest in his shift from narrated facts to a description of how it felt to remember the rejection in the context of Missouri.

Recalling fears about the status of his teenage soul and concerns that the Calvinist Presbyterians could be right about God saving or damning according to his will, and anxious to find evidence of a Methodist alternative, Joseph Smith remembered that he favored Methodism and wanted to join but felt paralyzed by the denominational competition. The epiphany that resulted from his reading of the invitation in James 1:5 to ask God for wisdom emerges often in Joseph's accounts but is especially pronounced in 1839, since it enabled him to transcend the clergy and sent him to the woods where he learned for himself.

In the 1839 document, Joseph Smith remembered not only sights, sounds, and the most intense thoughts and emotions of his experience, but he also made sense of his present position as the embattled president of a new church by noting how Protestant clergymen fought to redeem his soul, only to have their pretense exposed as sectarian strife.[27] He remembered in this context that when his vulnerable teenage self had asked the Son of God which of the churches he should join, the divine reply was "none of them, for they were all wrong, and the Personage who addressed me said that all their Creeds were an abomination in his sight, that those professors were all corrupt, that 'they draw near to me to with their lips but their hearts are far from me, They teach for doctrines the commandments of men, having a form of Godliness but they deny the power thereof.'"[28] He then describes his effort to share this heavenly message with a Methodist preacher, who "treated my communication not only lightly, but with great contempt, saying it was all of the devil."

Remembering his youthful rejection in the wake of war with Missouri made it seem to Joseph Smith that he had always been severely persecuted. In a present rife with concerted opposition often led by Protestant ministers, his mind was cued to search the past for the origins of persecution. He found it in the form of Protestants from whom he had unsuccessfully sought solace in his youth. He recounted his "serious reflection" on what he describes as a recurring thought that he had attracted so much unsolicited attention, though "an obscure boy." He described his "great sorrow" vividly.

An observer of the outward scene may not have interpreted these events nearly as intensely as Joseph did subjectively. Aside from the stinging rejection of the Methodist minister to whom he reported his vision, his memory of persecution in childhood was vague and notably impersonal. There is very little factual memory in this part of his 1839 narrative aside from the preacher's rebuff. In Joseph's interpretive memory, the preacher spoke for everyone else. It *seemed* like everyone had always been allied against him. In the middle of assigning this meaning to his memory, Joseph declared, as if responding to the preacher, that "it was nevertheless a fact, that I had seen a vision." He then returned to his interpretive mode, telling candidly how, subsequent to the vision itself, he found meaning in it by comparing his experience to St. Paul's before Herod Agrippa.[29] This portion of the autobiographical narrative especially shows how Joseph Smith's long-term consolidation of memory enabled him to find enlarged or at least varied meanings in his experience by 1839, meanings that made sense of his present as well as his past.

Joseph Smith continued to consciously interpret the experience over the years. In 1842 he added amendments to the 1839 document, including this interpretive memory: "It seems as though the adversary was aware at a very early period of my life that I was destined to prove a disturber & annoyer of his kingdom, or else why should the powers of Darkness combine against me, why the oppression & persecution that arose against me, almost in my infancy?"[30] The idea that Joseph Smith was persecuted as a toddler is not a factual memory for which one might find objectively verifiable evidence. It is an interpretive memory, for which the only archive is the mind of the rememberer. To the thirty-six-year-old Joseph Smith, embroiled at the time of the 1842 composition in efforts to extradite him from Illinois to Missouri, oppression and persecution *seemed* to have begun in infancy and to have lasted for a lifetime.

The Rearrangement of Memory

Joseph Smith's accounts of his experience are rich descriptions of his world, saturated with cognitive words and deeply emotional clauses. They are narrative descriptions of his experience, journeys inside of his *mind*, a word he used frequently when recounting the vision. As a result, Smith's accounts of his theophany are representative of a dynamic memory. His stories exhibit cognitive sophistication as well as a rich mixture of emotions. They reveal forgetting, as well as enduring, vivid memories of elements of the experience that deeply impressed him—anxious uncertainty prior to the vision, the epiphany that resulted from reading and reflecting on James 1:5, the feeling of love and redemption that followed being forgiven by God, and the reality of the vision itself. The accounts reveal that he consciously interpreted the experience and discovered meanings in it later that were not available to him when it occurred. The accounts are not, by Joseph's acknowledgment, a flawless recreation of the event, nor are they likely "a complete fabrication of life events."[31] Rather, they are products of Joseph Smith's subjective, constructive process of remembering.

There is no way to show, nor is there necessarily reason to assume, that Joseph's memories decrease in accuracy or increase in distortion in proportion to their historical distance from the vision itself. It seems best to regard each of them as a new memory, each a creation formed by an original connection of present cues and stored pieces of past experience. Each reveals some of the ways Joseph Smith integrated his past and ever-changing present in a continuous effort to make sense of both. Given what the study of memory has revealed, it seems unwise to read Joseph Smith's accounts as static pictures of a verifiable past or as complete fabrications of an experience that did not happen. Rather, they are evidence of what Richard Bushman called "the rearrangement of memory," or of what might be quite accurately called, simply, *remembering*.[32]

Additional Resources

The Church of Jesus Christ of Latter-day Saints. "First Vision Accounts." https://www.lds.org/topics/first-vision-accounts.

Davidson, Karen Lynn, David J. Whittaker, Richard L. Jensen, and Mark Ashurst-McGee, eds., *Histories, Volume 1: Joseph Smith Histories 1832–1844*. Volume 1 of the Histories Series of *The Joseph Smith Papers*, edited by Dean C. Jessee, Ronald K. Esplin, and Richard Lyman Bushman. Salt Lake City: Church Historian's Press, 2012.

Dodge, Samuel Alonzo, and Steven C. Harper, eds. *Exploring the First Vision*. Provo, UT: Religious Studies Center, 2012.

Harper, Steven C. "Suspicion or Trust: Reading the Accounts of Joseph Smith's First Vision." In *No Weapon Shall Prosper: New Light on Sensitive Issues*, edited by Robert L. Millet, 63–75. Provo, UT: Religious Studies Center; Salt Lake City: Deseret Book, 2011.

Harper, Steven C. *Joseph Smith's First Vision: A Seeker's Guide to the Historical Accounts*. Salt Lake City: Deseret Book, 2012.

Jessee, Dean C. *Personal Writings of Joseph Smith*. Salt Lake City: Deseret Book, 2002.

Jessee, Dean C., Mark Ashurst-McGee, and Richard L. Jensen, eds. *Journals, Volume 1: 1832–1839*. Volume 1 of the Journals Series of *The Joseph Smith Papers*, edited by Dean C. Jessee, Ronald K. Esplin, and Richard Lyman Bushman. Salt Lake City: Church Historian's Press, 2012.

Joseph Smith Papers. "Primary Accounts of Joseph Smith's First Vision of Deity." http://josephsmithpapers.org/site/accounts-of-the-first-vision.

Welch, John W. *Opening the Heavens: Accounts of Divine Manifestations, 1820–1844*. Provo, UT: Religious Studies Center; Salt Lake City: Deseret Book, 2011.

About the Author

Steven C. Harper is a historian in the Church History Department of The Church of Jesus Christ of Latter-day Saints. He earned a PhD in early American history from Lehigh University and was on the history and religion faculties at BYU–Hawaii for two years before joining the faculty of the Department of Church History and Doctrine at BYU for ten years. He has worked on The Joseph Smith Papers and as a document editor for BYU Studies and is the author of a book titled *Promised Land* (on colonial Pennsylvania) and of *Making Sense of the Doctrine and Covenants and Joseph*

Smith's First Vision. Among other projects, he is currently at work analyzing how Joseph Smith's First Vision has been remembered over time. He is married to Jennifer Sebring, and they have five children.

Notes

1. "Primary Accounts of Joseph Smith's First Vision of Deity," *Joseph Smith Papers*, http://josephsmithpapers.org/site/accounts-of-the-first-vision.

2. "History, circa 1832," *The Joseph Smith Papers*, http://josephsmithpapers.org/paperSummary/history-circa-summer-1832?p=1.

3. Doctrine and Covenants 85.

4. "History, circa 1832," *Joseph Smith Papers*.

5. "Journal, 1835–1836," *Joseph Smith Papers*, http://josephsmithpapers.org/paperSummary/journal-1835-1836?p=24.

6. "History, circa June 1839–circa 1841 [Draft 2]," *Joseph Smith Papers*, http://josephsmithpapers.org/paperSummary/history-circa-june-1839-circa-1841-draft-2?p=2.

7. Joseph Smith, "Latter Day Saints," in *An Original History of the Religious Denominations at Present Existing in the United States*, comp. I. Daniel Rupp (Philadelphia: J. Y. Humphreys, 1844), 404–10.

8. "'Church History,' 1 March 1842," *Joseph Smith Papers*, http://josephsmithpapers.org/paperSummary/church-history-1-march-1842?p=1.

9. Larry R. Squire, "Biological Foundations of Accuracy and Inaccuracy in Memory," in *Memory Distortion: How Minds, Brains, and Societies Reconstruct the Past*, ed. Daniel L. Schacter (Cambridge, MA: Harvard University Press, 1995), 211.

10. Daniel L. Schacter, *Searching for Memory: The Brain, the Mind, and the Past* (New York: Basic Books, 1996), 81–82.

11. Thomas J. Anastasio et al., *Individual and Collective Memory Consolidation: Analogous Processes on Different Levels* (Cambridge, MA: MIT Press, 2012), 30.

12. A. R. Damasio, "Time-locked Multiregional Retroactivation: A Systems-Level Proposal for the Neural Substrates of Recall and Recognition," *Cognition* 33 (1989): 25–62; Daniel L. Schacter, *Searching for Memory: The Brain, the Mind, and the Past* (New York: Basic Books, 1996), 88.

13. Dean C. Jessee, Mark Ashurst-McGee, and Richard L. Jensen, eds., *The Joseph Smith Papers: Journals, Volume 1: 1832–1839* (Salt Lake City: Church Historian's Press, 2008), 1:87–88 (hereafter *JSP*, J1).

14. *JSP*, J1:87–88.

15. Karen Lynn Davidson, David J. Whittaker, Mark Ashurst-McGee, and Richard L. Jensen, eds., *The Joseph Smith Papers: Histories, Volume 1: 1832–1844* (Salt Lake City: Church Historian's Press, 2012), 10–16 (hereafter *JSP*, H1).

16. Maurice Halbwachs and others have argued that all individual memory is in some sense collective, since it is socially mediated. See Anastasio et al., *Individual and Collective Memory Consolidation: Analogous Processes on Different Levels* (Cambridge, MA: MIT Press, 2012), 45–48.

17. Neal A. Lambert and Richard H. Cracroft, "Literary Form and Historical Understanding: Joseph Smith's First Vision," in *Journal of Mormon History* 7 (1980): 33.

18. *JSP*, H1:5, n. 11.

19. See D&C 76 and 84, "Doctrine and Covenants, 1844," *The Joseph Smith Papers*, http://josephsmithpapers.org/paperSummary/doctrine-and-covenants-1844.

20. Anastasio et al., *Individual and Collective Memory Consolidation*, 9.

21. Lambert and Cracroft, "Literary Form," 36–37.

22. JSP, H1:214–17.

23. Susan Engel, *Context Is Everything: The Nature of Memory* (New York: W. H. Freeman and Company, 1999), 9, 18–33, 48.

24. JSP, H1:10–16; Richard Lyman Bushman, *Joseph Smith: Rough Stone Rolling* (New York: Alfred A. Knopf, 2005), 69.

25. Bushman, *Rough Stone Rolling*, 389; see also Lambert and Cracroft, "Literary Form," 69.

26. JSP, H1:39.

27. JSP, H1:204–20.

28. JSP, H1:214.

29. JSP, H1:216–19.

30. JSP, H1:214–15.

31. C. R. Barclay, "Schematization of Autobiographical Memory," in *Autobiographical Memory*, ed. D. C. Rubin (Cambridge: Cambridge University Press, 1986), 97.

32. Bushman, *Rough Stone Rolling*, 69.

3

Translating the Book of Mormon

Brant A. Gardner

*J*OSEPH SMITH WAS CALLED OF GOD TO TRANSLATE THE GOLDEN PLATES, resulting in the Book of Mormon. The very idea that a New York farm boy with limited education might translate an ancient document is so unimaginable that it could only have occurred through, as Joseph himself declared, "the gift and power of God." Because Joseph told us nothing more about the way the translation occurred, modern readers and thinkers wonder and speculate. When we look back on the process of translation with our modern perspective, we often see more questions than answers. What was the method of translation, and why did it happen in the way it did?

In an unknown year after AD 400, the prophet Moroni buried the golden plates. What Mormon had begun, Moroni finished and entrusted to the Lord's care in the Hill Cumorah. Although the record was safe, there was still a crucial problem. When Moroni later died, the last person who could read what was written on those plates was gone. Moroni himself had declared, "none other people knoweth our language."[1] What was true when Moroni died was even more true when Joseph received those plates over fourteen hundred years later. No one had known the plate language for almost one and a half millennia. Translating the text on the plates would take a miracle.

Actually, it would take two miracles. Not only must an unreadable text be read, but a young man who, according to his wife, could barely compose a coherent letter would be asked to do it.[2] The Lord declared that he would "call upon the weak things of the world, those who are unlearned and despised, to thresh the nations by the power of my Spirit."[3] Before the translation miracle could occur, the Lord had to miraculously transform a young, unlearned, and despised weak thing of the world into a prophet of God.

The Faith to Translate and a Rock Called a Seer Stone

Joseph couldn't learn to read the text on the plates—there was no Nephite dictionary available. What God used to effect the transformation was yet another weak thing. God used the folk beliefs of the rural population that had been part of the way the world was understood for millennia. Even in Joseph's day the learned had come to despise them, but in the community where Joseph lived, those folk beliefs were alive and well.

For the Smiths and other rural families, the supernatural world was very real. At times and for specific purposes, Christian religion accessed and entreated the spiritual world. At other times and for other purposes, it could be accessed and manipulated more directly by people with particular talents. Each method had its place, and each assisted its believers in surviving their difficult circumstances. In churches on Sundays, Christian religion saved the soul. Every other day of the week, traditional Christian practices, which some have labeled magic, healed the sick, found the lost, and grew the crops.

One of the professions of this Christian magic, or Christian folk belief, was that of a seer, whose talent was to see something hidden. The seers in Joseph's day typically used unusually shaped stones they called seer stones, which were just the more recent instrument that a seer would use to see hidden objects, hidden meaning, or hidden futures. By contrast, in the Old Testament, the story of Joseph in Egypt describes a stratagem Joseph used to keep his brother Benjamin close. Joseph had his servants hide money in his brothers' bags, but a cup in Benjamin's. It was not an ordinary cup. Genesis 44:5 reports, "Is not this it in which my lord drinketh, and whereby indeed he divineth?" In the time and place of this story, seers would see their visions by pouring oil and water into a bowl or cup. When Joseph placed that particular cup in Benjamin's pack, it wasn't simply dinnerware. It was a very important religious object.[4]

By the time seers in England began appearing in the records (between the seventeenth and nineteenth centuries), the functions to which they applied their talents had evolved into two general forms: seeing a hidden future, seeing the location of lost things, or seeing the identity of the thief of stolen things.[5] The New England region of the relatively new United States of Joseph Smith's day inherited those English traditions. There were seers in Palmyra, and they used seer stones to find lost or hidden things, just as others had in England. In Joseph Smith's Palmyra, this ancient specialty not only survived but was widely practiced there and in neighboring communities that also perpetuated these ancient skills. Joseph was only one of several seers in that region.⁶ As a local seer, he was consulted to find things that were lost or to see into the future.⁷

Modern science has no good explanation for why such practices existed for so long. Nor does it have a good explanation for what the seers saw when they were successful. The actual effectiveness of seeing in the stone really isn't the important issue for the translation of the Book of Mormon. What is important is that Joseph believed that he could see hidden things that others could not, and there were others who believed that Joseph had that particular talent. It was Joseph's belief that he could see the unseeable that the Lord used as the fulcrum to leverage the village seer into a translator and then into a prophet of God.⁸

The meaning on the plates was certainly hidden and lost. Joseph could not translate as the scholars did. However, with God's help, he would do so using the instrument and methods he had successfully used before. This time he wasn't finding a lost object, but rather a lost meaning. Nevertheless, it wasn't the instrument that would translate, but the power of God. Joseph never claimed any other method of translating other than that it happened by "the gift and power of God."⁹

Joseph's faith in the process led him to use the seer stone to receive revelations in the early years of the Church. However, as Joseph grew into his calling as a prophet, he realized that *he* was the real instrument of revelation, not the stone. He stopped using it. Nevertheless, descriptions of Joseph receiving revelation show enough parallels to the descriptions of how he translated that we can be sure that it was always Joseph receiving revelation—the seer stone was simply the crutch the Lord used to prop up Joseph's nascent faith in his calling.¹⁰

Joseph's experience with seeing in a stone, however that had happened, was the trigger the Lord used to establish Joseph's faith that with the Lord's aid he could see the translation that was hidden in the unreadable characters on the plates. It was a method the Lord had used before when Mosiah was asked to translate the plates of Ether:

> Therefore he took the records which were engraven on the plates of brass, and also the plates of Nephi, and all the things which he had kept and preserved according to the commandments of God, after having translated and caused to be written the records which were on the plates of gold which had been found by the people of Limhi, which were delivered to him by the hand of Limhi;
>
> And this he did because of the great anxiety of his people; for they were desirous beyond measure to know concerning those people who had been destroyed.
>
> And now he translated them by the means of those two stones which were fastened into the two rims of a bow.

Now these things were prepared from the beginning, and were handed down from generation to generation, for the purpose of interpreting languages;

And they have been kept and preserved by the hand of the Lord, that he should discover to every creature who should possess the land the iniquities and abominations of his people;

And whosoever has these things is called seer, after the manner of old times.[11]

The Plates and the Translation Process

The descriptions of how Joseph used a seer stone prior to the Book of Mormon have him placing the stone in the crown of his hat and then drawing the hat to his face so that his vision was obscured. All methods of seeing with objects required some method whereby normal vision was masked. Perhaps this allowed the seer, and those who saw the seer work, to know that what was seen came from a different source than normal vision.

Placing the stone in a hat would have made it difficult to look at the plates and work out a translation. It is probable that for much of the translation process the plates were not visible. What, then, was the purpose of the plates if they were not to be used? Actually, they were used—just not in the way we may think they should have been. From the beginning, the physical presence of the plates declared the reality of the angelic revelation. Moroni had not been a dream. The plates Moroni gave to Joseph were real, and that tangible reality allowed Joseph's faith to deepen and develop. The physical plates became important again when witnesses were selected to view and handle them. They had text on them, and those who saw them could see the engravings. The plates provided the physical touchstone for the faith of the early believers in Joseph's mission. Seeing the plates and the characters on them demonstrated to those witnesses that there was information on the plates. What they could not do was read that text. What Joseph could not do, by himself, was read that text. No one could read that text. Only through the gift and power of God would the translation be known. No matter how many times Joseph looked at those characters, the translation would come through God and not the engravings. Knowing that there was something to translate required the plates. Translating through the gift and power of God did not.

A Seer Stone and the Urim and Thummim

The gift and power of God came to Joseph as the translator, not to a stone—whether the stone came from the Nephites or (as one of Joseph's stones did) from digging a well for a neighbor. During much of the early history of the Church, the two stones that accompanied the plates were called the interpreters. About the time of the publication of the Book of Commandments in 1833, W. W. Phelps began using the biblical term *Urim and Thummim* to describe both the interpreters and Joseph's seer stone. It was a reference of convenience that lent a more sophisticated feeling to the translation. Christians knew of the Urim and Thummim from the Bible, where they were connected with the high priest and receiving revelation.[12] Particularly for newer converts, that was a more familiar reference than the seer stones, and it soon became the way to refer to the process by which the translation occurred, even though the term was technically inaccurate.

The term *Urim and Thummim* was inserted later into sections of the Doctrine and Covenants. For example, in our current version, D&C 10:1 reads, "Now, behold, I say unto you, that because you delivered up those writings which you had power given unto you to translate by the means of the Urim and Thummim, into the hands of a wicked man, you have lost them." The same text from the 1833 Book of Commandments reads, "Now, behold I say unto you, that because you delivered up so many writings, which you had power to translate, into the hands of a wicked man, you have lost them."[13] The addition of the information about the Urim and Thummim is in the 1835 edition of the Doctrine and Covenants, and that meaning was firmly entrenched by that time.[14]

Although the use of *Urim and Thummim* is now pervasive among Church members, it is not the correct designation for the instruments used in the translation of the Book of Mormon. For a short period of time, the Nephite interpreters were used. For most of the translation, Joseph used one of the seer stones that he had used prior to his calling to receive the golden plates.

Why Don't the Artists Get It Right?

When Mosiah translated, he used "two stones which were fastened into the two rims of a bow."[15] That description matches the two stones that were given to Joseph along with the plates. His brother William remembered:

> [They were] set in two rims of a bow. . . . A silver bow ran over one stone and under the other, around over that one and under the first in the shape of a horizontal figure 8 much like a pair of spectacles. That they were much too large for Joseph and he could only see through one at a time using sometimes one and sometimes the other. By putting his head in a hat or some dark object it was not necessary to close one eye while looking though the stone with the other. In that way sometimes when his eyes grew tires [tired] he relieved them of the strain.[16]

When LDS artists depict the translation of the Book of Mormon, it doesn't look like William Smith's description of Joseph placing the interpreters, or the seer stone, in a hat and holding it to his face to block out the light. Most typical is a picture that has Joseph looking at the plates as he dictated—with some showing him moving his finger across the letters. How did the artists get it so wrong?

There is little mystery behind their art. They simply followed a very long tradition of imagining or reinterpreting the translation process. As early as 1836, Truman Coe, who was a Presbyterian minister living among the Saints in Kirtland, Ohio,[17] related the story of the translation as he understood it: "The manner of translation was as wonderful as the discovery. By putting his finger on one of the characters and imploring divine aid, then looking through the Urim and Thummim, he would see the import written in plain English on a screen placed before him. After delivering this to his emanuensi [scribe], he would again proceed in the same manner and obtain the meaning of the next character, and so on till he came to the part of the plates which were sealed up."[18]

Coe did not witness the translation, so he must have heard this story from the Saints in Kirtland, who constituted a fairly large colony by 1836. Although Coe certainly did not accept the story at face value, he seems to have reported it without sarcasm or distortion. Assuming that it represents the understanding of the Kirtland Saints—or at least of Coe's informant—it provides a picture of the translation that has endured from at least 1836 to modern times. Latter-day Saint artists who depict Joseph's finger on the plates are simply following a story about the translation that the Saints themselves were telling as early as 1836.

Modern historians have access to various documents that provide the information about the mechanism that produced the translation. The majority of Saints in Kirtland didn't have those documents. They had word of mouth, and that word of mouth transformed the less-than-familiar into the more common. By 1836 the world of the community seers was fading, and many of the converts had come from cities or other locations unfamiliar with that tradition. When they told the story of the translation, it was in terms that they could better understand, and moving a finger across the plates seemed obvious to them. That oral tradition became the standard explanation, not to intentionally disguise what had actually happened, but because it was simply the natural human process of the communal creation of their own history.[19] This natural human process repeats hearsay along with eyewitness accounts, and often *adapts* the stories to make them more understandable to the current community.[20] With the passage of time, those stories were codified into an official history. The process that led to the artists' depictions is simply the result of a different way of developing a historical understanding, one which developed differently from the way modern historians look back on earlier times.[21]

We live in the times of the modern historian, and we are now much more concerned with what we perceive to be an accurate picture of the past. Those historical interests are manifest in the recent description of the translation of the Book of Mormon found on the Church's official website:

> Joseph Smith and his scribes wrote of two instruments used in translating the Book of Mormon. According to witnesses of the translation, when Joseph looked into the instruments, the words of scripture appeared in English. One instrument, called in the Book of Mormon the "interpreters," is better known to Latter-day Saints today as the "Urim and Thummim." Joseph found the interpreters buried in the hill with the plates. Those who saw the interpreters described them as a clear pair of stones bound together with a metal rim. The Book of Mormon referred to this instrument, together with its breastplate, as a device "kept and preserved by the hand of the Lord" and "handed down from generation to generation, for the purpose of interpreting languages."
>
> The other instrument, which Joseph Smith discovered in the ground years before he retrieved the gold plates, was a small oval stone, or "seer stone." As a young man during the 1820s, Joseph Smith, like others in his day, used a seer stone to look for lost objects and buried treasure. As Joseph grew to understand his prophetic calling, he learned that he could use this stone for the higher purpose of translating scripture.[22]

Why Have There Been Changes in the Text?

Perhaps the most commonly misunderstood statement Joseph Smith ever made is that the Book of Mormon is "the most correct book." He said this, but it is misunderstood as meaning that Joseph thought the Book of Mormon was without error. When we find that there have been changes from the originally dictated text,[23] those who believe it should be without error point out this apparent contradiction.

It helps to know what Joseph actually meant by the phrase "most correct book." The more complete quotation states, "I told the brethren that the Book of Mormon was the most correct of any book on earth, and the keystone of our religion, and a man would get nearer to God by abiding by its precepts, than by any other book."[24] For Joseph, the correctness was in the precepts it taught, not in the absolute infallibility of the words on the page. We know that Joseph didn't consider the actual words to be perfect, because he himself participated in making editorial changes after the first edition.

Royal Skousen, a professor of linguistics and English language at Brigham Young University, has done the most extensive work examining all versions of the Book of Mormon from manuscripts through printed copies. He notes that because the original manuscript had no punctuation, all punctuation is technically a change from the original. Counting those, he indicates that "there are about 105,000 places of variation" from the earliest manuscript portion extant through all editions.[25] The proper question is not whether or not there have been changes, but what type of changes there have been. Changes in words are more interesting than changes in punctuation. Changes in words that might also change interpretation are the most interesting, and there are very few of those.[26]

But why should the text be changed at all? Wasn't it perfectly translated? Doesn't the "gift and power of God" assure a perfect translation? The answer to all of these questions depends entirely upon the precise method by which Joseph was able to translate using the gift and power of God. Unfortunately, Joseph never gave any more details than that. The process he used is open to speculation, but it is only speculation. One might speculate that because God inspired the translation that it should be without error. However, that is an assumption of what God would have done. The evidence for what God did do suggests that he worked through his human instrument—and Joseph, his human instrument, might have decided there was a better way to express the meaning of the plates in English. Perhaps Joseph even made a mistake that was later corrected. Even the inspired writers of the original text made human errors, enough that Moroni cautioned in the title page, "And now, if there are faults they are the mistakes of men."

Although we don't know how God was able to inspire Joseph to translate, we can piece together some information about the nature of the process by looking at the result of it. The most important lesson from looking at what Joseph produced is that he was willing to change words in the text after they had been dictated. In all important cases, the changes were made under Joseph's supervision. Both as the original translator and as a prophet, he was in a position to understand whether or not the words of the text accurately portrayed the meaning intended for the text.

Brigham Young interpreted the situation this way: "Should the Lord Almighty send an angel to re-write the Bible, it would in many places be very different from what it now is. And I will even venture to say that if the Book of Mormon were now to be re-written, in many instances it would materially differ from the present translation."[27] Brigham believed that the translation of the Book of Mormon was a miracle, but not that it was an infallible translation that could never be changed. It is the meaning that is most important in the Book of Mormon, not the words. That is the reason so many Saints have come to love the book in their native languages. The native meaning was translated into English, and that meaning continues to be translated into other languages. We believe that it can be translated because we believe that the meaning is much more important than the originally dictated words, which may not have an exact translation in another language.

Joseph Smith, Translator

The original title page of the Book of Mormon differed in one important concept from the one that we have today. Where today it lists Joseph Smith as the translator, the first title page had Joseph Smith as the author and proprietor. That was certainly not an indication that Joseph was the author, but rather a recognition of the copyright law in New York.[28] The law provided copyright protection only to the "author and proprietor." When the law no longer applied, the title page was changed to provide the more accurate relationship of Joseph to the text.

Joseph Smith Jr. did not author the Book of Mormon. Mormon was its principal author and compiler. Moroni also authored a portion. In addition, there are books that Nephi and Jacob authored. The authorship was ancient and the translation was modern. Although we do not know how Joseph translated, he was the one and only translator of the plates. It fell to Joseph to provide us with a text we could read that embodied the words and meaning that Mormon, Moroni, and others meant for us to have.

A small handful of Joseph's acquaintances had the opportunity to base their faith on the tangible presence of the plates. For the rest of us, it is the tangible presence of the text of the Book of Mormon that becomes our witness of Joseph's divine call. For many, the spirituality of the text speaks to their hearts and minds and declares the divine hand that gave us that text. For some, the presence of ancient literary forms testifies of the antiquity of the text. For others, the examination of the historical context that can be discerned for the Nephites and Lamanites provides sufficient connections to a real-world time and place that they see in the Book of Mormon—an unknown. However we as Saints may approach and understand the Book of Mormon, it stands as the cornerstone of our religion because it has become the tangible witness to the divine calling to Joseph Smith—first as a translator, and then as the first prophet of the restored Church established by Christ.

Additional Resources

The Church of Jesus Christ of Latter-day Saints. "Book of Mormon Translation." https://www.lds.org/topics/book-of-mormon-translation.

Anderson, Richard L. "The Mature Joseph Smith and Treasure Searching." *BYU Studies* 24, no. 4 (Fall 1984): 489–560.

Brown, Matthew B. *Plates of Gold: The Book of Mormon Comes Forth*. American Fork, UT: Covenant Communications, 2003.

Gardner, Brant A. *The Gift and Power: Translating the Book of Mormon*. Salt Lake City: Greg Kofford Books, 2011.

Mackay, Michael Hubbard, and Gerrit J. Dirkmaat. *From Darkness unto Light: Joseph Smith's Translation and Publication of the Book of Mormon*. Provo, UT: Religious Studies Center; Salt Lake City: Deseret Book, 2015.

Skousen, Royal. "Changes in the Book of Mormon." *Interpreter: A Journal of Mormon Scripture* 11 (2014): 161–76.

Skousen, Royal. *The Book of Mormon: The Earliest Text*. New Haven and London: Yale University Press, 2009.

About the Author

Brant A. Gardner earned a master's degree in anthropology and Mesoamerican ethnohistory from the State University of New York at Albany. He is the author of *Second Witness: Analytical and Contextual Commentary on the Book of Mormon* and *The Gift and Power: Translating the Book of Mormon*. He has presented papers at FairMormon conferences and published in the *FARMS Review* of the Neal A. Maxwell Institute at Brigham Young University as well as *Interpreter: A Journal of Mormon Scripture*.

Notes

1. Mormon 9:34.

2. Emma Smith Bidamon, "As Interviewed by Joseph Smith III (1879)," in *Opening the Heavens: Accounts of Divine Manifestations, 1820–1844*, ed. Jack Welch and Eric Carlson (Provo, UT: Brigham Young University Press; Salt Lake City: Deseret Book, 2005), 131: "Joseph Smith could neither write nor dictate a coherent and well-worded letter, let alone dictating a book like the Book of Mormon." Near the end of his life, Martin Harris told Simon Smith, "Joseph Smith's education was so limited that he could not draw up a note of hand." Martin Harris, "Martin Harris Interview with Simon Smith, 5 July 1875," in *Early Mormon Documents*, ed. Dan Vogel, 5 vols. (Salt Lake City: Signature Books, 1996–2003), 2:381.

3. D&C 35:13.

4. E. A. Speiser, "Genesis: Introduction, Translation, and Notes," in *The Anchor Bible* (Garden City, NY: Doubleday & Company, 1981), 333, n. 5.

5. Keith Thomas, *Religion and the Decline of Magic* (New York: Charles Scribner's Sons/Macmillan, 1971), 215, 217.

6. D. Michael Quinn, *Early Mormonism and the Magic World View* (Salt Lake City: Signature Books, 1987), 38: "Until the Book of Mormon thrust young Smith into prominence, Palmyra's most notable seer was Sally Chase, who used a greenish-colored stone. William Stafford

also had a seer stone, and Joshua Stafford had a 'peepstone' which looked like white marble and had a hole through the center."

7. Joseph found a lost wallet for a local judge. See Samuel D. Green, "Joseph Smith, the Mormon," *The Christian Cynosure* 10, no. 12 (December 20, 1877), http://www.sidneyrigdon.com/dbroadhu/IL/mischig.htm#122077.

8. The Church of Jesus Christ of Latter-day Saints, "Book of Mormon Translation," https://www.lds.org/topics/book-of-mormon-translation.

9. Joseph Smith Jr., *Book of Mormon* (1830; repr., Independence, MO: Herald House, 1970), 1.

10. Parley P. Pratt, *Autobiography of Parley P. Pratt*, ed. Parley P. Pratt Jr., 3rd ed. (Salt Lake City: Deseret Book, 1938), 62.

11. Mosiah 28:11–16.

12. Cornelis Van Dam, *The Urim and Thummim: A Means of Revelation in Ancient Israel* (Winona Lake, IN: Eisenbrauns, 1997), 27–31.

13. Joseph Smith Jr., *Book of Commandments, 1833* (repr., Herald Heritage 1972), 22. This is section IX in the Book of Commandments.

14. Joseph Smith Jr., *Doctrine and Covenants, 1835*, 163. This revelation is section 36 in this edition.

15. Mosiah 28:13.

16. J. W. Peterson, "William Smith, interview with J. W. Peterson and W. S. Pender, 1890," in Vogel, *Early Mormon Documents*, 1:508. For the practice of placing the stone in a hat, see "Martin Harris Interview with Joel Tiffany, 1859," in Vogel, *Early Mormon Documents*, 2:303; and Martin Harris, "Martin Harris as interviewed by Edward Stevenson, 1886," in Welch, *Opening the Heavens*, 136–37.

17. Matthew B. Brown, *Plates of Gold: The Book of Mormon Comes Forth* (American Fork, UT: Covenant Communications, 2003), 162.

18. Truman Coe, "Truman Coe to Mr. Editor, *Hudson Ohio Observer*, August 11, 1836," in Vogel, *Early Mormon Documents*, 1:47. See also Coe, "Truman Coe to Mr. Editor," in Welch, *Opening the Heavens*, 124.

19. Jan Vansina, *Oral Tradition as History* (Madison: University of Wisconsin Press, 1985), 8.

20. Vansina, *Oral Tradition as History*, 9.

21. William A. Wilson observes, "I consider folklore to be the unofficial part of our culture. When a Sunday School teacher reads to his class from an approved lesson manual, he is giving them what the Correlation Committee at least would call official religion; but when he illustrates the lesson with an account of the Three Nephites, which he learned from his mother, he is giving them unofficial religion. Folklore, then, is that part of our culture that is passed through time and space by the process of oral transmission (by hearing and repeating) rather than by institutionalized means of learning or by the mass media." William A. Wilson, "The Paradox of Mormon Folklore," *BYU Studies* 17, no. 1 (1976): 40.

22. Church of Jesus Christ, "Book of Mormon Translation."

23. Royal Skousen, *The Book of Mormon: The Earliest Text* (New Haven and London: Yale University Press, 2009). Skousen presents his reconstruction of what that earliest dictated text would have been. It is a study based on careful examination of the remaining text of the Original Manuscript, supplemented with the information in the Printer's Manuscript.

24. *History of the Church*, 4:461.

25. Royal Skousen, "Changes in the Book of Mormon," *Interpreter: A Journal of Mormon Scripture* 11 (2014): 162.

26. Skousen suggests that there are only five. He discusses each, and interested readers are directed to his online article for the specifics. Skousen, "Changes in the Book of Mormon," 169.

27. Brigham Young, in *Journal of Discourses*, 9:311 (July 13, 1862).

28. Royal Skousen, *Analysis of Textual Variants of the Book of Mormon*, 6 parts, The Critical Text of the Book of Mormon Series, 4 vols. (Provo, UT: FARMS, 2004), 1:35.

4

Anachronisms in the Book of Mormon

Brant A. Gardner

An anachronism is something that appears in a text prior to the time that it could have been present. When a clear anachronism is found in any document claiming to be an original historical record, it immediately marks the document as false. The reason is obvious. No writer could know to include something that had not yet been invented or had not yet happened. Many have assumed that anachronisms in the Book of Mormon should similarly prove that it must be false, and it is a modern text only posing as an ancient one. That would be as true for the Book of Mormon as it is for any other text if the Book of Mormon claimed to be an ancient text, but it does not. It claims to be a translation of an ancient text, and that is a very important difference. The fact that we have the Book of Mormon in translation doesn't mean that we can ignore the proposed anachronisms, but it does mean that we can, and should, carefully look to see if there are reasonable explanations for the proposed anachronisms.

Critics of the Book of Mormon have long noted what appear to be anachronisms in the text that Joseph Smith provided from what he claimed was a set of plates that contained the record of ancient inhabitants of the American continents. They have noted references to donkeys, bees, cattle, elephants, sheep, goats, silkworms, swine, wheat, and barley—all creatures and plants not associated with pre-Columbian America. Others identify biblical references that are either incorrect or would not have been available to the Nephites, such as the words of Malachi, New Testament text, Jerusalem as the site of Christ's birth, and references to the Holy Ghost before the birth of Christ. In addition, there are coins, a compass, and cement, which are objects and substances not associated with that era in America. Taken together, the stack of supposed anachronisms can seem quite daunting and disastrous to a historical claim regarding the authenticity of the Book of Mormon.

Evaluating Anachronisms

Though complete explanations for some of these seeming anachronisms are currently elusive, a careful study of one verse in Alma may serve as a model to approach the study of all such supposed anachronisms in the Book of Mormon. Alma 18:9 states, "And they said unto him: Behold, he is feeding thy horses. Now the king had commanded his servants, previous to the time of the watering of their flocks, that they should prepare his horses and chariots, and conduct him forth to the land of Nephi; for there had been a great feast appointed at the land of Nephi, by the father of Lamoni, who was king over all the land." The controversy focuses on the *horses* and *chariots* in this verse. Of course it is commonly believed there were no horses in the New World prior to the arrival of the Spanish, and there had never been chariots pulled by those non-existent horses in ancient America, so how is one to account for references to *horses* and *chariots* in the Book of Mormon?

Emerging Scientific and Archaeologic Evidence

LDS scholars have approached the issue of anachronisms in multiple ways,[1] and the verse with both *horses* and *chariots* provides a convenient way to describe the two major approaches. One explanation has been to search for reasons why the anachronism wasn't actually anachronistic. For example, contrasted to the common knowledge that there were no horses in the Americas prior to the Spanish Conquest, some scholars have argued that there were pre-Columbian horses.

In one way, the common understanding about horses is both right and wrong. There certainly were pre-Columbian horses, and fossil evidence provides a reasonable developmental history of the New World horse. However, these readily acceptable horses appear to have become extinct in the Pleistocene period. Appealing to those horses does not support the Book of Mormon because the Pleistocene ended long before the earliest parts of the Book of Mormon. However, researchers have found some anomalous remains that do appear to show that there were horses prior to the Spanish Conquest—both closer to and after Book of Mormon times.

Wade E. Miller, a retired paleontologist from the Department of Geology at Brigham Young University, notes results from recent studies: "Small scattered populations of horse and ass, especially in remote areas, probably survived in North America until shortly before they were reintroduced by the Spaniards. . . . The Carbon-14 dating involved was first instigated by Dr. Steven E. Jones, former physics professor at Brigham Young University.

I later worked with him on these."² Miller notes that horse fossils found in North America have been dated from 5,890 BC to 1,120 BC.³

This research suggests caution in the firm declaration that there were no horses during Book of Mormon times. Although not yet to the point that the evidence is widely accepted, the presence of the data introduces the possibility that the Book of Mormon horse might not be anachronistic after all. Others have also accepted that there would have been modern horses among the Nephites. LDS scholar Robert R. Bennett accepts that the word *horse* accurately represented that animal: "In short, the Book of Mormon claims only that horses were known to some New World peoples before the time of Christ in certain limited regions of the New World. Thus we need not conclude from the text that horses were universally known in the Americas throughout pre-Columbian history."⁴

Although some of the suggested anachronisms in the Book of Mormon might be resolved by the discovery that they really weren't anachronistic at all, it is not an approach that can explain all of the anachronistic terms. Returning to our verse from Alma, so far there is no archaeological discovery that explains *chariots*. To date, attempts to show that *chariots* are not anachronistic have centered on discussions of the wheel. Because a part of the argument against *chariots* has also been the presumed ignorance of the wheel and axle, LDS scholars have emphasized the evidence that the wheel and axle were known. Several small ancient ceremonial objects with wheels have been recovered.⁵ Although that shows there was pre-Columbian knowledge of the wheel and axle, it really doesn't tell us about *chariots* or any other larger wheeled vehicle, which are still unknown to exist during Book of Mormon times.

Word Choice in Translation

The use of words that have no counterpart in ancient culture is a larger category of potential anachronisms than the mention of plants and animals that are presently unknown to have been on the American continents before its European discovery in the late fifteenth century. These items have a better explanation in the fact that the Book of Mormon is a translation rather than an original document. It is entirely possible to have an anachronism in a translation that was not present in the original.

We need look no further than the King James translation of the Bible (KJV) for examples of anachronisms that occur only in the translation and not in the text being translated. The KJV frequently mentions candles,⁶ even though oil lamps provided light during both the Old and New Testament times. Technically, *candles* are an anachronism. No one suggests that the Old and New Testament must be false because they mention candles, even when candles were not yet used. The availability of the Hebrew and Greek source texts makes it clear that the original documents refer to the oil lamps rather than candles. The anachronism was the result of an assumption the translators made based on their time and culture. Candles were the common means of providing light in early seventeenth century when King James commissioned the English translation of the Bible.

Another anachronism cited by critics is the use of the French word *adieu*. Jacob, Nephi's brother, concludes his final remarks to his people with "I bid farewell, hoping that many of my brethren may read my words. Brethren, *adieu*."[7] Critics have jumped on this phrase as proof positive that the Book of Mormon is not authentic because the Nephites would be unaware of words in the French language, which is a relatively modern language and was nonexistent at the time of Jacob's death. This, however, like the use of *candles* in the KJV, is most likely the result of the translator using words common to his time to express concepts in the text.

This type of anachronism is not singular to books of translated scripture. William Whiston, translator of the autobiography of Flavius Josephus, which was written in the last decade of the first century AD, provides this translation of Josephus's opening lines: "Thus have I set down the genealogy of my family as I have found it described in the public records, and so bid *adieu* to those who calumniate me."[8] Though the French language was well known at the time Whiston was translating Josephus's memoir in the eighteenth century, it was not a language in Josephus's day when he was writing his authoritative history of the Jews and Romans. While scholars would balk at the idea that Josephus used the word *adieu* in his autobiography, they have not cried foul at Whiston's use of the word in the translation or indicated that Whiston changed, embellished, or made up the text. He was simply rendering the text into a new language for a new audience through the process of translation.

SHIFTING MEANINGS OF WORDS

The case of the use of *chariots* in the Book of Mormon presents another issue in translation in addition to the one mentioned above. All languages evolve over time as vocabulary is added and the meanings associated with words shift. Modern readers see the word *chariot* and may mentally conjure images of Egyptian or Roman chariots, which were two-wheeled conveyances. Nevertheless, the word *chariot* has also been applied to four-wheeled conveyances—specifically, the very wheeled figurines from Mesoamerica that some have used as support for pre-Columbian *chariots*.

William Henry Holmes (1846–1933), an anthropologist and archaeologist, recorded, "[Désiré] Charnay [1828–1915] obtained from an ancient cemetery at Tenenpanco, Mexico, a number of toy chariots of terra cotta, presumably buried with the body of a child, some of which retained their wheels."[9] Holmes had no problem using the same word that Charnay had used in his original text.[10] Holmes and Charnay wrote that there were chariots in Mesoamerica. They did not mean Old World war chariots. The use of *chariots* in the Book of Mormon translation need not either. Sometimes the translation anachronism might partially depend on changes in English meanings that make it appear that something was more anachronistic than it was at the time that Joseph translated the Book of Mormon.

Translation Anachronisms

There are two types of explanations for translation anachronisms in the Book of Mormon. The LDS scholars who propose one or the other make their selection on the basis of their understanding of the type of translation we see in the Book of Mormon. Those who understand a very literal, almost word for word translation from the plates to the English text will favor one approach. Those who see a less literal translation tend to favor the other.

Anachronisms Introduced by Authors

The first explanation of the presence of a translation anachronism suggests that the problem occurred with the Book of Mormon peoples, and Joseph accurately translated the linguistic anachronism the Book of Mormon peoples created. When people from different cultures and speaking different languages meet, there is a known phenomenon where unknown animals in the new culture receive names based on words and animals already known in one's own culture. For example, Latin speakers encountered a previously unknown animal in the Nile and called it a "river horse," which is now known as a hippopotamus. None of us would think a hippopotamus either looks or acts like a horse—but someone used that name to describe it. The Maya did not have a word for *horse* when the Spanish arrived, and they typically described horses with some version of the word for *deer*.[11] Again, we understand that there are major differences between deer and horses, yet when we read Maya language documents describing the Spaniard's horses, they are called deer.

The suggestion is that this labeling process generated the anachronistic names in the Book of Mormon. Nephites who knew horses from the Old World found some different animal in the New World and used an Old World name for it. This labeling attribution has been recorded so frequently in history that it is not implausible to believe that it could have happened when the Nephites settled on the American continent. In this scenario, the initial contact created the anachronistic term, which Joseph translated just as the word was found on the plates.

Anachronisms Introduced by Translators

The second explanation is based on a less literal translation method. Rather than suggest that Nephite linguistic labeling created the anachronism, the translation anachronisms came from Joseph as the translator. The vocabulary reflects Joseph's time and understanding in the same way that candles were the linguistic choice of the KJV translators.[12]

This explanation allows for a different way of seeing the anachronistic animals and provides an explanation for other phrases that are more appropriate to Joseph's time. For example, in 2 Nephi 9:47 we find: "Would I harrow up your souls if your minds were pure?" The verb *harrow* comes from the farm implement of that name that was used to break up ground for planting. It was an implement that was unknown in the New World, or even in the Old World, during Book of Mormon times.[13] The Book of Mormon exclusively uses the verb to describe emotions. It never describes the implement. Thus the concept being translated as *harrow up* could easily have been on the plates; the particular word Joseph chose depended upon his own time and understanding.

Understanding the difference between using *harrow up* and describing someone using a harrow is important. Using a harrow would still be anachronistic. Describing the emotion with *harrow up* is a translation anachronism only in the vocabulary—not in the meaning. The fact that an anachronism can exist in translation cannot simply dismiss all possible anachronisms in the Book of Mormon. As with *harrow up*, we can understand it as a translation anachronism only after examining how it is used in the text. Our initial examples of the *horses* and *chariots* provide an important test case.

Anachronisms in Context

The way words are used in a text tell us what the meaning of the words might have been when the text was written. For example, Jeremiah 51:21 states: "And with thee will I break in pieces the horse and his rider; and with thee will I break in pieces the chariot and his rider." It is abundantly clear that men ride horses and ride in chariots. Similarly, Jeremiah 46:9 declares, "Come up, ye horses; and rage, ye chariots; and let the mighty men come forth; the Ethiopians and the Libyans, that handle the shield; and the Lydians, that handle and bend the bow." Here both the horse and the chariot function in a military setting in which, again, men ride on horses and in chariots. The contexts justify our assumptions of what *horses* and *chariots* mean in those verses.

The problem comes when we use those assumptions to govern our reading of the text. For example, Deanne Matheny, a lawyer with archaeological training, notes, "Twice King Lamoni's horses and chariots are prepared for traveling.[14] Horses and chariots also are among the items that the Nephites assembled before their battle with the Gadianton robbers.[15] These references indicate that horses functioned in several areas to pull conveyances of some sort."[16]

The verses Matheny references are particularly interesting for the context in which she places them as opposed to their original context. For example, she says "horses and chariots are among the items with the Nephites assembled before their battle with the Gadianton robbers." That clearly intends to place horses and chariots in a military context. However, they are also used in nonmilitary contexts: "And it came to pass in the seventeenth year, in the latter end of the year, the proclamation of Lachoneus had gone forth throughout all the face of the land, and they had taken their horses, and their chariots, and their cattle, and all their flocks, and their herds, and their grain, and all their substance, and did march forth by thousands and by tens of thousands, until they had all gone forth to the place which had been appointed that they should gather themselves together, to defend themselves against their enemies."[17] Although the reason for gathering the material is a military situation, the actual context of the mention of horses and chariots is in a gathering of all their belongings: "and their cattle, and all their flocks, and their herds, and their grain, and all their substance." That is not a military context. When we examine the contextual data carefully, there is no such militaristic connection.[18]

In Alma 18:9, the servants explain, "Behold, he is feeding thy horses. Now the king had commanded his servants . . . that they should prepare his horses and chariots, and conduct him forth to the land of Nephi; for there had been a great feast appointed at the land of Nephi, by the father of Lamoni, who was king over all the land." This context explains that *horses* and *chariots* are near the palace and that *horses* must be fed. Lamoni is going to the land of Nephi on a formal state visit, but the role of the *horses* and *chariots* is not clear. We assume that the horse pulls the chariot because of the meaning of those words as we have learned them. However, it isn't the relationship between the meaning of the English words that is important but the discernible relationship between the use of *chariots* and *horses* in the text.

Rather than appear in the context of war, Book of Mormon *horses* and *chariots* are seen in the context of a formal state visit. *Horses* and *chariots* reappear in that setting when Ammon and Lamoni hear that Ammon's brothers are in prison: "Lamoni . . . caused that his servants should make ready his horses and his chariots"[19] for another state visit to the king of the land where they were held.

Chariots never appear in the context of Book of Mormon warfare. *Horses* only move and eat. They never explicitly pull anything. They are never ridden. There are no cultural innovations that followed the use of the horse in the Eastern hemisphere. If we replaced the word *horse* with a made-up word such as *glerk*, we would never suspect when reading the text that a *glerk* was a horse. Thus the text itself does not support *horse* as the only or even best translation for whatever word was on the plates.[20]

Even assuming that *horse* and *chariot* represent translation anachronisms, the nouns still represent textual placeholders for some animal and conveyance in the original plate language. Just as with the problem of the KJV translation of *candle*, there is some relationship to the original language. In that case, it is easy to see both the candle and the oil lamp as sources of light. We expect that both words will occur in contexts of providing light. Even if we didn't have the original, we could work our way back to oil lamps despite the translation anachronism.

In the case of horses and chariots, the proposed Mesoamerican location for the Book of Mormon provides a context in which we may see what might have been the underlying terms that had sufficient similarity to produce the translation anachronism of horses and chariots. The appropriate conveyance behind the word *chariot* would be a royal litter, carried on men's shoulders rather than pulled by an animal. Even the English of the text never mentions wheels, which were not know to be used for conveyance in ancient America. Our imagination supplies the wheels because of the word *chariot*. As translator, Joseph could have easily assumed wheels as we do, based on the common wheeled conveyances of his time.

As for the *horse*, it need not have pulled the *chariot*. The text never says that the *horse* pulls the *chariot*, only that *horses* and *chariots* are made ready. In Mesoamerica, the royal litter was also often associated with an animal. Freidel, Schele, and Parker—Maya researchers—commented on a scene found on one of the temples at Tikal. The king is "wearing the balloon headdress of Tlaloc-Venus warfare adopted at the time of the Waxaktun conquest, and holding the bunched javelins and shield.... He sits in majesty on the litter that carried him into battle, while above him hulks Waxaklahun-Ubah-Kan, the great War Serpent.... Graffiti drawings scratched on the walls of Tikal palaces, depicting the conjuring of supernatural beings from the Otherworld, prove that these scenes were more than imaginary events seen only by the kings.... They are the poorly drawn images of witnesses, perhaps minor members of lordly families, who scratched the wonders that they saw during moments of ritual into the walls of the places where they lived their lives."[21]

Karl Taube discusses the practice among the later lowland Maya: "Along with warriors and hunters, Maya kings had a distinct relation with the forest, as they were capable of passing beyond political and natural boundaries to visit or conquer distant realms. With this unique ability, they were identified with the jaguar (the "king" of the forest)—a concept vividly expressed by royal litters and palanquins topped by jaguar beings. First appearing on Stela 212 of Late Preclassic Izapa, such jaguar vehicles are common in Classic Maya art, including figurines.... The jaguar palanquins reveal that, during the Classic Maya period, Maya kings prowled the landscape as fierce beasts guarding and extending their domain."[22]

Both examples show that *chariots* and *horses* as used in the Book of Mormon text could refer to the type of animals and conveyances depicted in the artwork of ancient American cultures.

An Imperfect Translation

There is no way to know precisely what was on the plates. Nevertheless, the very fact that we have the Book of Mormon in translation requires that we look at anachronisms in the text carefully. What at first may appear like a clear mistake, when studied carefully, may just as rationally be interpreted as a rendering of an unknown element to its closest know representation in the language and understanding of the author or translator. In the vast majority of the cases, it is reasonable that we are seeing a translation anachronism rather than a historical anachronism, and translation anachronisms do not impugn the authenticity of the original.

Additional Resources

Clark, John E. "Archaeological Trends and Book of Mormon Origins." *BYU Studies* 44, no. 4 (2005): 83–104.

Gardner, Brant. *Second Witness: Analytical and Contextual Commentary on the Book of Mormon*. Draper, UT: Greg Kofford Books, 2011.

Miller, Wade E. and Matthew Roper. "Animals in the Book of Mormon: Challenges and Perspectives." *Interpreter: A Journal of Mormon Scripture*, http://www.mormoninterpreter.com/animals-in-the-book-of-mormon-challenges-and-perspectives/.

Miller, Wade E. *Science and the Book of Mormon: Cureloms, Cumoms, Horses & More*. Highland, UT: Miller Publishing, 2010.

Roper, Matthew. "Swords and 'Cimeters' in the Book of Mormon." *Journal of Book of Mormon Studies* 8, no. 1 (1999): 34–43.

Wright, Mark Alan. "The Cultural Tapestry of Mesoamerica." *Journal of the Book of Mormon and Other Restoration Scripture* 22, no. 2 (2013): 4–21.

About the Author

Brant A. Gardner earned a master's degree in anthropology and Mesoamerican ethnohistory from the State University of New York at Albany. He is the author of *Second Witness: Analytical and Contextual Commentary on the Book of Mormon* and *The Gift and Power: Translating the Book of Mormon*. He has presented papers at FairMormon conferences and published in the *FARMS Review* of the Neal A. Maxwell Institute at Brigham Young University as well as *Interpreter: A Journal of Mormon Scripture*.

Notes

1. A catalog of potential anachronisms and responses may be found at FairMormon, "Book of Mormon Anachronisms," FairMormon, http://en.fairmormon.org/Book_of_Mormon/Anachronisms.

2. Wade E. Miller, *Science and the Book of Mormon: Cureloms, Cumoms, Horses & More* (Highland, UT: Miller Publishing, 2010), 77.

3. Wade E. Miller and Matthew Roper, "Animals in the Book of Mormon: Challenges and Perspectives," *Interpreter: A Journal of Mormon Scripture*, http://www.mormoninterpreter.com/?s=Animals+in+the+book+of+Mormon.

4. Robert R. Bennett, "Horses in the Book of Mormon," Neal A Maxwell Institute for Religious Scholarship, http://publications.maxwellinstitute.byu.edu/fullscreen/?pub=1055&index=1.

5. Richard A. Diehl and Margaret D. Mandeville, "Tula, and Wheeled Animal Effigies in Mesoamerica," *Antiquity* 61, no. 232 (1987): 239–46; Paul R. Cheesman, *The World of the Book of Mormon* (Bountiful, UT: Horizon Publishers & Distributors, 1984), 172–73; Paul R. Cheesman, "The Wheel in Ancient America," *BYU Studies* 9, no. 2 (Winter 1969): 185–97; John L. Sorenson, "Wheeled Figurines in the Ancient World," *FARMS Preliminary Reports* (Provo, UT: FARMS, 1981).

6. Job 18:6, 21:17; Psalm 18:28; Proverbs 20:27, 24:20, 31:18; Jeremiah 25:10; Matthew 5:15; Mark 4:21; Luke 8:16, 11:33, 15:8; Revelation 18:23, 22:5.

7. Jacob 7:27; emphasis added.

8. William Whiston, trans., *The Life of Flavius Josephus—Autobiography*, http://sacred-texts.com/jud/josephus/autobiog.htm; emphasis added. The author thanks Stephen Smoot for this insight.

9. William Henry Holmes, *Handbook of Aboriginal American Antiquities* (Washington, DC: Government Printing Office, 1919), 20.

10. Désiré Charnay, *The Ancient Cities of the New World, Being Voyages and Explorations in Mexico and Central America from 1857–1882* (Charleston, SC: Nabu Press, 2010), 171.

11. The best explication of this concept is found in John L. Sorenson, *An Ancient American Setting for the Book of Mormon* (Provo, UT: FARMS, 1975), 295–99.

12. Brant A. Gardner, *The Gift and Power: Translating the Book of Mormon* (Draper, UT: Greg Kofford Books, 2011), 187–92.

13. The harrow was known to the KJV translators, who also used it anachronistically as both the implement and the verb. See 1 Chronicles 20:3 and Job 39:10 among others.

14. Alma 18:9–10, 20:6.

15. 3 Nephi 3:22.

16. Deanne G. Matheny, "Does the Shoe Fit? A Critique of the Limited Tehuantepec Geography," in *New Approaches to the Book of Mormon*, ed. Brent Lee Metcalfe (Salt Lake City: Signature Books, 1993), 305, n. 23.

17. 3 Nephi 3:22.

18. In 2 Nephi 12:7 and 2 Nephi 15:28, descriptions of horses and chariots functioning in Old Testament contexts are, in fact, Old Testament quotations from Isaiah.

19. Alma 20:6.

20. In contrast to the vocabulary issue with *horse*, the use of metal plates in the Book of Mormon is not an anachronism because the context refers to creating them with ore (1 Nephi 19:1; Mosiah 21:27; Mormon 8:5), and they were metal when delivered to Joseph Smith. The

process of identifying an anachronism to vocabulary choices cannot be used indiscriminately but must be based on evidence from the text.

21. David Freidel, Linda Schele, and Joy Parker, *Maya Cosmos: Three Thousand Years on the Shaman's Path* (1993; repr., New York: William Morrow Paperbacks, 1995), 311–13.

22. Karl Taube, "Ancient and Contemporary Maya Conceptions about Field and Forest," in *The Lowland Maya Area: Three Millennia at the Human-Wildland Interface*, ed. Scott Fedick et al. (Boca Raton, FL: CRC Press, 2003), 480.

5

THE TESTIMONIES OF THE BOOK OF MORMON WITNESSES

Alexander L. Baugh

*A*N IMPORTANT EPISODE ASSOCIATED WITH THE TRANSLATION AND coming forth of the Book of Mormon was the experience of two sets of witnesses—eleven total—who, among other things, claimed to have actually seen the gold plates, which were delivered by the angel Moroni to Joseph Smith. Following their respective experiences, the witnesses signed their names to a declaration testifying of the truthfulness of what they had seen and heard. However, skeptics who consider the Prophet's claims of being visited by divine personages and possessing ancient sacred plates to be a pretentious and deceptive hoax conclude that the experience and testimonies of the Book of Mormon witnesses could not be genuine either. In their attempts to explain away what actually occurred, skeptics and critics have put forward what essentially consists of psychological explanations to demonstrate that what the witnesses actually experienced was nothing more than a form of mental illusion. By so doing, they draw the conclusion that the events surrounding the coming forth of the Book of Mormon were part of a manufactured scheme by Joseph Smith to conjure individuals into believing his claims. But historical evidence does not support these claims, and the testimonies of the witnesses of the plates remain a powerful confirmation of their existence.

While engaged in the translation of the Book of Mormon, Joseph Smith learned from several passages in the record that witnesses selected to view the plates would testify to their authenticity. For example, a passage in the book of Ether indicated that the translator would be able to show the gold plates and other ancient artifacts to those who would "assist to bring forth this work." The scriptural text also specified the precise number: "And unto three shall they be shown by the power of God; wherefore they shall know of a surety that these things are true. And in the mouth of three witnesses shall these things be established; and the testimony of three and this work . . . shall . . . [show] forth the power of God and also his word."[1] Additional passages in the ancient record reiterated a similar injunction: "Wherefore, at that day when the book shall be delivered unto the man of whom I have spoken, the book shall be hid from the eyes of the world, that the eyes of none shall behold it save it be that three witnesses shall behold it, by the power of God, besides him to whom the book shall be delivered; and they shall testify to the truth of the book and the things therein."[2]

THE THREE WITNESSES

Each of the individuals chosen to be the primary witnesses—Martin Harris, Oliver Cowdery, and David Whitmer—received their designation by revelation. Harris was the first witness appointed. During the initial months of the translation (ca. April 12–June 14, 1828), Harris acted as a scribe to the Prophet before losing 116 pages of the translated manuscript. In March 1829, Harris visited Joseph Smith in Harmony, Pennsylvania, where he requested the privilege of seeing the plates and other ancient relics in the Prophet's possession. In spite of his previous negligence, Joseph Smith received a revelation informing Harris that if he humbled himself he would be granted "a view of the things which he desires to see."[3] However, an additional mandate was given. After viewing the relics, he would be under the obligation of bearing testimony of what he experienced: "And then he shall say unto the people of this generation: I have seen the things which the Lord hath shown unto Joseph Smith, Jun., and I know of a surety that they are true, for I have seen them, for they have been shown unto me by the power of God and not of man."[4]

On April 5, 1829, Oliver Cowdery, who had become acquainted with the Smith family in Manchester, New York, arrived in Harmony in company with Samuel Smith, Joseph Smith's younger brother, to offer his assistance. Two days later, the Prophet resumed the translation of the plates in earnest, with Oliver as the principal scribe for the second phase of the translation. In the first revelation received by Joseph Smith later that month in behalf of Oliver, two brief phrases possibly allude to his selection as one of the primary witnesses: "In the mouth of two or three witnesses shall every word be established" and "by the testimony which shall be given."[5]

While in Harmony, Oliver communicated with a close acquaintance, David Whitmer, who resided in Fayette, New York, about the work of translation. In May, because of heightened harassment and persecution against him and Joseph, Oliver wrote David to ask if they could finish the translation at the home of Peter Whitmer Sr., David's father. David agreed, and in late May or early June he traveled to Harmony and transported the translator and the scribe to Fayette.

It did not take David Whitmer long to recognize Joseph Smith's intuitive revelatory gift and request that the Prophet pronounce a revelation in his behalf. Like the first revelation given to Oliver, the revelation to David also implied that he would be selected as one of the Book of Mormon witnesses. A portion reads, "If you shall ask the Father in my name, in faith believing, . . . you may stand as a witness of the things of which you shall both hear and see."[6]

At or near the completion of the translation in late June 1829, Joseph Smith sought to comply with the revelatory directives in the Book of Mormon regarding the requirement that three witnesses be chosen to view the record and at the same time fulfill the promises given to Martin Harris, Oliver Cowdery, and David Whitmer, who had been specifically singled out in the Prophet's revelations for that privilege. Joseph later recalled that the three men were so eager to see the plates for themselves that they became "very solicitous, and teazed [*sic*] me so much, that at length I complied and through the Urim and Thummim I obtained [the word] of the Lord for them."[7]

The revelation not only promised them a view of the plates but also a view of the breastplate and the spectacles (sometimes referred to as the Nephite interpreters), the sword of Laban, and the Liahona—the miraculous directors given to Lehi in the wilderness.[8] However, several stipulations were also given: In order to see the sacred relics, the witnesses would have to rely upon the word of God "with full purpose of heart," and exercise faith, for they were told, "It is by your faith that you shall obtain a view of them." But this was not all: "And after . . . you have obtained faith, and have seen them with your eyes, you shall testify of them, by the power of God; and this you shall do that my servant Joseph Smith, Jun., may not be destroyed, that I may bring about my righteous purposes unto the children of men in this work."[9]

Not long after this directive was given, the promised witness was granted. Joseph, Oliver, David, and Martin secluded themselves in a wooded area a short distance from the Whitmer home. Upon finding an appropriate location, the party knelt down, whereupon Joseph commenced praying in behalf of the group, followed by each of the others in turn. This pattern was repeated a second time, but nothing transpired, at which time Martin "proposed that he should withdraw himself from us, believing . . . that his presence was the cause of our not obtaining the object of our desires at that time." Shortly after Martin's departure, an exceedingly bright light appeared and an angel stood before the other men: "In his hands he held the plates we had been praying . . . to have a view of," the Prophet recorded. "He turned over the plates one by one so that we could see them, and discern the engravings thereon distinctly." The voice of Jesus Christ was also heard: "These plates have been revealed by the power of God, and they have been translated by the power of God, the translation of them which you have seen is correct, and I command you to bear record of what you now see & hear." After the vision closed, Joseph Smith went in search of Martin. "I found [him] at a considerable distance," Joseph reported, "fervently engaged in prayer [and said] that he had not yet prevailed with the Lord, and earnestly requested me to join him in prayer that he also might realize the same blessings which we had just received." Moments later "the same vision was again opened," and Joseph and Martin saw a similar manifestation and heard the same heavenly injunction given previously to the others.[10]

Lucy Mack Smith, who was present at the Peter Whitmer Sr. home at the time the witnesses returned after experiencing their vision, wrote:

> It was between three and four o'clock p.m. Mrs. Whitmer, Mr. Smith, and myself, were sitting in a bedroom at the time. On coming in, Joseph threw himself down beside me and exclaimed, "Father, mother, you do not know how happy I am; the Lord has now caused the plates to be shown to three more besides myself. They have seen an angel, who has testified to them, and they will have to bear witness to the truth of what I have said, for now they know for themselves, that I do not go about to deceive the people, and I feel as if I was relieved of a burden which was almost too heavy for me to bear, and it rejoices my soul, that I am not any longer to be entirely alone in the world." Upon this, Martin Harris came in: he seemed almost overcome with joy, and testified boldly to what he had both seen and heard. And so did David and Oliver, adding, that no tongue could express the joy of their hearts, and the greatness of the things which they had both seen and heard.[11]

In an interview conducted by LDS Apostles Orson Pratt and Joseph F. Smith with David Whitmer at his home in Richmond, Missouri, in September 1878, Whitmer provided a number of significant details regarding the witnesses' experience:

> D. W. It was in June, 1829—the latter part of the month . . . the angel showed us (the three witnesses) the plates, as I suppose to fulfill the words of the book itself. Martin Harris was not with us at the time, he obtained a view of them afterwards, (the same day). Joseph, Oliver, and myself were together when I saw them. We not only saw the plates of the Book of Mormon but also the brass plates, the plates of the Book of Ether, the plates containing the records of the wickedness and secret combination of the people of the world down to the time of their being engraved, and many other plates. The fact

is, it was just as though Joseph, Oliver, and I were sitting just here on a log, when we were overshadowed by a light. It was not like the light of the sun nor like that of a fire, but more glorious and beautiful. It extended away round us . . . but in the midst of this light . . . there appeared as it were, a table with many records of plates upon it, besides the plates of the Book of Mormon, also the Sword of Laban, the directors—i.e., the ball which Lehi had, and the interpreters. I saw them just as plain as I see this bed . . . and I heard the voice of the Lord, as distinctly as I ever heard anything in my life, declaring that the records of the plates of the Book of Mormon were translated by the gift and power of God.[12]

Significantly, Whitmer stated he and the others saw additional plates on a table besides the plates from which the Book of Mormon was translated. He also specifically stated that they saw Laban's sword, the Liahona, and the interpreters—artifacts the witnesses were promised they would be permitted to view,[13] although no mention was made of the breastplate. Furthermore, he detailed the unusual light that surrounded them during the vision. And finally, he emphatically declared that they each heard an audible voice, even that of the resurrected Jesus Christ, affirming that the translation given by Joseph Smith was correct.

The Eight Witnesses

Even though the vision given to Cowdery, Whitmer, and Harris fulfilled the scriptural promise in the Book of Mormon that the record would be shown to three witnesses by the power of God, two passages in the sacred text suggested that additional witnesses might also have a view of the plates. Speaking to the translator, Moroni wrote, "And behold, ye may be privileged that ye may show the plates unto those who shall assist to bring forth this work."[14] And Nephi added, "And there is none other which shall view it, save it be a few according to the will of God."[15] Given this additional exception, Joseph Smith concluded that after the plates were shown to the Three Witnesses, it would be permissible for him to allow a few others to see the sacred record. He selected his father (Joseph Sr.) and his two adult brothers Hyrum and Samuel. The remaining witnesses came from the Whitmer family—brothers Christian, Jacob, John, Peter Jr., and Hiram Page, a brother-in-law—each of whom had supported and accommodated the Prophet and Oliver Cowdery during the final month of the translation at the Whitmer home.

The viewing of the plates by the Eight Witnesses was considerably less dramatic but exceptionally significant nonetheless. A few days following the Three Witnesses' manifestation, Joseph, Oliver, and several members of the Whitmer family came to Manchester to look into making arrangements to have the book printed when, according to Lucy Mack Smith, "all the male part of the company, with my husband, Samuel and Hyrum, retired to a place where the family were in the habit of offering up their secret devotions to God." She continued, "Here it was, that those eight witnesses, whose names are recorded in the Book of Mormon, looked upon them, and handled them."[16]

In 1878, P. Wilhelm Poulson interviewed John Whitmer, the last surviving member of the Eight Witnesses, and asked him a series of questions regarding what he recalled about seeing the plates. A portion of the interview reads:

> I [Poulson] said: I am aware that your name is affixed to the testimony in the Book of Mormon, that you saw the plates?
> He [Whitmer]—It is so, and that testimony is true.
> I—Did you handle the plates with your hands?
> He—I did so!
> I—Then they were a material substance?
> He—Yes, as material as anything can be.
> I—They were heavy to lift?
> He—Yes, and you know gold is a heavy metal, they were very heavy.
> I—How big were the leaves?
> He—So far as I recollect, 8 by 6 or 7 inches.
> I—Were the leaves thick?
> He—Yes, just so thick, that characters could be engraven on both sides.
> I—How were the leaves joined together?
> He—In three rings, each one in the shape of a D with the straight line towards the centre. . . .
> I—Did you see them covered with a cloth?
> He—No. He [Joseph Smith] handed them uncovered into our hands, and we turned the leaves sufficiently to satisfy us.[17]

Following this incident, Joseph Smith returned the plates and other sacred relics to the angel Moroni.

Shortly after seeing the plates, both the Three and the Eight Witnesses prepared formal statements attesting to the truthfulness and reality of what they experienced. Regarding the written declaration made by the Three Witnesses, Joseph Smith's history states, "Having thus through the mercy of God, obtained these glorious manifestations, it now remained for these three individuals to fulfil the commandment which they had received, viz: to bear record of these things; in order to accomplish which, *they drew up and subscribed the following document.*"[18] David Whitmer later said that he, Oliver, and Martin "each signed his own name" to the document.[19] The fact that each of the Three Witnesses personally signed his name to the official declaration suggests that the Eight Witnesses may have done the same and attached their handwritten signatures to their statement. Unfortunately, no document containing the actual signatures of either of two groups of witnesses is known to exist. But evidence suggests that the two statements, along with the personal signatures by each of the witnesses, were likely included at the very end of the original manuscript of the Book of Mormon. However, since most of the original manuscript did not survive, this would explain why the transcription of the original version of the testimonies given by both the Three Witnesses and the Eight Witnesses and their personal signatures no longer exists. Significantly, a word-for-word transcription of both the testimony of the Three Witnesses and that of the Eight Witnesses and their individual names appears at the end of the manuscript of the printer's copy of the Book of Mormon in the handwriting of Oliver Cowdery. Critics have argued that Cowdery actually "signed" their names for them, when in actuality all he was doing was copying the text and their signatures from the original manuscript of the Book of Mormon. The fact that both of the witnesses' testimonies were added at the end of the original Book of Mormon manuscript as well as the printer's copy would also explain why they appear on the last two pages of the first edition of the Book of Mormon, published in 1830.[20]

In their declaration, Oliver Cowdery, David Whitmer, and Martin Harris subscribe to the following statements: (1) their experience was a divine manifestation (namely, it was given to them "by the power of God, and not of man"), (2) an angel showed them the Book of Mormon plates and the engravings, and (3) the voice of God (Jesus Christ) was heard declaring that the translation of the sacred record was true and that they must bear testimony of what they had both seen and heard. In their declaration, the Eight Witnesses certify to the following: (1) Joseph Smith showed them the plates (as distinguished from the Three Witnesses, who were shown the plates by an angel), (2) the plates had the appearance of gold and were an "ancient work" of "curious workmanship," and (3) they saw the engravings, handled the leaves, and lifted the plates.

Additional Witnesses

In addition to Joseph Smith and the eleven witnesses seeing the plates, David Whitmer stated on at least three different occasions that in June 1829, soon after the Prophet and Oliver Cowdery arrived at the Peter Whitmer Sr. home in Fayette, New York, to work on the translation, Mary Whitmer, David's mother, was shown the plates by the angel.[21]

Several Smith family members acknowledged that Joseph had the plates in his possession, although they were always covered, and the family was never permitted to see them. After retrieving the plates from the

Hill Cumorah, the Prophet's father, mother, and sister Katherine were each reported to have handled the plates through a linen frock Joseph had concealed them in.[22] Emma said she moved the plates from place to place while doing housework. "The plates often lay on the table . . . wrapped in a small linen table cloth." She also felt the plates through the fabric and even traced their outline and shape. "They seemed to be pliable like thick paper, and would rustle with a metallic sound when the edges were moved by the thumb."[23] William Smith, the Prophet's younger brother, said that although he never saw the plates uncovered, he "handled them and hefted them while wrapped in a tow frock and judged them to have weighed about sixty pounds."[24]

Secular Explanations

Some secularists, or those who do not believe in the divine, have explained the experience of the Three Witnesses as being some sort of mental delusion, a metaphysical mystical abnormality, a psychological fantasy, or perhaps more simply, religious hypnosis or hallucination. To these types of subjective individuals, spiritual manifestations such as those experienced by Joseph Smith and his associates cannot be considered legitimate because they represent a supernatural manifestation that cannot be proven. These people therefore have concluded that the experience of the witnesses to the Book of Mormon had to have been psychologically induced.

One of the first individuals to propose the notion that Joseph Smith's spiritual manifestations were psychologically centered was I. Woodbridge Riley, a late-nineteenth and early-twentieth century academic who specialized in philosophy and psychology. Riley wrote and authored *The Founder of Mormonism: A Psychological Study of Joseph Smith*, which was published in 1903. To secular theorists such as Riley, the Prophet's visionary experiences were peculiar psychological experiences that resulted from a combination of physical illnesses and abnormalities; psychological elements stemming from his religious, cultural, and social environment and experiences; and possible psychosomatic mental disorders brought about by traumatic experiences from his childhood and youth.

In his assessment of the vision experienced by Oliver Cowdery, David Whitmer, and Martin Harris, Riley categorized it as a "subjective hallucination, induced by hypnotic suggestion."[25] Joseph Smith, the facilitator, provided "repetition, steady attention, absence of mistrust, self-surrender to the will of the principal,—all the requisites are present." The result, he concluded, was a "psychic mirage, complete in every detail."[26] In the case of the Eight Witnesses, Riley contended their vision was "collective hypnotization," which produced a "hallucination or an illusion . . . of an object where in reality there is nothing, or the false interpretation of some existing external object."[27]

In 1945, historian Fawn M. Brodie published *No Man Knows My History*, a psychoanalytical biography of Joseph Smith. In much the same manner as Riley's, Brodie's work was underscored with psychological explanations for the Prophet's religious claims and spiritual experiences. Given this context, it should not be surprising that in her analysis of Cowdery, Whitmer, and Harris seeing the angel and the ancient artifacts and hearing the heavenly voice, Brodie asserted that the three men were "victims of Joseph's unconscious but positive talent at hypnosis."[28] Perhaps not surprising is the fact that Brodie offered no expanded commentary about what was experienced by the Eight Witnesses, other than that Joseph was "not content with the testimony of the three witnesses," so a second testimony was drafted.[29]

More recently, Dan Vogel, an ardent critic of Joseph Smith and early Mormonism, took a page—actually many pages—out of Riley's and Brodie's books, so his argument was not new, although he attempted to bolster it with more historical sources. Vogel also propounded hypnosis as a possible explanation regarding how Joseph Smith was able to generate artificial spiritual manifestations, including that experienced by the Three Witnesses, but Vogel appeared to lean more to the experience being a hallucination. Vogel also made the case that group hallucination was possible, which he believed explains how Oliver, David, and Martin could each claim to have all seen the same scenes and objects in their so-called "vision." But Vogel added another interesting twist to the witnesses' story. Citing statements given later by several of the Eight Witnesses and others who interviewed or interrogated them, Vogel maintained that the collective viewing of the plates by the eight men was also extrasensory, much like that of the Three Witnesses. Vogel also believed that Joseph Smith made a set of fake tin plates, which he allowed the witnesses to lift in a box or handle while covered (either on a previous occasion or on the occasion of their shared witness experience), but the actual viewing of the plates was "visionary." It was not solely "physical," as their written testimony maintains.[30]

Grant Palmer, another critic, came to an interesting conclusion about the gold plates and what the witnesses actually saw. Palmer advanced the theory that the gold plates were not even a genuine relic from a previous ancient civilization, but a supernatural treasure that belonged "to another world rather than this one." Palmer also believed the Eight Witnesses "saw and scrutinized the plates in a mind vision," but unlike Vogel, who asserted that the eight men experienced a psychic encounter, Palmer considered it to have been an authentic, spiritual one.[31]

Religious opponents who speculate that what the Three or Eight Witnesses saw was merely some sort of hypnotic trance or psychic hallucination tend to support their argument by pointing out that the witnesses (and more precisely the Three Witnesses) sometimes described seeing the plates and other artifacts with their "spiritual eyes." In other words, they didn't really see them in a conscious state. While they did indeed occasionally speak of seeing the plates in a spiritual sense, we learn from scripture that individuals who experience heavenly visions or divine manifestations undergo a spiritual transformation, sometimes referred to as being transfigured or "quickened by the Spirit of God"[32] so they can actually "see" or observe the divine. For example, before receiving the vision of the degrees of glory, Joseph Smith and Sidney Rigdon recorded, "By the power of the Spirit our eyes were opened and our understandings were enlightened, so as to see and understand the things of God."[33] At the same time, this is not to suggest that the appearance of Moroni and his showing the plates to Oliver, David, and Martin completely excluded any type of physical element. From their personal descriptions and statements, each one clearly acknowledged the spiritual aspects of the manifestation but was also aware of the present surroundings and the physical conditions. It was a spiritual and physical reality. They saw and heard things in a spiritual dimension, but at the same time the angel and the plates and other artifacts were also physically present.

Speaking of those who do not believe in spiritual or divine manifestations, the Apostle Paul taught, "But the natural man receiveth not the things of the Spirit of God: for they are foolishness unto him: neither can he know them, because they are spiritually discerned."[34] Modern naturalistic thinkers would also discount Moses's divine encounters with Jehovah; Peter, James, and John's theophany on the Mount of Transfiguration; Stephen's heavenly vision of God the Father and the Son; and Paul's dramatic encounter with the risen Lord on the road to Damascus. When it comes to his own remarkable visionary claims, Joseph Smith is in good company.

Alternate Explanations are Flawed

There is no evidence that Joseph Smith ever engaged others in hypnotic activity, conjured up a trance or mental illusion, or possessed such mesmerizing gifts that allowed him to subjugate individuals into coming under some mystic group trance or spell. If the twenty-three-year-old Prophet had engaged in any kind of mind control with the witnesses—each of whom was a rational, sensible individual—any one of them could have recognized what took place; and when questioned about their experience, these men likely would have mentioned that Joseph Smith employed some type of manipulation, especially those who later became disillusioned with Mormonism. But none of the eleven men ever talked about or suggested that anything of the kind ever took place. Such accusations are completely nonexistent in the well-documented record of Joseph Smith's life because nothing of the sort ever occurred.

Recognizing the notable deficiencies in the psychological arguments put forward by the critics regarding the experience and testimony of the Three Witnesses, noted LDS scholar Richard L. Bushman has observed that doubters still cannot find any "plausible cause" to explain "the elaborate vision."[35] The same could be said about the secularist arguments put forward regarding the experience of the Eight Witnesses of seeing and handling the plates. Furthermore, close scrutiny by LDS scholars of the available historical documents and sources associated with the experiences and testimonies provided by the Book of Mormon witnesses shows that many of the explanations made by those critical of Mormonism are incongruent with the firsthand accounts made by the witnesses themselves. This is evident in the fact that one of the fatal flaws skeptical writers have made in their historical interpretations is that they have tended to accept hearsay reports by the witnesses (i.e., reports of what was purportedly said by a witness, some of which obscure firsthand statements) above the actual personal accounts.

Significance of the Testimonies of the Witnesses

In late 1837 and early 1838, four of the eleven witnesses to the Book of Mormon—Martin Harris, John Whitmer, Oliver Cowdery, and David Whitmer—were formally cut off from the Church, while Jacob Whitmer and Hiram Page became disaffected and left on their own. Two of these six eventually returned to the Church: Cowdery in 1848 and Harris in 1875. However, in spite of the personal objections they may have had toward Joseph Smith or the Church following their separation from Mormonism, none of these men ever asserted that Joseph Smith was a religious charlatan or deceiver, nor did they recant or revoke their testimony regarding the Book of Mormon or declare the sacred record to be a sham.

Richard Lloyd Anderson, the leading scholar on the witnesses, has written, "Perhaps their later alienation makes them even more credible witnesses, for no collusion could have withstood their years of separation from the Church and from each other." He then concludes, "The testimonies of the Three and Eight Witnesses balance the supernatural and the natural, the one stressing the angel and heavenly voice, the other, the existence of the tangible record on gold plates. To the end of their lives, each of the Three said he had seen the plates, and each of the Eight insisted that he had handled them."[36]

Critics will continue to cry foul and insist that Joseph Smith was a cunning manipulator of the witnesses who were victims of his deception. However, to individuals whose hearts and minds are open and attuned to the divine and who believe in spiritual manifestations and communication from heaven, the collective testimonies of the Three and Eight Witnesses stand as a powerful affirmation of the existence of gold plates and the truthfulness of the Book of Mormon as another testament of Jesus Christ.

Additional Resources

Anderson, Gale Yancey. "Eleven Witnesses Behold the Plates." *Journal of Mormon History* 38, no. 2 (Spring 2012): 145–62.

Anderson, Richard Lloyd. "Attempts to Redefine the Experience of the Eight Witnesses." *Journal of Book of Mormon Studies* 14, no. 1 (2005): 18–31.

———. *Investigating the Book of Mormon Witnesses*. Salt Lake City: Deseret Book, 1981.

Harper, Steven C. "Evaluating the Book of Mormon Witnesses." *Religious Educator* 11, no. 2 (2010): 37–49.

About the Author

Alexander L. Baugh is a professor in the Department of Church History and Doctrine at Brigham Young University, where he has been a full-time faculty member since 1995. He received his BS from Utah State University and his MA and PhD degrees from Brigham Young University. He specializes in researching and writing about the Missouri period of early LDS Church history (1831–39). He is the author, editor, or coeditor of seven books. In addition, he has published over seventy historical journal articles, essays, and book chapters. He is a member of the Mormon History Association and the John Whitmer Historical Association, having served as president of the latter from 2006 to 2007. He is also the past editor of *Mormon Historical Studies*. He currently serves as the codirector of research for the Religious Studies Center at BYU, and he is a volume editor for *The Joseph Smith Papers*. He is married to the former Susan Johnson. They are the parents of five children, and they have nine grandchildren. He and his family reside in Highland, Utah.

Notes

1. Ether 5:2–4.
2. 2 Nephi 27:12; see also 2 Nephi 11:3.
3. D&C 5:24.
4. D&C 5:25; see also vv. 26–29.
5. D&C 6:28, 31.
6. D&C 14:8.
7. Karen Lynn Davidson, David J. Whittaker, Mark Ashurst-McGee, and Richard L. Jensen, eds., *Histories, Volume 1: Joseph Smith Histories, 1832–1844*, vol. 1 of the Histories series of *The*

Joseph Smith Papers, ed. Dean C. Jessee, Ronald K. Esplin, and Richard Lyman Bushman (Salt Lake City: Church Historian's Press, 2012), 23 (hereafter *JSP*, H1).

8. D&C 17:1. In addition to seeing the Book of Mormon plates, David Whitmer stated on numerous occasions that the angel also showed them the breastplate, the spectacles, the sword of Laban, the Liahona, and even additional plates. See Lyndon W. Cook, ed., *David Whitmer Interviews: A Restoration Witness* (Orem, UT: Grandin Book, 1991), 11, 15, 20, 26, 34, 40, 86, 108, 127, 181, 184, 186, 198, 213.

9. D&C 17:3–4.

10. *JSP*, H1:318–20 ("Draft 2").

11. Lavina Fielding Anderson, *Lucy's Book: A Critical Edition of Lucy Mack Smith's Family Memoir* (Salt Lake City: Signature Books, 2001), 453.

12. Joseph F. Smith, letter to John Taylor, September 17, 1878, draft, Joseph F. Smith Papers, Church History Library, Salt Lake City (hereafter CHL). For a published version, see Orson Pratt and Joseph F. Smith, "Report of Elder Orson Pratt and Joseph F. Smith," *Deseret News*, November 27, 1878, 674.

13. See D&C 17:1.

14. Ether 5:2.

15. 2 Nephi 27:13.

16. Anderson, *Lucy's Book*, 455–56.

17. P. Wilhelm Poulson, letter to George Q. Cannon and Brigham Young Jr., *Deseret Evening News*, August 6, 1878, 2.

18. *JSP*, H1:320 ("Draft 2"); emphasis added.

19. Pratt and Smith, "Report of Elder Orson Pratt and Joseph F. Smith," 674.

20. Michael H. MacKay, Gerrit J. Dirkmaat, Grant Underwood, Robert J. Woodford, and William G. Hartley, eds., *Documents, Volume 1: July 1828–June 1831*, vol. 1 of the Documents series of *The Joseph Smith Papers*, ed. Dean C. Jessee, Ronald K. Esplin, Richard Lyman Bushman, and Matthew J. Grow (Salt Lake City: Church Historian's Press, 2013), "Appendix 4: Testimony of the Three Witnesses, Late June 1829," and "Appendix 5: Testimony of Eight Witnesses, Late June 1829," 378–87.

21. See Cook, *David Whitmer Interviews*, 13, 182, 214–18.

22. See William B. Smith, "The Old Soldier's Testimony," *Saints' Herald*, October 4, 1884, 643–44; Joel Tiffany, "Mormonism—No. II," *Tiffany's Monthly*, June 1859, 166; Herbert S. Salisbury, "Things the Prophet's Sister Told Me," July 2, 1945, typescript, 1, CHL.

23. "Last Testimony of Sister Emma," *Saints' Herald*, October 1, 1879, 290.

24. J. E. Peterson, "Statement of William Smith, Concerning Joseph, the Prophet," *Deseret Evening News*, January 20, 1894, 11.

25. I. Woodbridge Riley, *The Founder of Mormonism: A Psychological Study of Joseph Smith* (New York: Dodd, Mead, and Company, 1903), 226.

26. Riley, *Founder of Mormonism*, 228.

27. Riley, *Founder of Mormonism*, 230.

28. Fawn M. Brodie, *No Man Knows My History: The Life of Joseph Smith, the Mormon Prophet* (New York: Vintage Books, 1945), 77.

29. Brodie, *No Man Knows My History*, 78.

30. Dan Vogel, "The Validity of the Witnesses' Testimonies," in *America Apocrypha: Essays on the Book of Mormon*, ed. Dan Vogel and Brent Lee Metcalf (Salt Lake City: Signature Books, 2002), 79–121.

31. Grant Palmer, *An Insider's View of Mormon Origins* (Salt Lake City: Signature Books, 2002), 206.

32. See D&C 68:11–12.

33. D&C 76:12, 19; see also D&C 110:1; Moses 1:11.

34. 1 Corinthians 2:14.

35. Richard L. Bushman, "The Recovery of the Book of Mormon," in *Book of Mormon Authorship Revisited*, ed. Noel B. Reynolds (Provo, UT: FARMS, 1997), 33.

36. Richard Lloyd Anderson, "Book of Mormon Witnesses," in *Encyclopedia of Mormonism*, ed. Daniel H. Ludlow, 5 vols. (New York: Macmillan, 1992), 1:216.

6

The Restoration of the Priesthood

Ronald O. Barney

---

*T*HE PATTERN FOR DESIGNATING THOSE ON EARTH WHO REPRESENT GOD and his authority is clear in both the Old and the New Testaments. God called and then sanctioned those who were to act as his earthly delegates. In the book of Hebrews, this concept is clarified: "No man taketh this honor unto himself, but he that is called of God, as was Aaron."[1] Latter-day Saints believe that after the death of Jesus and his Apostles, the authority to act in God's name disintegrated and eventually disappeared. The Bible foretells of events that will occur before the Second Coming of Jesus[2] that require God's authority. The restoration of this authority, also known as priesthood power, came through the ministrations of heavenly messengers to Joseph Smith and Oliver Cowdery beginning in 1829 and during the early days of the Church.

Joseph Smith was "about the age of twelve years" when concerns about God and Jesus and his standing before them first stirred his soul.[3] He had grown up in a home with parents who disagreed on the matter of religion. His mother, Lucy Mack Smith, taught her children the traditional views then advocated by many Christian churches. Joseph's father's beliefs about God's earthly work were considered by local ministers as a perverted form of religion. Though Joseph leaned toward a particular denomination, the Methodists, he likely did not attend church regularly; he was not overly familiar with pulpits and pews. And, while he had been taught to read and believe in the Bible as a boy, he had not been saturated with religion as were other young people around him. Not surprisingly, as he grew older he also grew more confused about God and his work on earth, as well as his own spiritual welfare. But because Joseph acted on his yearnings for greater knowledge, what followed in his life led to seminal religious events, preparing the world for the Savior's Second Coming.

The Necessity of Angelic Delivery of Priesthood Powers

While Joseph was translating the Book of Mormon, the matter of God's earthly authority became a concern to the young Prophet and his scribe Oliver Cowdery. They had come across a discussion dealing with baptism and the remission of sins and wondered about the authority to perform the baptismal ordinance. As they were praying in the woods, an angel visited them and restored the authority to perform valid baptisms, authority that would later be defined as the Aaronic Priesthood.[4]

Some may wonder why Moroni did not transmit his priesthood authority during the many visitations preceding the delivery of the plates. Elder Orson Pratt, one of the Church's early Twelve Apostles, addressed this question: "A revelation and restoration to the earth of the *everlasting gospel* through the angel Moroni would be of no benefit to the nations, unless someone should be ordained with authority to preach it and administer its ordinances.... Did Moroni ordain Mr. [Joseph] Smith to the [priesthood and] apostleship, and command him to administer ordinances? No, he did not. But why not confer authority by ordination, as well as reveal the everlasting gospel? Because in all probability he had not the right to do so. All angels have not the same authority."[5] Apparently, Moroni was not given the authority to restore the lost priesthoods.

The Gradual Unfolding of the Restored Gospel

If Joseph Smith had made up the stories of his experiences with Deity and with other heavenly beings, he could have simplified his claims by reporting that Moroni not only gave him the golden plates but also authorized Joseph to do everything else required by God to restore and organize a church in the latter days. It would have been as believable as any other explanation. Instead, Joseph commented briefly over time on the sometimes complicated, step-by-step process involved in the Restoration of the gospel, which included the specific restoration of God's authority to the earth.

The understanding of priesthood authority developed in the same manner that we all gain understanding. Elder Neal A. Maxwell noted that the divine procedure of giving "unto the faithful line upon line, precept upon precept" creates a "gradual unfolding" that characterizes "the history of God's work."[6] Elder Boyd K. Packer clarified further that the entirety of the Restoration of the gospel, including the priesthood, must be considered in this light. He stated, "Some suppose that the organization was handed to the Prophet Joseph Smith like a set of plans and specifications for a building, with all of the details known at the beginning. But it did not come that way. Rather, it came a piece at a time as the Brethren were ready and as they inquired of God."[7] Even the concept of authority, as it was initially understood and later more broadly known as priesthood, crystalized over time in the mind of Joseph Smith through revelation and visitations by angelic beings. The surviving historical record confirms this understanding. It also sheds light on the delivery from heavenly messengers of the priesthood of God that at the beginning gave Joseph Smith power to organize a church and to perform authentic baptisms, followed later by other prophetic powers.

The "Lesser" or Aaronic Priesthood

In 1829, Joseph Smith and his wife of two years, Emma Hale Smith, lived in a small frame home in a village in northeastern Pennsylvania called Harmony. The Smith home, located near Emma's parents' home, which was near the Susquehanna River, became a particularly important site in the unfolding process of restoring the fulness of the gospel.[8] But Joseph and Emma were not alone in their efforts. Oliver Cowdery became acquainted with Joseph Smith's family in April 1829 while he was living near Palmyra, New York. He heard about Joseph's work, and after receiving a visitation from Jesus Christ declaring the work to be true,[9] Oliver moved from New York to Harmony and became Joseph's scribe. While they worked together in the middle of May 1829 translating the plates—Joseph dictating and Oliver transcribing—they arrived at the point in the story where Jesus appeared to the Nephites. Coincident to translating the book of 3 Nephi, Oliver realized that "it was easily to be seen, that amid the great strife and noise concerning religion, none had authority from God to administer the ordinances of the gospel."

Oliver recorded that after "writing the account given of the Savior's ministry" to those who lived "upon this continent," he and Joseph were visited by an angel:

> On a sudden, as from the midst of eternity, the voice of the Redeemer spake peace to us, while the vail was parted and the angel of God came down clothed with glory, and delivered the anxiously looked for message.... What joy! what wonder! what amazement! ... Our eyes beheld—our ears heard. As in the "blaze of day;" yes, more—above the glitter of the May Sun beam, which then shed its brilliancy over the face of nature! Then his voice, though mild, pierced to the center, and his words, "I am thy fellow servant," dispelled every fear. We listened—we gazed—we admired! 'Twas the voice of the angel from glory—'twas a message from the Most High! and as we heard we rejoiced, while his love enkindled upon our souls, and we were rapt in the vision of the Almighty! Where was room for doubt? No

where: uncertainty had fled, doubt had sunk, no more to rise, while fiction and deception had fled forever!"[10]

The angel's visitation, besides confirming to Joseph and Oliver their recognition that they were now part of something much larger than themselves, involved the actual bestowal of divine authority. Oliver continued, "We received under his hand the holy priesthood as he said, 'upon you my fellow servants, in the name of Messiah, I confer this priesthood and this authority, which shall remain upon earth that the sons of Levi may yet offer an offering unto the Lord in righteousness!' . . . The assurance that we were in the presence of an angel; the certainty that we heard the voice of Jesus, and the truth unsullied as it flowed from a pure personage, dictated by the will of God, is to me, past description."[11]

Now with the authorization to do so, "by the direction of the angel," Joseph Smith baptized his friend Oliver, "the first received into this church, in this day."[12] Joseph, in his own account of the visitation, prepared in 1838–39, said that following Oliver's baptism, "he baptized me."[13] When the baptisms were performed, Joseph continued, "I laid my hands upon his head and ordained him to the Aaronick [sic] priesthood, and afterward he laid his hands on me and ordained me to the same priesthood, for so we were commanded."[14]

The "Greater" or Melchizedek Priesthood

To the young men, the reception of heavenly power to perform the gateway ordinance of baptism at the time became of paramount importance. In Joseph Smith's portrayal of the event, which he noted occurred on May 15, 1829, the same angel, whom he identified as John the Baptist, promised that if Joseph Smith and Oliver Cowdery "continued faithful," besides the "priesthood of Aaron," they "should also have the Melchesidec [sic] Priesthood" given to them.[15] While both Oliver and Joseph created a brief narrative of their experience with John the Baptist, there is a lack of certainty as to whether it was their intent to recount the reception of the higher or greater priesthood from Peter, James, and John as they both did regarding the lesser priesthood. At any rate, such a portrayal was never prepared for publication.[16] This lack of documentation has led some critics to speculate that the Melchizedek Priesthood was not restored until after the organization of the Church in 1830, claiming it was not done under proper authority. The arguments for an earlier restoration are more compelling, however.

Despite the lack of written narrative, Oliver Cowdery affirmed that he, with Joseph, had indeed been visited by the "holy angles [angels] of God" who gave them the greater priesthood of Melchizedek.[17] In 1846, Oliver relayed to one of his close friends his experience with the angel: "Had you stood in the presence of John, with our departed Joseph, to receive the Lesser Priesthood—and in the presence of Peter, to receive the Greater

... you would feel what you have never felt."[18] Oliver, who had been out of sorts with the Church since 1838 and who could have denied the heavenly visitations, undermining more effectively than any other single person the truth claims of Joseph Smith, instead verified his and Joseph's experience with heavenly beings.

In October 1848, Oliver provided additional testimony. The Saints had temporarily relocated westward to the Missouri River en route to Utah after being driven from Nauvoo, Illinois, and were holding a regular conference. But as it turned out, the meeting became an unusual gathering. Oliver Cowdery, still out of the Church, apparently visited the conference unannounced, intent on reuniting with his former friends. Invited to speak before the audience, he declared to attendees: "I was present with Joseph when an holy angle [angel] from god came down from heaven and confered, or restored the Aronic priesthood. And said at the same time that it should remain upon the earth while the earth stands. I was also present with Joseph when the Melchizedek priesthood was confered by the holy angles [angels] of god."[19] Oliver was accepted by the Saints and was rebaptized shortly thereafter.

In Joseph Smith's account of the visitation of the ancient Apostles, he stated that once he and Oliver Cowdery had been ordained by Peter, James, and John, to the "greater" or Melchizedek Priesthood, they "for some time [had] made this [restoration of authority] a subject of humble prayer," surely uncertain about the scope of what they had experienced. Gathered at the home of Peter Whitmer Sr., where the Church would later be organized, "the Word of the Lord came unto us, in the Chamber commanding us, that I should ordain Oliver Cowdery to be an Elder in the Church of Jesus Christ, and that he also should ordain me to the same office, and that after having been thus ordained, we should proceed to ordain others to the same office."[20] The authority necessary to empower the Church to perform valid baptisms and to administer in the other functions of the priesthood, including organizing a church itself, had been given by heavenly messengers to Joseph Smith and Oliver Cowdery.

But this was not the final delivery of divine power to Joseph and Oliver. Again, had Joseph manufactured God's involvement with him, he could have bundled the entirety of God's authority in the person of Moroni. But not only did he define the separate functions and purposes of the "lesser" and "greater" priesthoods, he further described other specific priesthood powers that had been held by the ancient prophets of God.

Priesthood Restoration in the Kirtland House of the Lord

The "lesser" and "greater" priesthoods had empowered the Prophet Joseph and his associates since 1829. Much had been done to expand the growing

Church, particularly the gathering of the elect through missionary efforts.[21] After Church growth required relocation from New York to Ohio, other powers were then bestowed upon Joseph and Oliver. In northeastern Ohio, where the Saints had gathered at Kirtland, Joseph received a revelation that a house of the Lord, where God could further reveal important information, should be built.[22] After three years of sacrifice and difficulty, the house of the Lord, or temple, was completed and awaited dedication. The dedicatory services for the temple at the end of March and early part of April 1836 involved another of the important components of priesthood restoration to the early Church, though it is usually not described as such. There were, as witnessed by numerous attendees, remarkable spiritual events that accompanied the solemn assembly and the temple's dedication. But it was on April 3, when Joseph Smith and Oliver Cowdery were in the western pulpits of the temple, that the most-noted occurrence of the dedicatory period took place. It paralleled the great New Testament vision when Jesus participated in what occurred on the Mount of Transfiguration with the transfer of prophetic authority to Peter, James, and John.[23]

The remarkable event of April 3, 1836, was described in Joseph's own journal shortly after the event occurred, penned by Joseph's scribe at the time, Oliver Cowdery's brother Warren. After Jesus appeared to Joseph and Oliver to accept the labors of the Saints in constructing the house of the Lord, a singular event in itself, the account states that Joseph and Oliver acquired something that perhaps they did not expect: significant heavenly authority from heavenly messengers that opened more doors as part of the restoration of all things. "[T]he heavens were again opened unto us; and Moses appeared before us. . . . After this, Elias appeared. . . . After this vision had closed, another great and glorious vision burst upon us; for Elijah the prophet, who was taken to heaven without tasting death, stood before us."[24] Thus, after Jesus appeared, Joseph and Oliver were successively visited by Moses, Elias, and Elijah, all administering their particular priesthood powers held during their biblical ministries.

This great event was part of the larger restoration plan, described by Joseph to the Saints, where "in the ushering in of the dispensation of the fulness of times" it was required "that a whole and complete and perfect union, and welding together of dispensations, and keys, and powers, and glories should take place."[25] This restoration included revelations and bestowal of authority held by ancient prophets "from the days of Adam even to the present time." But, he told the Saints, "not only this, but those things which never have been revealed from the foundation of the world, but have been kept hid from the wise and prudent, shall be revealed unto babes and sucklings in this, the dispensation of the fulness of times." It was required that each of the prophetic figures give to Joseph Smith "their dispensation, their rights, *their keys*, their honors, their majesty and glory, and *the power of their priesthood*; giving line upon line, precept upon precept; here a little, and there a little."[26] The dramatic panorama of priesthood restoration may appear complicated, but the "dispensation" given to Joseph Smith required all of the power and authority held by the ancient prophets. Joseph Smith testified to the Saints that these priesthood keys had been restored.

Disclosure of Priesthood Restoration Accounts

There is one last factor to consider in understanding priesthood restoration. The inquirer may ask, "If priesthood restoration was of such consequence to the early Church, then why didn't Joseph Smith and Oliver Cowdery run to the local newspapers after their visitations and publish what had happened to them?" There are several explanations for the lack of documentation, only two of which will be given here. The first was given by Joseph himself just after recording his own 1838–39 account: "We were forced to keep secret the circumstances of our having been baptized, and having received this priesthood; owing to the spirit of persecution which had already manifested itself in the neighborhood."[27] Because both men desired to protect their divine experiences from public attention and ridicule, the disclosure of accounts revealing the events of priesthood restoration were initially kept in confidence.

This was consistent with the behavior of other prophetic figures who preceded them. During the course of translating the Book of Mormon, for example, Joseph repeated this significant passage to Oliver: "It is given unto many to know the mysteries of God; nevertheless they are laid under a strict command that they shall not impart, only according to the portion of his word which he doth grant unto the children of men."[28] In other words, those who receive revelation from God are "under a strict command" to keep it to themselves and share it only as appropriate. While receiving the revelation known as the Book of Moses, Joseph was twice counseled to be discreet: "show them not unto any except them that believe," and "see thou show them unto no man, until I command you, except to them that believe."[29] Clearly, there was a sensibility emphasized here that could not have escaped Joseph, which imposed restraint on sharing the revelations of God before it was appropriate.

Not only did Joseph understand this principle, but he also tried to teach this precept to Church leaders, helping them to understand that keeping sacred experiences sacred was expected of all to whom the Lord revealed such things. In November 1835, Joseph taught the newly called Quorum of the Twelve about the anticipated outpouring of spiritual gifts as they prepared for the solemn assembly associated with the dedication of the Kirtland Temple. Regarding their ministries, Joseph recorded, "We must be clean every whit. Let us be faithful and silent brethren, and if God gives you a manifestation, keep it to yourself."[30] Thus it is not surprising that Joseph Smith and Oliver Cowdery kept their sacred experiences to themselves until it was required and appropriate that they explain the essential restoration of the priesthood.

With the powers and priesthood that God gave to his ancient prophets now given to Joseph Smith and Oliver Cowdery, they could, under the direction of God, perform valid baptisms and give the gift of the Holy Ghost; confer the biblical spiritual gifts, such as healing and the working of miracles; share the priesthood with others; and organize a church. Joseph F. Smith said in 1894 of Joseph Smith:

> [W]e must not forget the fact that he was the man out of the millions of human beings that inhabited this earth at the time—the only man, that was called of God, by the voice of God Himself, to open up the dispensation of the Gospel to the world for the last time; and this is the great thing to bear in mind, that he was called of God to introduce the Gospel to the world, to restore the holy priesthood to the children of men, to organize the Church of Jesus Christ of Latter-day Saints in the world, and to restore all the ordinances of the Gospel, for the salvation not only of the living, but also of the dead....
>
> [H]e also communed with the Father and the Son and spoke with angels, and they visited him, and conferred blessings and gifts and keys of power upon him that were never before bestowed upon any human being other than the Son of God himself. No man yet that ever lived upon the earth had all the keys of the Gospel and of the dispensations bestowed upon him as were bestowed upon the Prophet Joseph Smith.[31]

The restoration of the priesthood played a central role in the Restoration of the gospel through Joseph Smith. It was not simply a delivery of the "lesser" and "greater" priesthoods to the Prophet and Oliver Cowdery in 1829. It was far more complex and impressive in scope than is generally recognized. The larger understanding of this perspective leads to a greater appreciation of Joseph Smith's significant role in the unfolding of the Lord's work in the "dispensation of the fulness of times."[32]

Additional Resources

Cannon, Brian Q., and BYU Studies staff. "Seventy Contemporaneous Priesthood Restoration Documents." In *Opening the Heavens: Accounts of Divine Manifestations, 1820–1844*, edited by John W. Welch and

Erick B. Carlson, 215–63. Provo, UT: Brigham Young University Press; Salt Lake City: Deseret Book, 2005.

Harrell, Charles R. "The Restoration of the Priesthood." In *Studies in Scripture*. Vol. 1, *The Doctrine and Covenants*, edited by Robert L. Millet and Kent P. Jackson, 86–99. Sandy, UT: Randall Book Co., 1984.

About the Author

Ronald O. Barney is the editor of *Mormon Historical Studies*. He was executive director of the Mormon History Association from 2011 to 2014. He was an archivist and historian for thirty-three years in the History Department of The Church of Jesus Christ of Latter-day Saints. While there, he was also associate editor of *The Joseph Smith Papers* and was creator and executive producer of the television series that complemented the project. He has written three books and served on the editorial boards of BYU Studies, *Western Historical Quarterly*, and the *Journal of Mormon History*. He and his wife, Marilyn, have three children and eleven grandchildren.

Notes

1. Hebrews 5:4.

2. Matthew 24.

3. Karen Lynn Davidson, David J. Whittaker, Mark Ashurst-McGee, and Richard L. Jensen, eds., "History, Circa Summer 1832," in *Histories Volume 1: Histories, 1832–1844*, vol. 1 of the Histories series of *The Joseph Smith Papers*, ed. Dean C. Jessee, Ronald K. Esplin, and Richard Lyman Bushman (Salt Lake City: Church Historian's Press, 2012), 11 (hereafter *JSP*, H1).

4. Joseph Smith–History 1:68–72; "History Drafts, 1838–circa 1841," Draft 2, in *JSP*, H1:294.

5. Orson Pratt, *Divine Authority, or the Question, Was Joseph Smith Sent of God?* (1848; repr., Liverpool: R. James, 1851), 4. See also Orson Pratt, "The Question Answered, Was Joseph Smith Sent of God?," *Frontier Guardian*, February 7, 1849.

6. Neal A. Maxwell, "Out of Obscurity," *Ensign*, November 1984, 8–11.

7. Boyd K. Packer, "The Twelve Apostles," *Ensign*, November 1996, 6.

8. Mark Lyman Staker, "Where was the Aaronic Priesthood Restored?: Identifying the Location of John the Baptist's Appearance, May 15, 1829," *Mormon Historical Studies* 12, no. 2 (Fall 2011): 143–59.

9. *JSP*, H1:16.

10. Oliver Cowdery, *Latter Day Saints' Messenger and Advocate*, 1 (October 1834): 14–16.

11. Oliver Cowdery, letter to W. W. Phelps, September 7, 1834, Norton, Ohio, *Messenger and Advocate* 1, no. 1 (October 1834): 15–16.

12. Cowdery, letter to Phelps.

13. "History Drafts, 1838–circa 1841," Draft 2, *JSP*, H1:294.

14. "History Drafts, 1838–circa 1841," Draft 2, *JSP*, H1:294.

15. "History Drafts, 1838–circa 1841," Draft 1, *JSP*, H1:326.

16. In the absence of a priesthood restoration narrative for the Melchizedek Priesthood, the precise date of its restoration is not known. See Larry C. Porter, "Dating the Restoration of the Melchizedek Priesthood," *Ensign*, June 1979, 4–10, for a discussion of localizing the lesser and greater priesthood reception dates to 1829. See also D. Michael Quinn, *The Mormon Hierarchy: Origins of Power* (Salt Lake City: Signature Books, 1994), 14–26; and Richard Lyman Bushman, *Joseph Smith: Rough Stone Rolling* (New York: Alfred A. Knopf, 2005), 116–18, for the argument that the Melchizedek Priesthood restoration occurred after the Church was organized in April 1830.

17. Reuben Miller, journal, October 21, 1848, Church History Library, Salt Lake City (hereafter CHL).

18. Oliver Cowdery, letter to Phineas Young, March 23, 1846, Tiffin, Seneca County, Ohio, CHL.

19. Reuben Miller, journal, October 21, 1848, CHL.

20. "History Drafts, 1838–circa 1841," Draft 1, *JSP*, H1:326.

21. See D&C 29:7; 33:6–12.

22. See D&C 88:119.

23. See Matthew 17.

24. Dean C. Jessee, Mark Ashurst-McGee, and Richard L. Jensen, eds., "Joseph Smith, journal, April 3, 1836," in *Journals, Volume 1: 1832–1839*, vol. 1 of the Journals series of *The Joseph Smith Papers*, ed. Dean C. Jessee, Ronald K. Esplin, and Richard Lyman Bushman (Salt Lake City: Church Historian's Press, 2008), 219–22 (hereafter *JSP*, J1).

25. D&C 128:18.

26. "Letter from Joseph Smith," *Times and Seasons*, October 1, 1842, 935–36; emphasis added. This letter became part of the 1876 edition of the Doctrine and Covenants as section 128 and was canonized in an 1880 Latter-day Saint general conference. The cited language can be found in verses 18, 20–21.

27. "History Drafts, 1838–circa 1841," Draft 2, *JSP*, H1:294.

28. Alma 12:9.

29. Moses 1:42; Moses 4:32.

30. "Joseph Smith, journal, November 12, 1835," in *JSP*, J1:98; clear text transcription, punctuation and capitalization standardized.

31. Joseph F. Smith, "Recollections of the Prophet," in *Collected Discourses*, 5 vols., comp. and ed. Brian H. Stuy (Burbank and Woodland Hills, CA: B.H.S. Publishing, 1987–92), 5:27–29.

32. See D&C 121:31.

7

Isaiah in the Book of Mormon

Kent P. Jackson

*E*ARLY IN THE NARRATIVE OF THE BOOK OF MORMON, THE PROPHET Nephi was led by revelation to obtain an ancient record he called the plates of brass. It contained "the five books of Moses," "a record of the Jews from the beginning," and "the prophecies of the holy prophets" down to his own time.[1] It was the Old Testament as it existed in Nephi's day, only it was larger than what we have of that record now.[2] Book of Mormon authors quoted liberally from the writings of Isaiah that they found on the plates of brass. Those quotations play an important role in the book's message, but they have also attracted the attention of critics of the Book of Mormon for two reasons: First, the Isaiah sections appear to be straight out of the King James translation, with minor variations. Second, some of the chapters of Isaiah in the Book of Mormon are considered by scholars to have been written not by Isaiah but by other prophets who wrote after the time Lehi left Jerusalem. Some critical writers have attempted to exploit these two issues, but neither can bring the Book of Mormon's authenticity into question. As we examine the issue of Isaiah authorship and the process by which the Nephite record was translated, we can see that there are sound arguments in defense of the Isaiah material in the Book of Mormon.

Nephi set the pattern, later followed by other Book of Mormon authors, of quoting from the plates of brass. When he did, his emphasis was on passages that taught God's covenant with Israel and the promises God made with members of that family. Nephi's own sense of identity was that he and his people were a branch of a large tree. It was true that they were separated from Israel's main trunk, but they were nonetheless still part of the family, and they were heirs to its inheritance.³ To teach that message to his descendants, Nephi transcribed many prophecies of Isaiah into his own record, and Jacob did the same. Between them, they placed all or parts of twenty-four chapters of Isaiah into the Book of Mormon.⁴

The Book of Mormon's use of Isaiah is instructive and very interesting to Latter-day Saints. But it would not be a point of controversy except for the two issues mentioned above: the King James language and the presence of chapters thought to have been written after Lehi's time.

KING JAMES LANGUAGE IN BOOK OF MORMON ISAIAH

There is no question that the Isaiah passages in the Book of Mormon are in the language of the King James translation of the Bible. It seems that if Nephi had copied them from the plates of brass in Hebrew onto his own record and that if Joseph Smith had then received the English translation by the gift and power of God, the Isaiah passages would read more like the 1830 Book of Mormon and less like the 1611 King James Bible. After all, Nephi and Isaiah were native speakers of the same language, so one might expect that Isaiah in the Book of Mormon would resemble Nephi more than it does. Instead, the Book of Mormon Isaiah passages reproduce most of the King James wording intact and include archaic vocabulary from the King James text instead of using the "plain"⁵ words that are more characteristic of the English of the Book of Mormon. Latter-day Saint scholars are well aware of this and have explored different explanations for it.⁶

One possibility that has been proposed is that during the translation process, the Prophet and Oliver Cowdery, his scribe, simply transcribed the Isaiah text out of a printed copy of the King James Bible. According to this point of view, when Joseph Smith came to Isaiah material, recognizing that equivalent text was in the Bible, he dictated from the pages of a printed Bible rather than translating the material anew, making changes to the text when necessary. The idea here is that because there was already a usable translation available in English, there was no need to make a new one of the same material.⁷

The value of this proposal is that it explains why there is verbatim King James text in the Book of Mormon. And we now know of other examples where the Prophet did essentially the same thing with a translation. When he came to Isaiah 29 while working on his New Translation of the Bible (the Joseph Smith Translation), he simply copied 2 Nephi 27 from the 1830 Book of Mormon—Nephi's recitation of Isaiah 29—onto the pages of his Bible translation.⁸

But recent research on the translation process has raised some questions about this explanation. For one thing, none of those who witnessed the translation process mentioned a Bible being used. BYU professor Royal Skousen's study of the Book of Mormon manuscripts has led him to conclude, based on textual evidence, that the Prophet did not have a Bible with him while working on the translation. He includes as evidence the fact that the Isaiah material on the Book of Mormon manuscripts is not divided into the Bible's chapter divisions but into larger, content-based units. This suggests to him that a printed King James Bible was not involved in the process of translating the Isaiah passages in the Book of Mormon.[9]

Latter-day Saints come to various conclusions on why the Book of Mormon's Isaiah passages are in the form of the King James translation. It is a question asked by sincere seekers of understanding, and better explanations may yet be found. For now, I would propose the following in response to the question:

1. Because it was the common Bible in the English language in 1830, accepted by virtually all English-speaking believers, God intended the Book of Mormon's Isaiah passages to be in the words of the King James translation. Today we may look at this as an oddity or an anachronism, but that would not have been the case among many of Joseph Smith's contemporary readers. Having biblical texts in the Book of Mormon in different wording than they knew from the Bible may have hurt the book's credibility in the eyes of many potential converts.
2. We cannot rule out the possibility that the Prophet drew passages from a printed Bible.
3. Joseph Smith did not *translate* the Book of Mormon. The evidence both from the original manuscript and from the earliest witnesses is clear that the words of the translation were shown to him by revelation. He *saw* them in the interpreters and dictated to his scribes the words he saw.[10] If the Prophet did not read and dictate the Isaiah passages from a printed Bible, then they were shown to him visibly in the interpreters. And, by divine design, they were shown in the form of the common Bible of his time and place—the King James translation.

Authorship of Isaiah

A second major question is sometimes raised about the Isaiah material in the Book of Mormon. Some scholars believe that some of the chapters of the current book of Isaiah were not written by that prophet but by one or more different authors long after Isaiah's time—in fact, after the time that Lehi and his family left Jerusalem. So how could those chapters have been on the plates of brass and included in the record of Nephi before they were even written?[11]

From the outset, it must be made clear that multiple-authorship theories for the book of Isaiah have no support from any ancient manuscripts or traditions. The earliest known translation of Isaiah (the Greek Septuagint) is from the third century BC, and it includes all the material now found in the book of Isaiah. The same is true of the earliest existing manuscript of Isaiah, from the second century BC, found among the Dead Sea Scrolls. No ancient document—including the New Testament and the rabbinic literature—shows any hint that readers in antiquity questioned Isaiah's authorship of the entire book. Some modern scholars, however, see features within the text of the book that cause them to conclude that in its present state, it is not the product of one author but of two, three, or perhaps more.[12]

Here is the most common system for dividing the book:

"First" Isaiah—Chapters 1–39: From Isaiah son of Amoz, ca. 740–700 BC. This includes chapters 1–35 plus an excerpt from 2 Kings that is found in chapters 36–39.

"Second" Isaiah—Chapters 40–55: From an anonymous prophet during the Jews' exile in Babylonia, ca. 540 BC.[13]

"Third" Isaiah—Chapters 56–66: From one or more anonymous disciples of "Second" Isaiah after the return of the Jews from exile, ca. 515 BC. Some commentators include these chapters under "Second" Isaiah. According to the proponents of multiple authorship, the anonymous "Second" and "Third" Isaiah materials became attached to the writings of Isaiah because the succeeding writers were of the same school of thought as Isaiah, and the entire collection was viewed as representing one specific branch of prophetic tradition. Scholars who hold to the theory generally do so for the following major reasons:

1. "First" Isaiah mentions Isaiah son of Amoz and provides biographical material regarding him and others of his time. These chapters clearly fit within the period of time in which they purport to have been written, in the late eighth century BC. The prophecies in "Second" and "Third" Isaiah, on the other hand, make no mention of Isaiah's name and give no other biographical clues that would link them to him.
2. Most scripture has a historical setting that is recognizable, to some degree, in how the text is written and what it emphasizes. The historical setting of "Second" and "Third" Isaiah is different from that of "First" Isaiah. This is seen in the following examples: (a) Cyrus, a Persian king who lived over a century after Isaiah, is mentioned by name; (b) emphasis is placed on the power of the Babylonians, who in Isaiah's day were neither powerful nor very important for the Israelites; (c) the cities of Judah and the temple in Jerusalem are already described as being destroyed, seemingly reflecting circumstances a century after Isaiah; (d) the Judahites are described as already being punished and exiled, which took place after 586 BC.
3. The theological perspective is different between the early chapters and the later chapters. Chapters 1–35 place much emphasis on

judgment, and the later chapters place greater emphasis on forgiveness and reconciliation.
4. The literary style of chapters 40–66 differs from that of the earlier chapters.

Latter-day Saint scholars agree that the observations presented above, for the most part, represent accurately the change in tone that begins in Isaiah 40. Scholars who believe in the essential unity of the book acknowledge the changes, but they do not see them as grounds for denying the material in chapters 40–66 to Isaiah son of Amoz. If the Book of Mormon did not quote from "Second" Isaiah, the discussion of authorship would have little meaning for Latter-day Saints; it would not matter to us either way. But because there is material after chapter 39 in the Book of Mormon, the issue is important.

A Scriptural Perspective

There are legitimate academic arguments for the unity of the book of Isaiah. But even more importantly, there are sound reasons for rejecting the assumptions of those who insist that the Isaiah chapters in the Book of Mormon could not have been written before Lehi's time.

Prophetic Biography

While it is true that Isaiah's name is never mentioned after chapter 39, neither do the later chapters ascribe authorship to anyone else. The lack of biographical inferences does not argue either for or against Isaiah as the author. Almost all of the sixteen prophetic books in the Old Testament identify the author by name at the beginning of the book.[14] This is true of Isaiah, in that the entire sixty-six chapters of the book are under one heading: "The vision of Isaiah the son of Amoz, which he saw concerning Judah and Jerusalem in the days of Uzziah, Jotham, Ahaz, and Hezekiah, kings of Judah."[15] Nowhere are there different headings to tell readers otherwise, and because the book has been a unified whole as far back as its existence can be traced, the burden of proof is on those who choose to assign the later chapters to other ancient writers.

Speaking to a Later Generation

The material in chapters 40–66 does seem to address, to a degree, historical circumstances different from those of Isaiah's day. Because envisioning multiple settings is a characteristic of much prophetic writing in the Old Testament, the matter is hardly unique to Isaiah. In the Book of Mormon, we find a similar situation. President Ezra Taft Benson reminded the Church that the Book of Mormon "was written for our day," echoing the words of the book's authors.[16] Moroni explained, "Behold, I speak unto you as if ye were present, and yet ye are not. But behold, Jesus Christ hath shown you unto me, and I know your doing."[17]

As the Nephite writers saw and understood our time, they also wrote to meet our needs, not exclusively those of their contemporaries, who would never see the Book of Mormon as we have it. In the book of Isaiah is a striking parallel: Isaiah saw and understood the circumstances of his countrymen beyond his own lifetime, and through the inspiration of heaven he wrote in their behalf, as he also did for his contemporaries. He also saw our own latter-day setting, and the powerful witness that he left in his record speaks to our generation as well, when appropriately "likened" to us.[18]

From Judgment to Reconciliation

There is indeed a significant shift in tone and subject matter that begins in chapter 40, and the shift was deliberate. In the prophetic books of the Old Testament, as a general rule, prophecies of judgment and punishment precede those of blessing and restoration. This is true within individual prophecies and chapters as it is in the organization of entire books. This order of things mirrors real life, particularly the history of the house of Israel. God's judgment would be the inevitable consequence of Israel's rebellion, but in the latter days, Israel would be gathered and restored and would enjoy full reconciliation with God. It seems likely that Isaiah's prophecies were meant to follow the same sequence. We should not be surprised if he prepared two collections of revelations (or if his followers arranged them later). The first collection, chapters 1–35, is the "Book of Judgment." The second collection, chapters 40–66, is the "Book of Reconciliation."[19]

Literary Continuity

Even conservative scholars who argue for the unity of the entire book note some stylistic differences between "First" and "Second" (and "Third") Isaiah. More significant, however, is the fact that even critical scholars who argue for multiple authorship see a great deal of Isaiah son of Amoz throughout the entire collection, pointing to language and themes that were carried on in the later chapters.[20] It is important to note that the vast majority of Isaiah is written in poetry, and Hebrew poetry has sufficient flexibility to allow an author a wide range of literary options. In fact, the literary variations within chapters 1–35 are such that if one wanted to, one could argue for multiple authors within that section alone. Thus arguments defending multiple authorship based on different literary styles are inconclusive, especially since we do not know the history of Isaiah's words once they left his mouth or his pen.

Prophetic Vision

But the fundamental issue that underlies the idea of multiple authors within the book of Isaiah is not centered on biographical references or literary style.

It is centered on this basic question: Can a prophet see beyond his own time? One's answer to the question necessarily determines whether one can accept the book being in place when Nephi acquired it or whether one must date parts of it to a later time. Those who begin with the assumption that people cannot see beyond their own day must logically conclude that Isaiah could not have written those sections of the book that speak to a different historical setting than his own.

In contrast, those who understand the true nature of revelation and prophetic foresight have no trouble with prophecies of future events. Latter-day Saints are blessed with abundant revealed evidence that God can indeed inspire his servants with views of future days. The Book of Mormon provides us with ample proof of that.

For me, the evidence that matters most is the reality of the Book of Mormon. It is a record of people who left Jerusalem in 600 BC that contains excerpts from both "First" and "Second" Isaiah. Thus the passages Lehi and his sons quoted in the Book of Mormon must be dated before their departure, and those revelations were identified then to be the writings of Isaiah, decades before "Second" Isaiah was supposed to have been written. This is the most important piece of evidence for Isaiah's authorship of later chapters.

But we must be careful to understand what we can and cannot conclude from the available evidence. From "Second" Isaiah on the plates of brass, the Book of Mormon attests only to chapters 48–51, 53, and a few verses of chapters 40 and 55.[21] The Book of Mormon thus makes no statement regarding the other chapters and cannot be used as proof that all of "Second" Isaiah comes from Isaiah son of Amoz. In this context, it should be noted that the passage mentioning the Persian King Cyrus (Isaiah 44:28) is not included in the Nephite record. Also, because the Book of Mormon's Isaiah quotations do not include anything from "Third" Isaiah (chapters 56–66), it cannot tell us anything about the history and authorship of those chapters.

Latter-day Saints who accept the evidence from the Book of Mormon and believe that prophets can see beyond their own time should have no difficulty accepting the idea that the Isaiah chapters in the Book of Mormon were compiled before 600 BC. But this does not mean that all our questions have been answered. The great Old Testament scholar W. F. Albright pointed out that the prophetic books are not really books but rather "anthologies of oracles and sermons."[22] This description certainly fits the book of Isaiah. Like the Bible itself, it is a collection. And, as with the Bible, the circumstances under which it was written and compiled are not clearly known. Did Isaiah record his prophecies himself, or did he dictate them to scribes? If they were dictated, was Isaiah responsible for their poetic structure, or were others? Did Isaiah gather and compile the revelations himself, or did others do it—even after his lifetime?[23] Were Isaiah's words edited or reworded by later scribes? Who is responsible for the final order of the prophecies in the book? And what is the book's history in the century between Isaiah's death and Nephi's acquisition of the plates of brass?

The answers to these questions are not critical for our understanding of Isaiah's message. But the questions show us that we cannot speak with certainty on many issues related to how and when the book of Isaiah became what it is today. What we do know is that Lehi and his sons had at least part of the book with them when they left Jerusalem and that Isaiah's words are "great" because "all things that he spake have been and shall be, even according to the words which he spake."[24]

Additional Resources

Harrison, R. K. *Introduction to the Old Testament*, 371–78. Grand Rapids, MI: Eerdmans, 1969.

LaSor, W. S., D. A. Hubbard, and F. W. Bush. *Old Testament Survey*. Grand Rapids, MI: Eerdmans, 1982.

Sperry, Sidney B. "The 'Isaiah Problem' in the Book of Mormon." In *Book of Mormon Compendium*, 493–512. Salt Lake City: Bookcraft, 1968.

Welch, John W. "Authorship of the Book of Isaiah in Light of the Book of Mormon." In *Isaiah in the Book of Mormon*, edited by Donald W. Parry and John W. Welch, 423–37. Provo, UT: FARMS, 1997.

About the Author

Kent P. Jackson has two primary academic interests. The first is the intersection of the Bible and Latter-day Saint history and beliefs. The second is the Middle East—ancient, medieval, and modern. He is a former chair of Near Eastern Studies at the David M. Kennedy Center for International Studies at BYU and former associate dean of Religious Education. He has been a faculty member at the BYU Jerusalem Center for Near Eastern Studies five times. He is the author or editor of several books and has published over a hundred articles.

Notes

1. 1 Nephi 5:11–13.

2. See 1 Nephi 13:23.

3. See 1 Nephi 10:12–14; 15:12–16; 19:24.

4. Nephi and Jacob included all or parts of the following chapters of Isaiah in 1 and 2 Nephi: 2–14, 28–29, 40, 48–51, 55. See Monte S. Nyman, *"Great Are the Words of Isaiah"* (Salt Lake City: Bookcraft, 1980), 283–87.

5. 2 Nephi 31:2–3.

6. See, for example, B. H. Roberts, "Bible Quotations in the Book of Mormon; and Reasonableness of Nephi's Prophecies," *Improvement Era* 7, no. 3 (January 1904): 183–84, 191; Grant Hardy, *Understanding the Book of Mormon: A Reader's Guide* (New York: Oxford University Press, 2010), 66–68.

7. This is the point of view in Roberts, "Bible Quotations," and in Daniel H. Ludlow, *A Companion to Your Study of the Book of Mormon* (Salt Lake City: Deseret Book, 1976), 141–42.

8. See Robert A. Cloward, "Isaiah 29 and the Book of Mormon," in *Isaiah in the Book of Mormon*, ed. Donald W. Parry and John W. Welch (Provo, UT: Foundation for Ancient Research and Mormon Studies), 227–32.

9. See Royal Skousen, "Textual Variants in the Isaiah Quotations in the Book of Mormon," in *Isaiah in the Book of Mormon*, 369–90. The current Bible-matching chapter-and-verse divisions were added in the 1879 edition of the Book of Mormon.

10. Royal Skousen, "How Joseph Smith Translated the Book of Mormon: Evidence from the Original Manuscript," *Journal of Book of Mormon Studies* 7, no. 1 (1998): 22–31; Michael Hubbard MacKay and Gerrit J. Dirkmaat, *From Darkness into Light: Joseph Smith's Translation and Publication of the Book of Mormon* (Provo, UT: Religious Studies Center, 2015), 79–104, 119–39.

11. Latter-day Saint approaches to this question include Sidney B. Sperry, *Book of Mormon Compendium* (Salt Lake City: Bookcraft, 1968), 493–512; John W. Welch, "Authorship of the Book of Isaiah in Light of the Book of Mormon," in *Isaiah in the Book of Mormon*, 423–37.

12. See Joseph Blenkinsopp, *Isaiah 1–39: A New Translation with Introduction and Commentary*, vol. 19 of the Anchor Bible Series (Garden City, NY: Doubleday, 2000), 87; Shalom M. Paul, *Isaiah 40–66: Translation and Commentary* (Grand Rapids, MI: Eerdmans, 2012), 1–3; accessible responses to the issue are provided in W. S. LaSor, D. A. Hubbard, and F. W. Bush, *Old Testament Survey* (Grand Rapids, MI: Eerdmans, 1982), 371–77; R. K. Harrison, *Introduction to the Old Testament* (Grand Rapids, MI: Eerdmans, 1969), 764–80.

13. Some authors also assign chapters 34–35 to "Second" Isaiah. See Marvin A. Sweeney, *TANAK: A Theological and Critical Introduction to the Jewish Bible* (Minneapolis, MN: Fortress, 2012), 270–71.

14. The books of Daniel and Jonah do not begin this way because they are primarily narratives *about* the prophets rather than collections of prophecies. (But see Daniel 7:1; 8:1; 9:2; 10:1–2; 11:1.)

15. Isaiah 1:1.

16. Ezra Taft Benson, "The Book of Mormon—Keystone of Our Religion," *Ensign*, November 1986, 6.

17. Mormon 8:35.

18. See 1 Nephi 19:23.

19. Chapters 36–39, excerpted from 2 Kings 18:13–20:19, provide a bridge between the "Book of Judgment" and the "Book of Reconciliation."

20. See, for example, David Carr, "Reaching for Unity in Isaiah," in *Journal for the Study of the Old Testament* 18, no. 57 (1993): 61–80. Also note the extensive bibliography in notes 3–5.

21. Abinadi's quotation of Isaiah 53 (in Mosiah 14), with the implied criticism of his audience for not understanding that revelation, shows that it was on the plates of brass. Jesus quoted from Isaiah 52 and 54 (3 Nephi 16:18–20; 20:32–45; 22:1–17), but there is no

indication that those revelations were on the plates of brass. See the discussion in Welch, "Authorship of the Book of Isaiah," 433–34.

22. William F. Albright, *From the Stone Age to Christianity: Monotheism and the Historical Process*, 2nd ed. (Garden City, NY: Doubleday/Anchor, 1957), 275.

23. A rabbinic tradition (*Baba Bathra* 15a) states that the book was compiled by "Hezekiah and his company." Hezekiah was the king of Judah during a significant portion of Isaiah's lifetime.

24. 3 Nephi 23:3.

8

THE EXPLANATION-DEFYING BOOK OF ABRAHAM

Kerry Muhlestein

THE BOOK OF ABRAHAM HAS BEEN A SOURCE OF CONTROVERSY SINCE some Egyptologists called its authenticity into question in the mid-nineteenth and early twentieth centuries. Though an initial firestorm brewed after Egyptologists labeled Joseph Smith's interpretation of the facsimiles fraudulent, the furor soon settled. However, criticism about the interpretation's authenticity began again soon after portions of the Joseph Smith papyri were obtained by the Church in the late 1960s. When it was discovered that the text surrounding Facsimile 1 did not match the text in the Book of Abraham, detractors argued that the translation by Egyptologists substantiated their claims that Joseph Smith was a fraud. However, this discovery actually substantiated nothing about how, when, or from what source the Book of Abraham originated. These details continue to unfold as we learn more about Abraham from the existing papyri, the research in the field of Egyptology, and other sources independent of the Bible. While we do not yet fully understand its origins, we are sure that the Book of Abraham provides light and knowledge regarding such matters as the life of Abraham, the premortal existence, and the purpose of our earthly existence.

The Book of Abraham is an amazing book of scripture that continues to defy attempts to explain how or when it came about. As we try to better understand and appreciate it, I have found a useful analogy. At one point physicists were certain all matter could be classified as either a wave or a particle; nothing could be both. The difficulty was that as more and more investigations were conducted, scientists found that some evidence pointed toward light behaving as a particle while other evidence demonstrated that it behaved as a wave. This puzzled scientists. As Albert Einstein stated, "It seems as though we must use sometimes the one theory and sometimes the other, while at times we may use either. We are faced with a new kind of difficulty. We have two contradictory pictures of reality; separately neither of them fully explains the phenomena of light, but together they do."[1] It was only when light was paradoxically accepted as both a particle and a wave that physicists made further progress in understanding it. Similarly, there are many things about the Book of Abraham that do not fit tidily into the little boxes we have created regarding scripture and how it is revealed and recorded. It is a unique type of revelation just as light is a unique type of matter. The Book of Abraham is not typical scripture, so we should not be surprised that it was revealed by unprecedented means. Accepting the Book of Abraham as unique scripture enables readers to embrace its beauty, meaning, and validity.

History of the Papyri

Describing the unusual—even miraculous—nature of the Book of Abraham begins with its discovery. The papyri that sparked its translation were only found because of an exponential increase in excavations in Egypt after the Napoleonic invasion of 1798. As Egypt became more open to western countries and cultures, it experienced several years of large-scale exploration and exploitation, wherein thousands of objects were exported to other countries. During this short time period, some papyri found in Thebes were among the first Egyptian antiquities to arrive in the United States, working their way to Kirtland, Ohio, of all places. That such antiquities would show up in a small town and would be presented to an unlearned, upstart religious leader in July of 1835, facilitating the revelation of key doctrines concerning covenants, premortality, the purpose of life, and creation, is astonishing.

Upon receiving the papyri, Joseph Smith immediately began translating, proclaiming the papyri contained the writings of Joseph of Egypt and of Abraham. The Prophet spent time translating in July, focusing his attention on the writings of Abraham. He stopped in August and September in order to take care of Church business and then began translation again in October. In both July and October, Joseph Smith, Oliver Cowdery, and W. W. Phelps also tried to create an Egyptian Alphabet and Grammar. In November the Prophet spent a few weeks intensively working on the translation. As December began, the opportunity to begin a formal study of Hebrew arose, and all efforts to translate Egyptian or create a guide to Egyptian grammar were abandoned as they undertook Hebrew.

During the following years, Joseph often expressed a desire to do more translation of the papyri, but he was not able to do so seriously until 1842 when he became the editor of the Church's newspaper *Times and Seasons*. In early March of 1842 he used that newspaper to publish Facsimile 1 and

Abraham 1:1–2:18. He spent a few days in March translating the papyri and then, later in that month, published Facsimile 2 and the rest of the Book of Abraham that we now have. In May he published Facsimile 3. He said that he would publish more of the Book of Abraham but did not do so before he was killed.

After Joseph Smith was martyred, his mother, Lucy Mack Smith, inherited the papyri. She supported herself by charging people to see them and the mummies Joseph had acquired at the time he purchased the papyri. When Lucy died, Emma Smith inherited the antiquities and quickly sold them. The new owner, Abel Combs, sold most of the papyri and mummies to the St. Louis Museum, which sold them to a museum in Chicago that burned in the Great Chicago Fire of 1871. The mummies and papyri in the museum were destroyed by the fire.

While it was not known at the time, Abel Combs had not sold all of his papyri to the St. Louis Museum. He had given a small collection of mounted fragments to his housekeeper. This housekeeper's descendants later sold them to the Metropolitan Museum of Art in New York City. In 1967, the Church of Jesus Christ of Latter-day Saints acquired the papyri from the museum. The resurfacing of these papyrus fragments reignited interest in the Book of Abraham and its translation.

Which Papyri Were Translated?

Because it was almost universally assumed that all of the papyri Joseph Smith had once owned had been destroyed in the Great Chicago Fire, many were surprised when the papyri resurfaced in 1967. The fragment that drew the most interest was the one that contained the vignette or drawing that was the original source of Facsimile 1.[2] Part of the reason this fragment drew so much attention was because of the possibilities it presented. It seemed that perhaps we could now test Joseph Smith's revelatory abilities. Many members of the Church *assumed* that the text on the papyri that surrounded the original of Facsimile 1 was the source of the Book of Abraham. It seemed this might give them the chance to demonstrate Joseph Smith's translating abilities. Anti-Mormons also *assumed* that the text adjacent to that drawing was the source of the Book of Abraham and were excited about the opportunity to disprove Joseph Smith's prophetic abilities.[3] Sadly, neither of these groups took the time to carefully examine their assumptions. Thus, when the text was translated and was found to be a fairly common Egyptian funerary document called the Book of Breathings, many felt they could now demonstrate that Joseph Smith was not an inspired prophet. This, probably more than anything, has caused confusion regarding the Book of Abraham. Much of this confusion comes because so many don't even realize they have made an assumption about the source of the Book of Abraham. For them, it is simply a given that Joseph Smith translated the text adjacent to Facsimile 1 as the Book of Abraham.

So how could we test this assumption? The first step would be to examine the text itself to see if it contains any clues about its relationship with its associated pictures. The second would be to examine similar papyri from the same time period to see if the texts and their vignettes were typically adjacent to each other. The third way to test this assumption would be to examine the accounts of eyewitnesses who saw the papyri and knew from what material Joseph Smith said he was translating. Of course, modern speculations about the role of the extant papyri in the translation of the Book of Abraham would be less important than evidence from eyewitnesses.[4]

A test of these assumptions provides some useful insight. A study of the text reveals that Abraham 1:12 and 14 refer to the drawing known as Facsimile 1. Yet they refer to the drawing as being "at the beginning" of the text, which strongly suggests that it was not right next to the text. Thus, test one—examining the text itself—indicates that the drawing is probably not adjacent to the text.[5] Examining similar papyri from the same period reveals a similar pattern. Frequently, the drawing associated with a text is not adjacent to the text. Consequently, the second test indicates that the assumption may or may not be true but makes it clear that we are not safe in assuming that the text adjacent to Facsimile 1 is by default the source of the Book of Abraham.

When reading accounts of eyewitnesses who saw the papyri and heard from Joseph Smith or his close companions about them, we learn that most of these people say nothing at all about the source of the Book of Abraham. When they do, they refer to a distinct portion of the papyri, identified as the long roll, which was burned in the Great Chicago Fire, as that source.[6] Therefore, the long roll, not portions now in our possession, was identified as the source of the Book of Abraham by Joseph's contemporaries. To argue otherwise would be to argue against the historical record. Although the relationship between what was written on the physical papyri known as the long roll and what was recorded as the Book of Abraham is not clear, we can say that the text adjacent to Facsimile 1, which we now have in our possession, was not the source.

What was Joseph Smith's Translation Process?

Questions about *what* Joseph Smith was translating naturally lead to asking *how* he translated. For most people, the idea of translating is fairly straightforward. Conventionally, translators read a document in one language they understand and render it into another language they understand. The difficulty in assessing the Book of Abraham is that while Joseph Smith says he "translated" the Book of Abraham, he hardly ever used that word in the conventional way. Therefore, it will be helpful to first look at the other ways Joseph Smith used the word *translate*.

Joseph Smith's first translation project was the Book of Mormon. It was written in a language he clearly did not claim to know. Instead, he said he was given the ability to translate by the gift and power of God. We don't know a lot about the Book of Mormon translation process. We know that the Prophet used the seer stones we call the Urim and Thummim, as well as another seer stone he found in his youth. While the exact details are unknown, it seems he often was not looking at the gold plates at all when translating. Therefore, Joseph Smith translated a document written in a language he didn't know into a language he did know (English) without looking at the physical text that recorded the unknown language.

Joseph's next translation project took place while he was in the midst of finishing the Book of Mormon translation. As he and Oliver Cowdery asked a question, the Prophet was shown in vision a parchment written on by John.[7] Again, it was written in a language Joseph Smith did not understand. This time he never physically saw the words he translated—he only saw a document in vision. In fact, it is not clear whether or not he even saw the words written on the parchment. It is possible that he did and at the same time was given the translation of those words. However, it is also possible that he may have seen that the parchment existed and then had the translation of it come to him after the vision.

The Prophet's third translation had very little to do with what most people call *translating*. He studied an English version of the Bible and provided us with another English version of the text that contained a *translation* of things that enhanced the text. Although he called it the "New Translation of the Bible," we call it the Joseph Smith Translation. In this case, the text came to him as pure revelation and was not dependent at all on the physical text he had in front of him. This process began about two months after Joseph Smith published the Book of Mormon.

The next translation project was the Book of Abraham, which the Prophet began in 1835, several years after he had started working on his "New Translation of the Bible." This process began after he acquired some Egyptian papyri, as outlined earlier. While some later confidants of the Prophet spoke of his using the Urim and Thummim while translating,[8] the exact nature of this process is unknown. There is no doubt that the translation was spurred on by the physical possession of the papyri, although he certainly did not know the original language of the text. It is also clear that Joseph Smith and many of the Saints spoke of the writings of Abraham being on the papyri, intimating that the process may have been similar to the translation of the gold plates.

At the same time, some clues suggest there was something of a revelatory process akin to that which the Prophet utilzed in the translation of the Bible.

For example, in Joseph Smith's journal it is recorded, "This after noon labored on the Egyptian alphabet, in company with [Bros.] O[liver] Cowdery and W[illiam] W. Phelps: The system of astronomy was unfolded."[9] Perhaps this refers to the Prophet's coming to understand the meaning of Facsimile 2 or translating Abraham 3. Either way, the language suggests a revelatory experience in which the papyrus served only as some kind of catalyst for the revelation of the English text. Joseph's mother reported that he could translate portions of the papyrus that had been broken off, comparing his ability to translate to Daniel's ability to interpret a dream he was not told about.[10]

Based on the Prophet's translation history and the evidence we have, there seems to be at least four possible scenarios for the translation process:

1. By the power of God, Joseph Smith translated a text that was written on the long scroll of papyri by Abraham.
2. As Joseph opened his mind to God because of his curiosity about the text on the papyri, he received revelation about an ancient text not on the papyri but written by Abraham.
3. Joseph received revelation from God "about key events and teachings in the life of Abraham,"[11] unrelated to any specific ancient document, in a revelatory process.
4. A combination of the above choices also seems quite possible, meaning that Joseph translated something on the papyri and received revelation regarding other teachings as well.

Grammar of the Egyptian Alphabet and Language

There is a group of documents that makes understanding the translation process all the more complicated. Joseph Smith and his scribes left behind some sheets of paper they called a Grammar and Alphabet of the Egyptian Language, which contain various Egyptian characters alongside explanations of those characters. A few connected documents bear different titles but contain similar information. They also created a few copies of the text of the Book of Abraham that have some Egyptian characters in the margin. The latter characters seem to come from the fragments of papyrus that contain Facsimile 1. Some have postulated that Joseph Smith used the Egyptian Alphabet to translate the characters on the Book of Abraham manuscripts and that this was both the source of the Book of Abraham and the method of its translation.

If this explanation were true, it would certainly simplify the questions we have been trying to answer. Unfortunately, this theory does not fit the evidence we have. As we look at the Egyptian Alphabet, it is clear that Joseph Smith, Oliver Cowdery, and W. W. Phelps were products of their time when it came to their knowledge of Egyptian. In the early nineteenth century, the Egyptian language was in the process of being deciphered by scholars such as the Frenchman Jean-François Champollion and others, but many people thought that Egyptian was a cryptic language, with each character conveying varied meanings based on the amount of knowledge possessed by the reader. It was only after Egyptologists gained the ability to translate Egyptian using conventional methods that this notion about the language was dispelled. The Prophet and his colleagues were just hoping to figure out something that worked. Nevertheless, they failed, producing a document that makes little sense. This is not surprising considering none of the authors claimed to know or understand Egyptian and the translation of Egyptian characters had stumped scholars for centuries.

Yet some have supposed that the Egyptian Alphabet was the tool used to create the translation. In order to assess whether this could be the case or not, I conducted research to test the assumption. First, I located all of the phrases in the Egyptian Alphabet that also appear in the Book of Abraham. I then compared the Egyptian characters next to those phrases to the Egyptian characters adjacent to the matching lines in the early Book of Abraham manuscripts. Of the twenty-one times I found text in the Egyptian Alphabet that matched text in the Book of Abraham, I found only one time that the corresponding Egyptian characters matched, four times when part of the characters matched, and sixteen times in which there was no match whatsoever. Clearly the Egyptian alphabet was not used to translate the papyri, nor is there any demonstrable relationship between the characters on the papyri and the text of the Book of Abraham. This is not surprising since the characters come from fragments of papyri that eyewitnesses noted were not the source of the Book of Abraham.

How Do Joseph Smith's Interpretations Compare to Modern Discoveries?

Many people ask how Joseph Smith's explanations of the facsimiles compare to the interpretation an ancient Egyptian would have given that same drawing. This is a question worth asking but not simple to answer. Part of the reason this question is difficult to answer is because it is not necessarily the right question to ask. For example, as we compare Facsimile 1, or any of the facsimiles, with similar Egyptian vignettes, we are probably studying the wrong audience. Maybe we shouldn't be looking at what Egyptians thought the facsimiles meant at all but rather at how Joseph Smith would have viewed them as part of the spiritual interpretation needed in modern times. Or perhaps the Prophet was telling us how a group of ancient Jews would have interpreted the drawings.[12] Another possibility is that he was telling us how a small group of Egyptian priests who were collecting biblical stories would have interpreted the drawings. At this time in history, we know there was mutual adopting of religious figures between the Egyptian and Israelite cultures. The adopted figures would be given new meaning by the fostering religion,[13] which makes it difficult to know what we should compare Joseph Smith's interpretations of the facsimiles to. Sometime vignettes were used later in ways never intended in the original usage.

Typically when people have asked what the Egyptians would say these drawings meant, and how this compares with what Joseph Smith said they meant, they actually end up comparing it to what modern Egyptologists say they mean. This is, of course, understandable because we do not have access to any ancient Egyptians, and we assume modern Egyptologists are reliable replacements. But we know that Egyptologists, including myself, are often wrong regarding what ancient Egyptians would have said on a subject. In fact, one study demonstrated that in the few instances where we have found Egyptian labels about various figures in hypocephali (like Facsimile 2), they hardly ever match up with what Egyptologists said they meant.[14] It can therefore be problematic to look to modern Egyptologists for what ancient Egyptians would have said various drawings represented. Thus any conclusions reached by making such comparisons must be tentative and should not be the basis for any conclusions regarding the larger issues.

Still, what happens when we do compare the facsimiles with Egyptological interpretations? For example, it is tempting to say that Facsimile 1 is a common funerary scene because it has some elements in common with a funerary scene. It is, however, different in many of its elements. It is also clearly not a scene commonly associated with the Book of Breathings, though many have claimed it is. There are actually no other instances of this scene being adjacent to the Book of Breathings, though some continually insist that there are, regardless of lack of evidence to support the claim.[15]

There are elements that make Joseph Smith's interpretation of Facsimile 1 plausible. The story of Abraham's actions and his near sacrifice by a priest associated with Egypt have long caused pause among people who did not believe that the Egyptians practiced human sacrifice. However, we have since learned that they absolutely did.[16] Furthermore, the situations that prompted such action align perfectly well with the story presented in the Book of Abraham and Facsimile 1 because Abraham was trying to disrupt the worship of Egyptian gods, and disruption of official cultic worship was punishable by sacrifice.[17] We also know that in the international religious amalgamation some Egyptian priests were engaged in, they did sometimes associate a somewhat similar scene with Abraham.[18]

There are a number of elements in Facsimile 1 that do match well with what Joseph Smith said the drawing represented.[19] Do all of Joseph Smith's interpretations of Facsimile 1 match up with either a standard Egyptological interpretation or with one that has been demonstrated through more specialized research? No. Neither do all the elements of the vignette match with what Egyptologists would say about the representations. Clearly we have progress yet to make in arriving at both a better Latter-day Saint interpretation and an Egyptological understanding of this drawing.

This is also true of Facsimile 2. Again, many elements of Joseph Smith's interpretations do not align well with an Egyptological point of view;[20] however, a surprising amount are supported by good Egyptological research.[21] Additionally, using the kind of drawing represented in Facsimile 2, a hypocephalus, in such a way is strikingly similar to the use of the zodiac in synagogues in Roman Palestine, such as at Sepphoris or Bet Alpha. In these cases, ancient Jews took a Greek representation of the cosmos (Facsimile 2 is an Egyptian representation of the cosmos) and used it in a uniquely Jewish fashion with a uniquely Jewish interpretation, just as it appears is happening with Facsimile 2. Moreover, some ancient Egyptians associated Abraham with this kind of drawing.[22] Again, while none of these things prove that Joseph Smith was correct, they do demonstrate plausibility.

Facsimile 3 is similar. It has received the least amount of scholarly study and attention,[23] so it has the smallest amount of disagreement or agreement attached to it. There are some elements I do not understand from either an Egyptological or a Latter-day Saint point of view. Yet we do know that this very type of drawing was associated with Abraham by some ancient Egyptians.[24]

Egyptian and Jewish Religious Representations in the Facsimiles and the Book of Abraham

This discussion leads to one striking observation. While the international culture in Egypt at the time the papyri were created was such that we should expect *many* Egyptian religious representations to be correlated to Jewish religious elements, we should not expect that *every* Egyptian religious representation would be. Yet each of the three Egyptian representations, or facsimiles, Joseph Smith said were associated with Abraham actually *was* associated with him by ancient Egyptians. While this does not prove the Prophet to be a prophet, it does defy other proposed explanations. Critics who are quick to point out understandable inconsistencies with his explanations of the facsimiles do not even try to deal with these significant instances of consistency. This is true of studies about the Book of Abraham as a whole as well. While plausible explanations have been proposed that account for the inconsistencies, besides acknowledging the power of God, no plausible explanations have been posed for the many striking consistencies in the Book of Abraham with nonbiblical traditions regarding Abraham.[25]

A few such traditions that were not known in Joseph Smith's day but which agree with the Book of Abraham are that those who were disrupting the worship of idols in Abraham's society were killed; Abraham prayed for deliverance when he was about to be killed because of his disruption of idol worship; the priest or leader who was trying to kill him was killed instead; Abraham was heir to the priesthood because of his fathers; Abraham possessed a Urim and Thummim; Abraham possessed records of his fathers; there was a famine in Abraham's homeland; and Haran died in the famine.[26] The fact that Joseph Smith did not know of these details, and other similarities from ancient sources, yet they agree so well with ancient sources, is striking.

When we look candidly at the known facts, we are left with a number of elements about the facsimiles and text of the Book of Abraham that are puzzling, a number that are quite plausible, and a number that are compelling. In other words, we are again unable to explain the process using the theories or methods of men. We are forced to admit that, just as we had to adjust our thinking about matter because light behaves as both a particle and a wave, we will have to look for something that goes beyond our current understanding about how scripture is revealed if we are to account for everything we know about the Book of Abraham.

More Study Is Needed

While there are many more fascinating questions surrounding the Book of Abraham and dozens of similarities with known ancient history and literature that we could highlight, space does not permit detailing these things more fully here. What should be clear by now is that the Book of Abraham and the story that surrounds it are amazing. The serendipitous arrival of the papyri in Kirtland in 1835 is hard to accept as mere coincidence. In addition, no theories discussed can account for everything we know about its translation, its source, its similarities to ancient and medieval sources, and, most especially, the power and profoundness of its message.

While people from different backgrounds may disagree regarding some of my assessments, I believe we all can agree that the origin of the Book of Abraham currently defies explanation. It would be unfortunate to make assumptions regarding the things we don't know and then condemn Joseph Smith or the Book of Abraham based upon those assumptions. On the other hand, how interesting it is to explore the mystery of the translation of the Book of Abraham, which continues to reveal answers as it simultaneously elicits further questions. Regardless of how it was received, the Book of Abraham reveals sublime information about the premortal existence, the Creation, the importance of our mortal experience, and many more great and wonderful truths—which is the best evidence of its truthfulness.

Additional Resources

The Church of Jesus Christ of Latter-day Saints. "Translation and Historicity of the Book of Abraham." https://www.lds.org/topics/translation-and-historicity-of-the-book-of-abraham.

Gee, John. "Some Puzzles from the Joseph Smith Papyri." *FARMS Review* 20, no. 1 (2008): 113–37.

Muhlestein, Kerry. *Understanding the Book of Abraham, a Guided Tour*. 3 CDs. Salt Lake City: Covenant Communications, 2013.

———. "Egyptian Papyri and the Book of Abraham: A Faithful, Egyptological Point of View." In *No Weapon Shall Prosper: New Light on Sensitive Issues*, edited by Robert L. Millett, 217–43. Salt Lake City: Deseret Book, 2011.

Tvedtnes, John A., Brian M. Hauglid, and John Gee, comps. and eds. *Traditions about the Early Life of Abraham*. Provo, UT: FARMS, 2001.

About the Author

Kerry Muhlestein received his BS from BYU in psychology with a Hebrew minor. As an undergraduate he spent time at the BYU Jerusalem Center for Near Eastern Studies in the intensive Hebrew program. He received an MA in ancient Near Eastern studies from BYU and his PhD from UCLA in Egyptology. He taught courses in Hebrew and religion part-time at BYU and the UVSC extension center as well as in history at Cal Poly Pomona and UCLA. He also taught early-morning seminary classes and classes at the Westwood (UCLA) Institute of Religion. His first full-time appointment was a joint position in religion and history at BYU–Hawaii. He is the director of the BYU Egypt Excavation Project. He was selected by the *Princeton Review* in 2012 as one of the best 300 professors in the nation (the top .02 percent of those considered). He and his wife, Julianne, are the parents of six children, and together they lived in Jerusalem while Kerry taught there. He has served as the chair of a national committee for the American Research Center in Egypt and serves on their Research Supporting Member Council. He has also served on a committee for the Society for the Study of Egyptian Antiquities and currently serves on their board of trustees and as a vice president of the organization. He is also involved with the International Association of Egyptologists.

Notes

1. David Harrison, "Complementarity and Copenhagen Interpretation of Quantum Mechanics," UPSCALE, http://www.upscale.utoronto.ca/GeneralInterest/Harrison/Complementarity/CompCopen.html.

2. For more information, the reader can listen to a series of lectures by the author, available on CD. Kerry Muhlestein, *Understanding the Book of Abraham, a Guided Tour*, 3 CDs (Salt Lake City: Covenant Communications, 2013).

3. See Jerald and Sandra Tanner, *The Case Against Mormonism* (Salt Lake City: Utah Lighthouse Ministry, 1968), 2:159; 3:330. An example of Latter-day Saint ideas is found in Hugh Nibley, "A New Look at the Pearl of Great Price," *Improvement Era*, January 1968–May 1970; reprinted in Hugh Nibley, *Abraham in Egypt*, 2nd ed. (Provo, UT: FARMS, 2000); Hugh Nibley, *An Approach to the Book of Abraham* (Provo, UT: FARMS, 2009).

4. On the Kirtland Egyptian Papers, see Brian M. Hauglid, *A Textual History of the Book of Abraham: Manuscripts and Editions* (Provo, UT: Neal A. Maxwell Institute for Religious Scholarship, 2010); Brian M. Hauglid, "Thoughts on the Book of Abraham," in *No Weapon Shall Prosper: New Light on Sensitive Issues*, ed. Robert L. Millet (Salt Lake City: Deseret Book, 2011), 242–53.

5. Kerry Muhlestein, "Egyptian Papyri and the Book of Abraham," *Religious Educator* 11, no. 1 (2010): 90–106; Kerry Muhlestein, "Egyptian Papyri and the Book of Abraham: A Faithful, Egyptological Point of View," in *No Weapon Shall Prosper*, 217–41.

6. For some examples, see Charlotte Haven, letter to her mother, February 19, 1843, cited in "A Girl's Letters from Nauvoo," *Overland Monthly*, December 1890, 624; Jerusha W. Blanchard, "Reminiscences of the Granddaughter of Hyrum Smith," *Relief Society Magazine*, September 1922, 9; "M," *Friends' Weekly Intelligencer* 3, no. 27, October 7, 1846, 211. For a summary on this point, see Kerry Muhlestein, "Papyri and Presumptions: A Careful Examination of the Assumptions and Eyewitness Accounts Associated with the Joseph Smith Papyri," *Journal of Mormon History*, forthcoming.

7. See D&C 7.

8. At this point, they referred to the Prophet's seer stone as a Urim and Thummim.

9. Dean C. Jessee, Mark Ashurst-McGee, and Richard L. Jensen, eds., *Journals, Volume 1: 1832–1839*, vol. 1 of the Journals series of *The Joseph Smith Papers*, ed. Dean C. Jessee, Ronald K. Esplin, and Richard Lyman Bushman (Salt Lake City: Church Historian's Press, 2008), 67.

10. William S. West, *A Few Interesting Facts, Respecting the Rise Progress and Pretensions of the Mormons* (N.p.: 1837), 4–5.

11. "Translation and Historicity of the Book of Abraham," The Church of Jesus Christ of Latter-day Saints, https://www.lds.org/topics/translation-and-historicity-of-the-book-of-abraham.

12. Kevin L. Barney, "The Facsimiles and Semitic Adaptation of Existing Sources," in *Astronomy, Papyrus, and Covenant*, ed. John Gee and Brian M. Hauglid (Provo, UT: Brigham Young University, 2006), 107–30.

13. Kerry Muhlestein, "The Religious and Cultural Background of Joseph Smith Papyrus I," *Journal of the Book of Mormon and Other Restoration Scripture* 22, no. 1 (2013): 20–33.

14. John Gee, "Towards an Interpretation of Hypocephali," in *"Le lotus qui sort du terre": Mélanges offerts à Edith Varga*, Bulletin du Musée Hongrois des Beaux-Arts Supplément–2001 (Budapest: Musée Hongrois des Beaux-Arts, 2001), 325–34; Muhlestein, "Egyptian Papyri and the Book of Abraham," 98.

15. Muhlestein, "Egyptian Papyri and the Book of Abraham," 99–100.

16. See Kerry Muhlestein, *Violence in the Service of Order: the Religious Framework for Sanctioned Killing in Ancient Egypt*, British Archaeological Reports International Series 2299 (Oxford: Archaeopress, 2011); and Kerry Muhlestein, "Royal Executions: Evidence Bearing on the Subject of Sanctioned Killing in the Middle Kingdom," in *Journal of the Economic and Social History of the Orient* 15, no. 2 (2008). See also "Death by Water: The Role of Water in Ancient Egypt's Treatment of Enemies and Juridical Process," in *L'AcquaNell'anticoEgitto: Vita, Rigenerazione, Incantesimo, Medicamento*, ed. Alessia Amenta, Michela Luiselli, and

Maria Novella Sordi (Rome: L'Erma di Bretschneider, 2005), 173–79; Kerry Muhlestein, "Smashing, Stomping and Spitting: The Protection of Egypt through the Execration Ritual," lecture, Society for the Study of Egyptian Antiquities Annual Scholars Colloquium, Royal Ontario Museum and University of Toronto, November 2007.

17. Kerry Muhlestein and John Gee, "Egyptian Middle Kingdom Contexts for Human Sacrifice," in *Journal of Book of Mormon and Other Restoration Scripture* 2, no. 2 (2011): 70–77; Muhlestein, "Egyptian Papyri and the Book of Abraham," 216–43.

18. See John Gee, "Research and Perspectives: Abraham in Ancient Egyptian Texts," *Ensign*, July 1992, 60–62; and John Gee, "References to Abraham Found in Two Egyptian Texts," *Insights: An Ancient Window* (September 1991): 1, 3.

19. See Muhlestein, "Egyptian Papyri and the Book of Abraham," 90–106; and Muhlestein, "A Faithful, Egyptological Point of View," 217–41.

20. On the Egyptological point of view, see John Gee, "Towards an Interpretation of Hypocephali," 325–34.

21. Michael D. Rhodes, "The Joseph Smith Hypocephalus . . . Twenty Years Later" (Provo, UT: FARMS, 1994). See also John Gee, "Some Puzzles from the Joseph Smith Papyri," *FARMS Review* 20, no. 1 (2008): 136.

22. See Rhodes, "The Joseph Smith Hypocephalus."

23. John Gee, "Facsimile 3 and the Book of the Dead 125," in *Astronomy, Papyrus, and Covenant*, 95–106.

24. John Gee, "A New Look at the *ankh p' by* Formula," in *Proceedings of IXe Congroes International des Études Démotiques*, Paris, 31 août–3 septembre 2005, ed. Ghislaine Widmer and Didier Devauchelle (Cairo: Institut Français Archéologie Orientale, 2009), 133–44.

25. John A. Tvedtnes, Brian M. Hauglid, and John Gee, comps. and eds., *Traditions about the Early Life of Abraham* (Provo, UT: FARMS, 2001), xxii.

26. Information compiled by Bethany Jensen using Tvedtnes, Hauglid, and Gee, *Traditions about the Early Life of Abraham*.

9

Joseph Smith and the Kinderhook Plates

Don Bradley and Mark Ashurst-McGee

In the spring of 1843, a group of men dug into an Indian mound near Kinderhook, Illinois—about seventy-five miles downriver from Nauvoo. Several feet into the mound, they found human bones and a set of six brass plates covered with inscriptions. These "Kinderhook plates" were soon brought to Nauvoo. The official History of the Church *records that Joseph Smith examined the plates and translated from them. Many years later, two of the men present when the plates were uncovered revealed that the plates had been a hoax. The leader of the excavation had made the plates with some help from the village blacksmith and planted them in the mound just prior to their discovery. In 1980, the one surviving plate was examined and determined to be a modern forgery. This finding has been used to impugn Joseph's credibility as a prophet and translator of ancient scripture. The argument, however, ignores the historical context of Joseph Smith's personal interest in languages. A close investigation of the episode indicates that his "translation" from the Kinderhook plates was an attempt at traditional translation. He had not attempted a translation with divine aid, as he had with the Book of Mormon and the Book of Abraham, and he did not lead others to believe he had. His incorrect translation of the Kinderhook plates was simply a mistake—something he had never thought himself above.*

Robert Wiley, known as a "respectable merchant" in the small village of Kinderhook, Illinois, told others that he had dreamed three nights in a row that there was treasure buried in one of the nearby Indian mounds.[1] Wiley dug down several feet into a mound and uncovered "a flat rock that sounded hollow beneath."[2] On April 23, 1843, he gathered several others with him to remove the stone and see what lay beneath.[3]

When the stone was removed, the group found human bones and a set of six brass plates, each bell-shaped and nearly three inches in height. There was a hole near the top of each plate and a ring that connected them together—although the ring quickly broke and the plates were removed from it. The plates were covered with inscriptions—both illustrations and what appeared to be an ancient language.[4] At the time of the discovery, there were two local Latter-day Saints among the crowd. Wilbur Fugate recounted that when the plates were discovered, one of the Latter-day Saints "leaped and shouted for joy."[5]

It is not hard to guess why this Latter-day Saint jumped for joy. The Church of Jesus Christ of Latter-day Saints rests on the claims of Joseph Smith that an angel revealed to him the location of an ancient record, inscribed on plates of gold, and that God had given him power to translate the language on the plates, known as the Book of Mormon.[6] The plates found near Kinderhook could be seen as providing evidence for the golden plates of the Book of Mormon.

The plates were soon brought to Nauvoo and shown to Joseph Smith by a man named Moore. This was apparently George Moore, a Unitarian minister based in Quincy, Illinois—located between Kinderhook and Nauvoo.[7] Joseph Smith kept them at his house for a few days and attempted to translate a part of them. Under the date of May 1, 1843, the official *History of the Church* reads: "I [Joseph Smith] insert fac-similes of the six brass plates found near Kinderhook, in Pike county, Illinois, on April 23, by Mr. Robert Wiley and others, while excavating a large mound [the history includes images of the facsimiles].... I have translated a portion of them, and find they contain the history of the person with whom they were found. He was a descendant of Ham, through the loins of Pharaoh, king of Egypt, and that he received his kingdom from the Ruler of heaven and earth."[8]

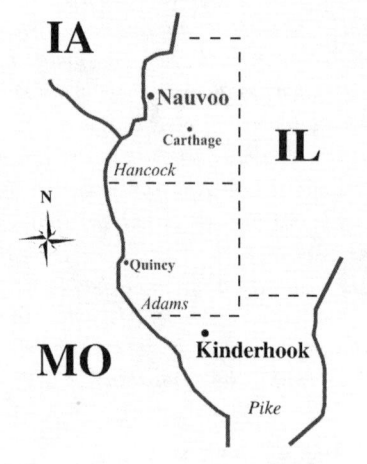

Western Illinois. Courtesy of Brian Hales.

Apostles John Taylor and Wilford Woodruff, publishers of both the *Times and Seasons* (the Church newspaper) and the *Nauvoo Neighbor* (the

Two sides of the surviving Kinderhook plate. Courtesy of Chicago History Museum.

city newspaper), printed an article in both papers about the discovery of the plates.[9] They also published a broadside with facsimiles of the twelve sides of the six Kinderhook plates. The broadside declared, "The contents of the Plates, together with a Fac-Simile of the same, will be published in the 'Times and Seasons,' as soon as the translation is completed."[10]

During the pioneer period of Mormon history, Apostle Orson Pratt and other Latter-day Saint authors occasionally republished the facsimiles and information about the plates as evidence for the reality of the golden plates of the Book of Mormon. These members clearly believed the plates were authentic.[11]

THE KINDERHOOK PLATES ARE FORGERIES

Toward the end of the nineteenth century, suspicions began to arise regarding the authenticity of the plates. In the 1870s, Wilbur Fugate, one of the men who unearthed the plates, wrote letters revealing that the plates were part of a hoax. He claimed that he, Robert Wiley, and the village blacksmith had made the plates, and he had planted them in the mound the night before their discovery. One of Fugate's letters was published in an anti-Mormon book in 1886.[12] In 1912, the Illinois State Historical Society published an earlier letter written by W. P. Harris, also present when the plates were unearthed, confirming what Fugate had written. Harris's 1855 letter said he had initially believed in the discovery but later discovered that it was a prank.[13]

For over a century now, critics of Mormonism have been publicizing this evidence—insisting that if the plates are fraudulent, then Joseph Smith

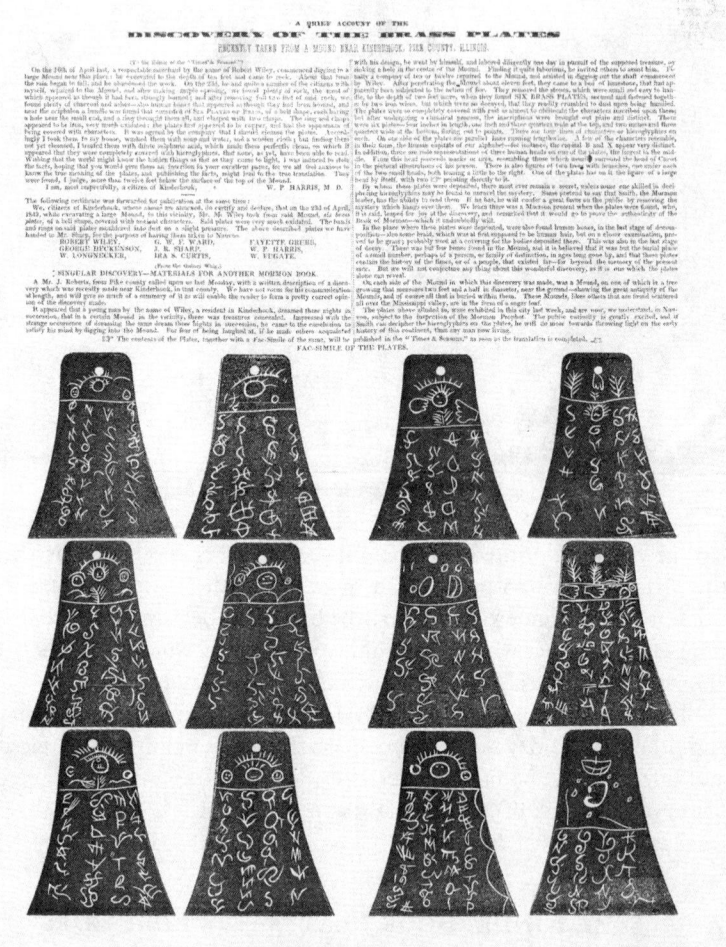

Broadside of Kinderhook plates published in Nauvoo. Courtesy of Church History Library.

must have produced a fraudulent translation.[14] An anti-Mormon writer named Charles Shook coined a catchy phrase that has been quoted repeatedly: "Only a bogus prophet translates bogus plates."[15] In response to such attacks, Mormon historians argued for several decades that Fugate and Harris were lying in order to make Joseph Smith look bad. They attempted to defend Joseph Smith by insisting on the authenticity of the plates.[16]

Scientific Examination

Clearly, what was needed was a careful examination of the Kinderhook plates to determine whether they were ancient artifacts or modern forgeries.

In one of Fugate's letters, he wrote, "I made the hieroglyphics by making impressions on beeswax and filling them with acid and putting it on the plates," a process of etching that had been developed in Europe in the Middle Ages. If the Kinderhook plates had been created in the Americas before European contact, they would most likely have been engraved with a stylus or some other sharp tool.

Five of the six plates have been lost, but one remaining plate is housed at the Chicago History Museum.[17] In 1980, Mormon historian Stanley B. Kimball received permission to have this plate tested by D. Lynn Johnson, a professor of materials science and engineering at Northwestern University. Testing with a scanning electron microscope showed that the characters on the plates were etched with acid, not engraved, and testing with a scanning auger microscope found traces of etching acid in the character grooves. Destructive testing showed that the metal inside the plate was a fine alloy, consistent with nineteenth-century manufacturing techniques and unlike the crude alloys of ancient times. These results determined conclusively that the Kinderhook plates were of modern manufacture.[18]

Kimball also noted that the characters on the plates were not authentic. They bear little-to-no resemblance to any known language. In fact, they do not resemble language at all because they have almost none of the character repetition found in genuine script. When Wiley and Fugate etched the inscriptions, they apparently just made up the characters on the spot.[19] So there actually is no way to translate anything from the plates.

An Argument against a Translation

In the same article, Kimball argued that Joseph Smith never claimed to translate from the Kinderhook plates. In fact, he showed that Joseph Smith had not actually written that he translated the plates, as it seems he did in the official *History of the Church*. The mid-nineteenth-century Church historians who compiled "The History of Joseph Smith," later published as *The History of the Church*, had taken entries from Joseph Smith's journal, entries from other journals, and other documents and combined them into a continuous narrative that reads as if written by Joseph Smith. This kind of historical writing was common before the early twentieth century.[20] Stanley Kimball argued that the information on the Kinderhook plates in the *History of the Church* was unreliable because it was not taken from Joseph Smith's journal but rather from William Clayton's.[21]

William Clayton served as Joseph Smith's private secretary and in several clerical capacities in the Church and in Nauvoo's city government.[22] While carrying out his duties, Clayton often worked closely with Joseph Smith. James B. Allen, a Mormon historian who wrote a biography of Clayton, explained that "beginning in early 1842, William Clayton found himself involved in nearly every important activity of Nauvoo, but especially the private concerns of Joseph Smith. For two and a half years, until Joseph's death in 1844, they were in each other's company almost daily."[23] Over time, they became good friends. Because William Clayton was so close to Joseph Smith, his journal contains valuable information about the things the Prophet said and did. This is why the early Church historians felt comfortable utilizing entries from Clayton's journal.

On May 1, 1843, William Clayton traced the edges of one of the plates in his journal, and wrote about them:

> I have seen 6 brass plates which were found . . . by some persons who were digging in a mound. They found a skeleton. . . . The plates were on the breast of the skeleton—This diagram shows the size of the plates being drawn on the edge of one of them. They are covered with ancient characters of language containing from 30 to 40 on each side of the plates. Prest J. has translated a portion and says they contain the history of the person with whom they were found & he was a descendant of Ham through the loins of Pharaoh king of Egypt, and that he received his kingdom from the ruler of heaven & earth.[24]

On May 7, 1843, Apostle Parley P. Pratt wrote about the Kinderhook plates in a letter to one of his cousins. Pratt wrote:

> Six plates having the appearance of Brass have lately been dug out of a mound by a gentleman in Pike Co. Illinois. they are small and filled with engravings in Egyptian language and contain the genealogy of one of the ancient Jaredites back to Ham the son of Noah[.] his bones were found in the same vase (made of cement) part of the bones had crumbled to dust & the other part were preserved[.] the bones were 15 feet underground. . . . A large number of Citizens here have seen them and compared the Characters with those on the Egyptian papyri which is now in this city.[25]

Stanley Kimball questioned the reliability of Clayton's journal entry by pointing out its differences with this letter by Pratt.[26] Clayton and Pratt disagreed on a few points regarding the unearthing of the plates. But neither man had been present when the plates were unearthed—they were just reporting what they had heard. They were better positioned to know what Joseph Smith had said about the plates. Kimball wrote that "Clayton said that the plates gave a history of an Egyptian; Pratt mentioned a Jaredite."[27] Actually, Clayton never referred to the skeletal remains found with the plates as belonging to an Egyptian. Rather, he wrote the man was "a descendant of Ham through the loins of Pharaoh, king of Egypt." Pratt wrote that the plates contained "the genealogy of one of the ancient Jaredites back to Ham the son of Noah." So Pratt actually concurred with Clayton that this person was a descendant of Ham, supporting the credibility of Clayton's report.

Kimball also argued that we do not know for certain where Clayton got his information. When Clayton wrote that Joseph Smith had "translated a portion" of the plates, he did not write that he had seen Joseph Smith translating or state directly that Joseph Smith had said he translated. The journal entry's text and tracing of one of the plates do show, however, that Clayton was with Joseph Smith in the Smith home, had access to the plates there, and had his journal with him.

Another assertion Kimball promoted was that Clayton may have been exaggerating—that what Clayton called the results of translation may have just been a speculative comment.[28] But nothing in the entry indicates speculation, and this would not have been typical of Clayton. Modern historians recognize Clayton as one of the most accurate and important Nauvoo sources on Joseph Smith. James B. Allen, Clayton's biographer, wrote that Clayton "delighted in the specific and the concrete, which helps account for his success as a scribe and a clerk. . . . [A]s a diarist and historian he described what he saw around him, usually with skill and great descriptive power but seldom with any interpretive imagination."[29] Church leaders trusted his reporting of Joseph Smith's teachings enough to canonize Clayton's report of some of these teachings, taken with little change from his journal entries, as what are now sections 130 and 131 of the Doctrine and Covenants.[30] Clayton's entry about Joseph Smith's statements and actions regarding the Kinderhook plates is likely accurate.

Kimball's main argument that Joseph Smith did not translate is that "the expected translation did not appear."[31] But Clayton said Joseph Smith had translated only "a portion" of the Kinderhook plates. And a translation of or from the "portion" Smith worked on did "appear"—in Clayton's journal. Although Joseph Smith himself did not write that he had translated from the Kinderhook plates, we still have to account for what Clayton wrote—which to all appearances is reliable. Consequently, as believing Latter-day Saints, we need to be able to explain how Joseph Smith could have translated from fraudulent plates.

Some may feel that we also need to account for Joseph Smith believing the plates were genuine. Although he was a prophet, he was a man who could make mistakes. Joseph Smith believed that the Holy Ghost could warn him of trouble and help him discern truth from falsehood,[32] but he also admitted that he could be tricked by others. For example, he explained that when the Missouri state militia took him and others as prisoners in 1838 it was because George Hinkle, a fellow Latter-day Saint whom they trusted, had taken them to negotiate with the militia and, as Smith wrote, "decoyed us unawares."[33] Because Joseph Smith never claimed that he could not be deceived, his mistaken belief that the Kinderhook plates were genuine does not detract from his prophetic claims. Moreover, Joseph Smith's belief that the Kinderhook plates were genuine could be used to argue that he was a true prophet. It suggests that he believed in real buried records, as one would expect if he had found such a record himself. The only real problem for Latter-day Saints is how or why Joseph Smith *translated* from the Kinderhook plates.

The Problem of Translation

It should be noted that the problem of Joseph's translation of the Kinderhook plates is not in how much he translated but rather whether he translated at all. If Joseph Smith only translated a single character from the plates, we would still need to explain how this could be if there was nothing to translate.

Since 1981, when Stanley Kimball published his article on the Kinderhook plates, his evidence that the plates were forgeries has been uniformly accepted. Nearly all devout Latter-day Saints who have written about the plates have also accepted Kimball's argument that Joseph Smith did not translate from them. Latter-day Saints have been inclined to accept Kimball's argument that Joseph Smith did not translate the plates. They likely want to defend Joseph Smith as a true prophet, and they believe this means that he could not have translated anything from the fraudulent Kinderhook plates. Critics claim that since the plates were fake, Joseph Smith was a false prophet, and they have used this as evidence that he deceived others about having the gift of translation. What both these positions share in common is the assumption that Joseph Smith would have been acting as a prophet while translating from the Kinderhook plates.[34]

The assumption is a natural one, given that Joseph Smith brought forth the Book of Mormon through a process he described as translation "by the gift and power of God."[35] It is reasonable to place the Kinderhook-plates episode in the same context as the Book of Mormon—that Joseph Smith was either translating or pretending to translate the Kinderhook plates by the power of God. The problem with this common assumption is that it ignores the evidence that Joseph Smith had a personal interest in languages, that he spent considerable time studying languages, that he engaged in traditional translation without claiming divine aid, and that he approached the Kinderhook plates in precisely this fashion.

Joseph Smith and Translation by Revelation

Joseph Smith's interest in language grew naturally out of his earlier prophetic projects. He had translated the Book of Mormon in 1828 and 1829.[36] According to the Book of Mormon, the golden plates had been written using "reformed Egyptian" characters to express the Hebrew language.[37]

From the time he translated this passage forward, Joseph Smith may have seen a relationship between the Hebrew and Egyptian languages.

From 1830 to 1833, Joseph Smith and his scribes worked on a "new translation" of the Bible. Starting with the King James Version, they made several expansions and hundreds of revisions to the text, some by revelation and others, such as small grammatical changes, which may have been considered to be the result of human reason rather than revelation.[38] In the summer of 1835, Joseph Smith and others in Kirtland, Ohio, purchased four Egyptian mummies and a collection of papyri. Using the papyri, Joseph Smith translated the Book of Abraham by the divine gift of revelation.[39] He translated Abraham 1:1–2:18 in Kirtland; then he resumed his translation several years later in Nauvoo. His journal reports that he was "translating" the Book of Abraham and then "translating and revising" on March 8–9, 1842—about one year before he translated from the Kinderhook plates. Some of the explanations of the illustrations that accompanied the published Book of Abraham used Hebrew words—again linking Hebrew and Egyptian.[40]

Joseph Smith and Traditional Translation

Joseph Smith's translation work with the Egyptian papyri in 1835 heightened his more traditional interest in ancient languages. In addition to the Egyptian papyri themselves and the Book of Abraham translation manuscripts, there are several other manuscripts from this period that are clearly related to both. These documents, commonly called the "Kirtland Egyptian Papers," are in the handwriting of Joseph Smith and others who were helping him at the time. One of these documents is a bound volume titled "Grammar & Alphabet of the Egyptian Language," with a spine labeled "Egyptian Alphabet." The "Egyptian Alphabet" is really more of a lexicon—a sort of dual-language dictionary with Egyptian characters and corresponding definitions or interpretations in English.[41]

It is uncertain why or how these documents were made, but many of the character interpretations are clearly related to content in the Book of Abraham. Because of this, some people view the documents as the translation key for Egyptian by which Joseph Smith produced the English text of the Book of Abraham. Critics of Mormonism especially favor this hypothesis because the English interpretations of the Egyptian characters do not match the definitions given by Egyptologists.[42] Another hypothesis is that Joseph Smith first received the Book of Abraham by revelation and then tried to figure out how to translate Egyptian by matching papyri characters to the Book of Abraham text. Before Joseph Smith acquired the papyri, scholars in New York and Philadelphia had tried to translate them but could not.[43] Champollion, the French linguist, was just beginning to figure out how to translate Egyptian using the Rosetta Stone. Perhaps Joseph Smith

"Egyptian Alphabet." Courtesy of Church History Library.

was attempting the same process, using the revealed Book of Abraham and the papyri as his "Rosetta Stone."[44]

A problem for either theory is that despite the overlapping content, neither document could have been wholly derived from the other. The "Egyptian Alphabet" contains much that is not in the Book of Abraham, and thus could not have been entirely derived from it. Additionally, the Book of Abraham contains a great deal that is not in the "Egyptian Alphabet" and thus could not have been translated by solely using it. Another possibility is that Joseph Smith received initial impressions of some concepts in the Book of Abraham as he and his scribes attempted to figure out the papyri for themselves. These concepts, along with the group's larger intellectual effort, were recorded in the "Egyptian Alphabet." Such a process could account for why the "Egyptian Alphabet" and translated Book of Abraham share some content even though neither could have been simply derived from the other. These enigmatic documents remain a subject of great controversy in Mormon history.

Joseph Smith began a serious study of biblical languages in late 1835. His journal notes that he began his studies with "a Hebrew bible, lexicon & Grammar, also a Greek Lexicon and Webster's English Lexicon."[45] He and others soon began an intensive Hebrew class with a Jewish instructor, meeting almost daily for the next eight weeks.[46] The students read from the Old Testament in Hebrew and practiced translating. Joseph wrote enthusiastically of these studies, recording in his journal: "I attended the school and read and translated with my class as usual, and my soul delights in reading the word of the Lord in the original, and I am determined to pursue the study of languages until I shall become master of them, if I am permitted to live long enough, at any rate so long as I do live I am determined to make

Title page of "Egyptian Alphabet." Courtesy of Church History Library.

this my object."[47] Smith never mastered Hebrew, but he studied in earnest and did gain some rudimentary proficiency with the language.

True to his intentions, Joseph Smith maintained a passion for and intermittent study of languages for the rest of his life. In addition to Hebrew, he studied Greek, and in Nauvoo he occasionally cited the Greek New Testament in his sermons.[48] He also frequently used Latin phrases in sermons and letters.[49] Toward the end of his life, he made a serious study of the German language.[50] During the April 1844 general conference, just a few months before he died, he discussed Hebrew, Greek, Latin, and German translations of the Bible in his famous King Follett Discourse and drew on his knowledge of Hebrew to give a translation of Genesis 1:1.[51]

Joseph Smith continued his language studies throughout his busy life as occasion would permit. In a sermon about a month after encountering the Kinderhook plates, he drew on his knowledge of biblical languages and introduced his comments by saying, "I will turn linguist."[52] This shows explicitly that he saw himself occasionally taking on the role of a linguist. It is quite possible that he attempted to translate the Kinderhook plates, not as a prophet, but as a linguist.

The fact that the characters on the Kinderhook plates did not match any known language was not necessarily a deterrent to such an attempt. Stephen Williams, who wrote a history of amateur archaeology, explains there was no professional field of archaeology in Joseph Smith's day: "Archaeology was open to anyone, and the data could be interpreted almost any way and . . . usually was."[53] Enthusiastic amateurs were eager to try to decipher ancient script.[54] Even in the twentieth century, examples can be given from within the field of archaeology of mistranslations, mistaking non-linguistic patterns for actual language, and translating forgeries—all in good faith.[55]

It is easy to imagine Joseph Smith—as someone interested in both language and the archaeology of ancient America—trying to translate the Kinderhook plates as would any linguist or archaeologist. It is also easy to imagine Joseph Smith—as the prophet who translated the Book of Mormon and the Book of Abraham—trying to translate from the Kinderhook plates by revelation. So, when Joseph Smith attempted to translate from the Kinderhook plates, was he acting as a prophet or was he acting as an amateur linguist? An unbiased examination of the Kinderhook plates episode would have to consider both possibilities and follow the evidence wherever it leads.

Charlotte Haven and Translation by Revelation

One source that suggests the method by which Joseph Smith translated from the Kinderhook plates is a letter written by Charlotte Haven, a young woman who visited Nauvoo in 1843. Haven, a Unitarian, wrote to her "dear home friends" about the Kinderhook plates. She reported that "Mr. Moore," apparently the Reverend George Moore, had shown her the plates and that they were "half a dozen thin pieces of brass, apparently very old, in the form of a bell about five or six inches long." Haven continued: "When he showed them to Joseph, the latter said the figures or writing on them was similar to that in which the Book of Mormon was written, and if Mr. Moore could leave them, he thought that by the help of revelation he would be able to translate them. So a sequel to that holy book may soon be expected."[56] Haven's account does not describe how Joseph Smith translated from the Kinderhook plates, but it does purport to tell how he initially expected to translate: by revelation.

Haven's account is plausible. George Moore wrote in his diary the previous June that Joseph Smith had shown him a transcript of characters from the golden plates of the Book of Mormon.[57] That earlier encounter, and similarities Moore perceived between the Book of Mormon characters and some of the Kinderhook plates characters, could account for why Moore brought the plates to Joseph Smith. If Joseph Smith also perceived these or other similarities, he may have concluded that he could translate the characters on the Kinderhook plates just as he had been able to translate those on the golden plates.

While this scenario is plausible, its accuracy is uncertain. Although Haven was largely accurate in reporting Nauvoo events, she occasionally displayed a tendency toward overstatement—such as reporting that the Kinderhook plates were about twice as large as their actual size.[58] Haven, in turn, was restating what she had heard from Moore about what he had heard from Joseph Smith. And it is difficult to assess how accurately Moore understood Joseph Smith's statements and transmitted them to Haven. So, although there is a plausible scenario in which Joseph Smith might naturally have discussed the idea of translating the Kinderhook plates by revelation, as he had the Book of Mormon, the available sources do not settle this with certainty.

This, however, is not a barrier to further inquiry. Ultimately, the question is not whether Joseph Smith believed he could translate the Kinderhook plates by revelation but what method he actually used to translate the "portion" Clayton reported he translated. And on this question, we do not have to rely on Charlotte Haven's third-hand report of what Joseph Smith may have said prior to his actual translation effort. We have better sources to work with—sources that describe his translation activities and demonstrate how he derived the translation content.

Joseph Smith's Translation of the Kinderhook Plates

On May 7, 1843, Joseph Smith and several others examined the Kinderhook plates. From this event, we have three sources that corroborate each other and indirectly corroborate Clayton's journal entry from a few days earlier. A close examination of these sources indicates that Joseph Smith attempted to translate from the Kinderhook plates by traditional methods. The first of these is Parley P. Pratt's letter discussed earlier, which reported that Joseph Smith displayed both the Kinderhook plates and the characters from his Egyptian papyri to his visitors, allowing them to compare the two. The second is Joseph Smith's own journal, where he notes that either William Smith or Willard Richards (depending on how the abbreviated entry is read) was sent to get a "Hebrew Bible & lexicon." That one of the Apostles was reportedly dispatched to get a Hebrew lexicon suggests that the men who were examining the Kinderhook plates may have been comparing their characters to Hebrew as well as Egyptian characters, languages connected by both the Book of Mormon and Book of Abraham. All of this further suggests that the group was taking a traditional approach to translation.

The third of the three sources is a letter one of the group wrote to the editor of the *New York Herald*. It was common in early America for people writing letters to newspapers to use an obvious pseudonym. With tongue in cheek, this correspondent, who was apparently not a Latter-day Saint, wrote from Nauvoo under the name "A Gentile." The *New York Herald* published his letter about the Kinderhook plates, which reported in part: "The plates are evidently brass, and are covered on both sides with hieroglyphics. They were brought up and shown to Joseph Smith. He compared them in my presence with his Egyptian alphabet, which he took from the plates from which the Book of Mormon was translated, and they are evidently the same characters. He therefore will be able to decipher them."[59] According to this witness, Joseph Smith compared the characters on the Kinderhook plates to the characters in his "Egyptian Alphabet." Perhaps the "Gentile" made an understandable mistake in associating the "Egyptian Alphabet" with the Book of Mormon instead of the Book of Abraham because Joseph Smith was so much better known for the Book of Mormon. Joseph Smith had displayed a transcript of Book of Mormon characters to George Moore several months earlier. So it is not unlikely that Joseph Smith displayed it again on May 7, along with the "Egyptian Alphabet" volume, when visitors came to see the Kinderhook plates. In that case, the juxtaposition of Egyptian characters from both the Book of Mormon and the Book of Abraham could have easily added to his "Gentile" guest's confusion over which Book of Mormon scripture the "Egyptian Alphabet" characters came from.

The "Gentile" correspondent to the *New York Herald* watched Joseph Smith comparing characters from the plates and from the "Egyptian Alphabet" in a method typical of traditional translation. And, as he wrote, "they are evidently the same characters." The characters were not only compared but compared favorably. Joseph Smith and others believed they had found matching characters. As the author of the letter put it: "He therefore will be able to decipher them."

This naturally leads to the question: Which characters in the "Egyptian Alphabet" were found to match characters on the Kinderhook plates and what were the corresponding English definitions for those characters in the "Egyptian Alphabet"? William Clayton's journal gives us evidence of one such character. A few days earlier, when Clayton wrote that Joseph Smith had translated a portion of the plates, he also wrote that Joseph Smith had said they contained "the history of the person with whom they were found, and he was a descendant of Ham through the loins of Pharaoh, king of Egypt, and that he received his kingdom from the Ruler of heaven and earth." This information bears remarkable resemblance to one of the character interpretations in the "Egyptian Alphabet." The character named "Ha e oop hah" was given the following interpretation: "honor by birth, kingly power by the line of Pharoah. possession by birth one who riegns upon his throne universally—possessor of heaven and earth, and of the blessings of the earth."[60] A careful comparison of this interpretation with the information in William Clayton's journal reveals their parallel content. In the table below, the parallels are printed with corresponding emphasis:

Comparison of Translation to "Egyptian Alphabet" Character

Joseph Smith told William Clayton	"Ha e oop hah" defined
He was *a descendant of* Ham **through the loins of Pharaoh** <u>king</u> of Egypt,	Honor *by birth*, <u>kingly</u> power **by the line of Pharaoh**; possession *by birth*;
and ... *received his kingdom* from the **ruler of heaven & earth**.	one who *reigns upon his throne* universally—**possessor of heaven and earth**, and of the blessings of the earth.

The character named "Ha e oop hah" has the shape of a closed half circle. It could be said to resemble a boat in shape. This character bears some resemblance to one of the characters on the Kinderhook plates.

Of course there are some obvious differences between these two characters. The character on the Kinderhook plates is a closed half circle with four additional lines added to it. However, to put this in historical context, it must be noted that Joseph Smith and those who helped him with the Kirtland Egyptian papers had the understanding that the Egyptian characters on the papyri could be dissected into parts that had meaningful definitions of their own. This linguistic theory is explained in the opening pages of the "Egyptian Alphabet," just before "Ha e oop hah" is defined.[61] If the extraneous

108   Don Bradley and Mark Ashurst-McGee

Kinderhook plate character (left) and "Egyptian Alphabet" character (right). Courtesy of Church History Library.

lines are dissected from the boat-shaped character, it bears a close resemblance to the "Ha e oop hah" character in the "Egyptian Alphabet." On the Kinderhook plates, the boat-shaped character is relatively large and prominently placed at the top of one of the plates. The plates had originally been fastened with a ring, maintaining any intended order. But the ring broke open as the plates were unearthed, and it is doubtful that any sense of order or arrangement was conveyed to Joseph Smith when the plates were lent to him. If Joseph Smith had any guess as to the order of the plates, he would likely have been inclined to begin his translation attempt at the presumed beginning of the inscriptions.

From the facsimiles printed by the Church newspaper, it can be seen that the characters and illustrations on each of the Kinderhook plates are divided by an inscribed line—with a more illustrative section at the top of the plate and with characters inscribed below on the main body of the plate. One of the sides of one of the plates—the last one illustrated in the broadside—differs from the others, rendering the area above the line significantly larger. Also, whereas most of the headings to the plates are filled with illustrations—particularly suns with faces—the plate side with the larger heading features two large characters. The first of these characters is the boat-shaped figure.

Because this side of this plate had a larger heading, and a heading with characters, it would have been a natural place to begin translating. And if Joseph Smith looked for a boat-shaped character in the "Egyptian Alphabet," it would not have taken him long to find it. This character appears on the fourth page of the volume, which is the second page of characters and their assigned definitions.

Facsimile of Kinderhook plate with boat-shaped character at the top. Courtesy of Church History Library.

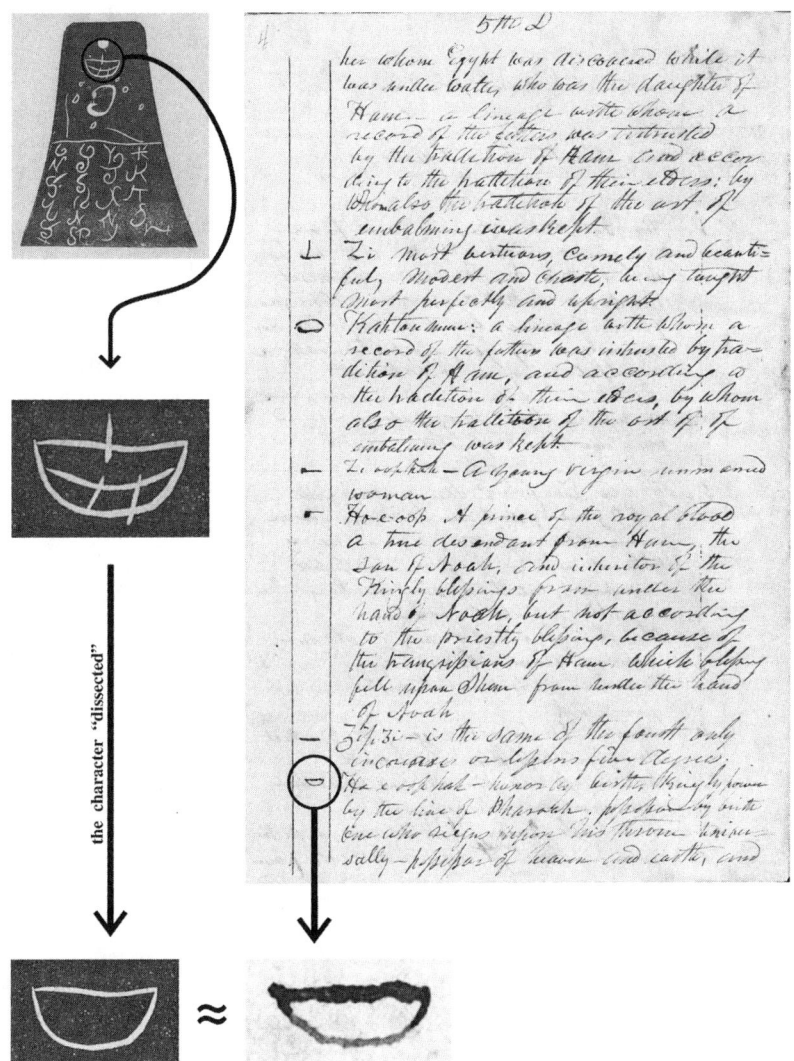

Comparison of characters from the Kinderhook plates and Joseph Smith's "Egyptian Alphabet."

The character named "Ha e oop hah" in Joseph Smith's "Egyptian Alphabet" can be seen as the same character featured prominently on the top of one of the Kinderhook plates, and the reported content of Joseph Smith's translation from the Kinderhook plates can be substantially drawn from that character's definition in the "Egyptian Alphabet." It may be that the "portion" of the Kinderhook plates that Joseph Smith translated on or before May 1, 1843, was no more than this single character from the top of one of the plates. It appears that Joseph Smith shared this same translation with the group of men who met a few days later.

What Do We Learn from the Kinderhook Plates?

Taken together, these sources indicate that Joseph Smith was attempting to translate the Kinderhook plates by ordinary methods of traditional translation. Furthermore, they show that he was doing so openly, in the company of a group of Church members and nonmembers. In contrast, there is no mention of Joseph Smith using the Urim and Thummim or a seer stone or divine revelation of any kind in any of the sources close to the event. William Clayton mentioned nothing about revelation in his journal entry about the translation of the plates.

As it turned out, the Kinderhook plates were not what they appeared to be. With the benefit of hindsight and modern scientific testing equipment, we see the plates differently than Joseph Smith did. Time has shown that he was mistaken. He mistakenly accepted the Kinderhook plates as authentic artifacts; he mistakenly identified their characters as Egyptian; and he mistakenly thought that he had translated one or more of these characters. However, there is no evidence that Joseph Smith believed he had experienced a revealed translation or that he led others to believe he had.

For over a century, many have argued as to whether the Kinderhook plates episode revealed Joseph Smith as a true or false prophet. Yet a closer examination of the relevant historical sources reveals Joseph Smith acting neither as an inspired prophet nor as a fraudulent imposter. Instead, it reveals an enthusiastic, yet amateur, linguist.

There is a more general lesson to be learned here. Many arguments for and against Joseph Smith's prophetic claims, upon closer examination, turn out to be much more complex than originally framed, or simply fall apart, because they are based on assumptions that turn out to be incorrect. A careful and historically grounded approach is best in evaluating such arguments.

Additional Resources

Blumell, Lincoln H., Matthew J. Grey, and Andrew H. Hedges, eds., *Approaching Antiquity: Joseph Smith and the Ancient World.* Provo, UT: Religious Studies Center; Salt Lake City: Deseret Book, 2015.

Hauglid, Brian M. "Did Joseph Smith Translate the Kinderhook Plates?" In *No Weapon Shall Prosper: New Light on Sensitive Issues*, edited by Robert L. Millet, 92–103. Provo, UT: Religious Studies Center; Salt Lake City: Deseret Book Company, 2011.

Jessee, Dean C. "The Writing of Joseph Smith's History." *BYU Studies* 11 (Spring 1971): 439–73.

Kimball, Stanley B. "Kinderhook Plates Brought to Joseph Smith Appear to Be a Nineteenth-Century Hoax." *Ensign*, August 1981, 66–74.

Peters, Jason Frederick. "The Kinderhook Plates: Examining a Nineteenth-Century Hoax." *Journal of the Illinois State Historical Society* 96, no. 2 (Summer 2003): 130–45.

Smith, Joseph. *The Joseph Smith Papers.* www.josephsmithpapers.org.

Zucker, Louis C. "Joseph Smith as a Student of Hebrew." *Dialogue* 3, no. 2 (Summer 1968): 41–55.

About the Authors

Don Bradley is a writer, editor, and researcher specializing in Latter-day Saint history and scripture. He performed an internship with the Joseph Smith Papers Project and is completing his thesis toward a master's degree in history at Utah State University. He has published on the translation of the Book of Mormon, plural marriage before Nauvoo, and Joseph Smith's "grand fundamental principles of Mormonism." Don's first book, *The Lost 116 Pages: Rediscovering the Book of Lehi*, is forthcoming from Greg Kofford Books. He is married to the former Michaelann Gardner and is the father of Donnie and Nicholas Bradley.

Mark Ashurst-McGee is a historian and documentary editor with the Joseph Smith Papers Project at the Church History Library. He holds a PhD in history and has trained at the Institute for the Editing of Historical Documents. He specializes in document analysis and documentary editing methodology. He has coedited several volumes of *The Joseph Smith Papers* and is the author of scholarly articles on Joseph Smith and early Mormon history. He and Angela Ashurst-McGee are the parents of six children. They live in West Jordan, Utah. The author would like to thank the Neil A. Maxwell Institute for Religious Scholarship for a research grant.

Notes

1. W. P. Harris, letter to the editor of the *Times and Seasons*, as published in *Times and Seasons*, Nauvoo, Illinois, May 1, 1843, 186; See also "Singular Discovery—Materials for Another Mormon Book," *Quincy Whig*. Quincy, Illinois, May 3, 1843, 3.

2. Wilbur Fugate, letter to Mr. James Cobb, June 30, 1879; quoted in William Wyl, *Mormon Portraits, or the Truth about Mormon Leaders from 1830 to 1886, Joseph Smith the Prophet, His Family and His Friends: A Study Based on Fact and Documents* (Salt Lake City: Tribune Printing and Publishing, 1886), 207–8.

3. Statement, in *Times and Seasons*, May 1, 1843, 186.

4. "A Brief Account of the Discovery of the Brass Plates Recently Taken from a Mound near Kinderhook, Pike County, Illinois," *Nauvoo Neighbor*, June 24, 1843.

5. Wilbur Fugate, letter to Mr. James Cobb, June 30, 1879, in W. Wyl, *Mormon Portraits*, 208–11.

6. On the Book of Mormon, see Richard Lyman Bushman, *Joseph Smith: Rough Stone Rolling* (New York: Alfred A. Knopf, 2005), 57–83; Terryl L. Givens, *By the Hand of Mormon: The American Scripture That Launched a New World Religion* (Oxford and New York: Oxford University Press, 2002).

7. *Times and Seasons*, May 1, 1843, 186. Charlotte Haven, a young woman who visited Quincy and Nauvoo in 1843, reported in a letter to "dear home friends" on May 2, 1843, that the plates had been brought to Nauvoo by "Joshua Moore." But this "Mr. Joshua Moore, who passes through that place and this in his monthly zigzag tours through the State, traveling horseback," seems to be identical to George Moore, the traveling minister she names in subsequent letters. George Moore's name may have been mistakenly written by Haven or erroneously transcribed by the publisher of her letters. "A Girl's Letters from Nauvoo," *Overland Monthly*, December 1890, 630, spelling standardized.

8. Joseph Smith Jr., *History of the Church of Jesus Christ of Latter-day Saints: Period I. History of Joseph Smith, the Prophet. By Himself*, with an Introduction and Notes by Brigham H. Roberts (repr.; Salt Lake City: Deseret Book, 1967), 5:372–78.

9. "Ancient Records," *Times and Seasons*, May 1, 1843, 186; "Ancient Records," *Nauvoo Neighbor*, May 10, 1843.

10. "A Brief Account of the Discovery of the Brass Plates Recently Taken from a Mound in the Vicinity of Kinderhook, Pike County, Illinois," *Nauvoo Neighbor*, June 24, 1843.

11. For examples, see "Fac-Simile of Plates with Engraved Characters taken out of an Ancient Mound in Illinois, in 1843," in Orson Pratt, *A Series of Pamphlets* (Liverpool: R. James, 1851); "Fac Similes of the Plates," *Deseret News*, September 3–10, 1856; "American Antiquities, Corroborative of the Book of Mormon," *Latter-day Saints' Millennial Star*, May 7, 1859, 306–7.

12. Wilbur Fugate, letter to Mr. James Cobb, June 30, 1879; quoted in W. Wyl, *Mormon Portraits*, 207–8. See also Wilbur Fugate, letter to James Cobb, April 8, 1878, Theodore Albert Schroeder Papers, 1845–1901, Wisconsin Historical Society, Madison, Wisconsin.

13. W. P. Harris, Barry, Pike County, Illinois, letter to Mr. Flagg, Moro, Illinois, April 25, 1855; quoted in "A Hoax," *Journal of the Illinois State Historical Society* 5 (July 1912): 271–73.

14. For examples, see James D. Bales, *Book of Mormon?* (Rosemead, CA: Old Paths Book Club, 1958), 89–102; Ed Decker and Dave Hunt, *The God Makers* (Eugene, OR: Harvest House Publishers, 1984), 99–100; *Joseph Smith and the Kinderhook Plates* [tract pamphlet] (Salt Lake City: Utah Lighthouse Ministry, n.d.).

15. Charles A. Shook, letter to James D. Bales; quoted originally in Bales, *Book of Mormon?*, 98.

16. For examples, see B. H. Roberts, *The Book of Mormon*, New Witnesses for God series, 3 vols. (Salt Lake City: Deseret News, 1951), 2:58–64; Welby W. Ricks, "The Kinderhook Plates," *Improvement Era*, September 1962, 636–60.

17. The extant plate is at the Chicago History Museum.

18. Stanley B. Kimball, "Kinderhook Plates Brought to Joseph Smith Appear to Be a Nineteenth-Century Hoax," *Ensign*, August 1981, 68–70.

19. Paul R. Cheesman, "An Analysis of the Kinderhook Plates," 1970, Special Collections, Harold B. Lee Library, Brigham Young University, Provo, Utah, 8–9; Kimball, "Kinderhook Plates," 74, n. 17.

20. Dean C. Jessee, "The Writing of Joseph Smith's History," *BYU Studies* 11 (Spring 1971): 439–73.

21. Kimball, "Kinderhook Plates," 67–68.

22. Clayton served as the Nauvoo temple recorder, as Nauvoo city treasurer, and as secretary of Nauvoo's Freemasonry lodge. Clayton, "History of the Nauvoo Temple," 18, 30–31; Joseph Smith, Journal, 29 June 1842; Nauvoo City Council Minute Book, 9 September 1842, 101; Nauvoo Masonic Lodge Minute Book, 10 November 1842. All sources found at the Church History Library (hereafter CHL).

23. James B. Allen, *No Toil nor Labor Fear: The Story of William Clayton* (Provo, UT: Brigham Young University Press, 2002), 73.

24. William Clayton, journal, quoted in Allen, *No Toil nor Labor Fear*, 393.

25. Parley P. Pratt, letter to John Van Cott, May 7, 1843, CHL.

26. Kimball, "Kinderhook Plates," 73.

27. Kimball, "Kinderhook Plates," 73.

28. Kimball, "Kinderhook Plates," 73.

29. Allen, *No Toil nor Labor Fear*, 62.

30. Clayton kept a journal for Joseph Smith during the last month of his life, presumably at Smith's request. William Clayton, Daily Account of Joseph Smith's Activities, 14–22 June 1844," Appendix 2 in Andrew H. Hedges, Alex D. Smith, and Brent M. Rogers, eds., *May 1843–June 1844*, vol. 3 of the Journals series of *The Joseph Smith Papers*, ed. Ronald K. Esplin and Matthew J. Grow (Salt Lake City: Church Historian's Press, 2015), 331–39.

31. Kimball, "Kinderhook Plates," 73.

32. For some examples, see Truman G. Madsen's discussion of Joseph Smith and the spiritual gift of discernment. Truman G. Madsen, *Joseph Smith the Prophet* (Salt Lake City: Bookcraft, 1989), 41–42, 90.

33. Joseph Smith, letter to Emma Smith, November 4, 1838, Archives of the Community of Christ, Independence, Missouri.

34. For examples, see Allen, *No Toil nor Labor Fear*, 112–13; Richard E. Turley Jr., *Victims: The LDS Church and the Mark Hofmann Case* (Urbana: University of Illinois Press, 1992), 10–11; Jerald and Sandra Tanner, *Mormonism: Shadow or Reality?*, enlarged edition (Salt Lake City: Utah Lighthouse Ministries, 1982), 125, G–I; John E. Hallwas, *Western Illinois Heritage* (Macomb: Illinois Heritage Press, 1983), 77–79.

35. "The Author" [Joseph Smith], "Preface," in *The Book of Mormon: An Account Written by the Hand of Mormon, upon Plates Taken from the Plates of Nephi* (Palmyra, NY: E. B. Grandin, 1830), iii–iv.

36. Welch, "The Miraculous Translation of the Book of Mormon," in *Opening the Heavens: Accounts of Divine Manifestations, 1820–1844*, ed. John W. Welch with Eric Carlson (Provo, UT: BYU Studies, 2005), 77–213.

37. See Mormon 9:32–33.

38. Robert J. Matthews, *"A Plainer Translation": Joseph Smith's Translation of the Bible: A History and Commentary* (Provo, UT: Brigham Young University Press, 1985), 39–40, 252–53.

39. See H. Donl Peterson, *The Story of the Book of Abraham: Mummies, Manuscripts, and Mormonism* (Salt Lake City: Deseret Book, 1995), 119–24.

40. "A Fac-Simile from the Book of Abraham. No. 1," Fig. 12, in *Times and Seasons*, March 1, 1842, 703 (Book of Abraham, Facsimile 1, explanation 12); "A Fac-Simile from the Book of Abraham, No. 2," Fig. 4, in *Times and Seasons*, March 15, 1842, foldout between pages 720 and 721 (Book of Abraham, Facsimile 2, explanation 4).

41. "Grammar and Alphabet of the Egyptian Language," 1835, Kirtland Egyptian Papers, CHL.

42. See, for example, Charles M. Larson, *By His Own Hand upon Papyrus: A New Look at the Joseph Smith Papyri,* rev. ed. (Grand Rapids, MI: Institute for Religious Research, 1992), chapter 9; Christopher C. Smith, "The Dependence of Abraham 1:1–3 on the Egyptian Alphabet and Grammar," *John Whitmer Historical Association Journal* 29 (2009): 38–54.

43. Oliver Cowdery, letter to William Frye, December 22, 1835, Huntington Library, San Marino, California, excerpted in appendix A of Stanley R. Gunn, *Oliver Cowdery: Second Elder and Scribe* (Salt Lake City: Bookcraft, 1962), 235–39.

44. See, for example, John Gee, *A Guide to the Joseph Smith Papyri* (Provo, UT: FARMS, 2000), 19–23.

45. Joseph Smith, journal, November 2, 1835, CHL.

46. See entries throughout January, February, and March 1836 in Joseph Smith, journal, Joseph Smith Collection, CHL.

47. Joseph Smith, journal, February 17, 1836; spelling standardized.

48. Andrew F. Ehat and Lyndon W. Cook, comps. and eds., *The Words of Joseph Smith: The Contemporary Accounts of the Nauvoo Discourses of the Prophet Joseph* (Orem, UT: Grandin Book, 1991), 244, 351, 354, 358, 366, 380.

49. See, for example, Joseph Smith, "Journeying," letter to The Church of Jesus Christ of Latter Day Saints, September 6, 1842, Revelations Collection, CHL; see also D&C 128:11.

50. This was especially so within the half year preceding his encounter with the Kinderhook plates. Joseph Smith, journal, various entries from January 1–June 3; also Alexander Neibaur, journal, May 24, 1844, CHL.

51. Stan Larson, "The King Follett Discourse: A Newly Amalgamated Text," *BYU Studies* 18, no. 2 (Winter 1978): 202–3, 207.

52. Joseph Smith, journal, June 11, 1843.

53. Stephen Williams, *Fantastic Archaeology: The Wild Side of North American Prehistory* (Philadelphia: University of Pennsylvania Press, 1991), 78–79.

54. Williams, *Fantastic Archaeology*, 12, 13.

55. Archaeologists are unsure whether some cylinder seal patterns are lingual or not. Dominique Collon, *First Impressions: Cylinder Seals in the Ancient Near East* (Chicago: The University of Chicago Press, 1987), 105–6. Noted biblical scholar James Charlesworth claimed to have translated a newly discovered ancient text into prose, but it was later shown to be a basically meaningless writing exercise including some miscellaneous letters, words, and names. Joseph Naveh, "A Medical Document or a Writing Exercise? The So-called 4Q Therapeia," *Israel Exploration Journal* 36, nos. 1–2 (1986): 52–55. Charlesworth later admitted his error. James H. Charlesworth, "A Misunderstood Recently Published Dead Sea Scroll," *Exploration* 1, no. 2 (1994): 2.

56. Charlotte Haven, letter to "My dear home friends," May 2, 1843 as published in "A Girl's Letters from Nauvoo," *The Overland Monthly*, December 1890, 630. As noted above, Haven referred to Moore here as "Joshua," but likely intended Unitarian minister George Moore.

57. George Moore wrote in his diary for June 3, 1842, that he had called on Joseph Smith, and "He showed me some specimens of the hieroglyphics, such as, he says, were on the gold

plates." Moore's diary has been published in Donald Q. Cannon, "Reverend George Moore Comments on Nauvoo, the Mormons, and Joseph Smith," *Western Illinois Regional Studies* 5 (Spring 1982): 6–16.

58. Haven also seems to have misstated information about the Egyptian mummies and papyri. Charlotte Haven, letter to "My Dear Mother," February 19, 1843, as published in "A Girl's Letters from Nauvoo," *Overland Monthly*, December 1890, 628. Peterson, *The Story of the Book of Abraham*, 191–202.

59. "A Gentile," letter to James Gordon Bennett, May 7, 1843, as published in "Late and Interesting from the Mormon Empire on the Upper Mississippi," *New York Herald*, May 30, 1843.

60. "Grammar and Alphabet of the Egyptian Language," 1835, CHL.

61. See "Grammar and Alphabet of the Egyptian Language," 1–2.

10

The Practice of Polygamy

Brian C. Hales and Laura Harris Hales

In Old Testament times, patriarchs like Abraham and Jacob practiced polygamy, which allowed them to have multiple wives. In the early nineteenth century, there were some fringe religious groups who toyed with the practice, but in general it was foreign and repugnant to most pre-Victorian Americans. Nevertheless, in Nauvoo in the 1840s, Joseph Smith taught that God commanded polygamy to be practiced by the Latter-day Saints. He described plural marriage as one part of a much grander doctrine called celestial marriage, which allows God's children to be eternally married and to become like our exalted Heavenly Parents. This exaltation is offered to all righteous couples sealed in the new and everlasting covenant of marriage and is not conditional on a plurality of wives, which is sometimes authorized by the Lord.

As far as historians can determine, Joseph Smith concluded that polygamy could be a divinely sanctioned practice in 1831, while reviewing the Old Testament accounts about patriarchs who practiced plural marriage. The Prophet told a few close associates that three years later an angel appeared to him and commanded him to reestablish the practice upon the earth, but he did not immediately act on this instruction. Erastus Snow, a friend, recalled: "The Prophet Joseph had said . . . 'I have not been obedient enough to this holy law and the Lord was angry with me and an angel met me with a drawn sword but I pled with the Lord to forgive me and he did so and I made the sacrifice required of my hand and by the help of the Lord I will obey his Holy Law.'"[1]

In 1840, Joseph Smith began teaching the practice of *polygamy*, or *plurality of wives*, to select members of the Church in Nauvoo, Illinois. At his death on June 27, 1844, over a hundred men and women had been married in plural matrimonies. Hundreds more were aware of the principle even though the practice was not openly taught or acknowledged until years later. In the twenty-first century, the practice of plural marriage may seem strange and perhaps difficult to accept. Unfortunately, Joseph Smith only left one document to help us understand his plural marriage teachings (section 132 of the Doctrine and Covenants), but it contains three reasons why plural marriage is sometimes allowed by God.

To Provide Bodies for Premortal Spirits by "Multiplying and Replenishing the Earth"

One reason given in the revelation for the practice of plural marriage is the need for polygamous couples to multiply and replenish the earth. It explains, "They [plural wives] are given unto him [their husband] to multiply and replenish the earth, according to my commandment . . . that they may bear the souls of men."[2]

A teaching that is generally unique to The Church of Jesus Christ of Latter-day Saints is that we lived as premortal spirits before we were born on earth. Nauvooan Charles Lambert recalled: "The Prophet used to hold meetings in a log house of his sometimes. . . . At one of these he said he wished he had a people that he could reveal to them what the Lord had shown to him. But one thing I will say, there are thousands of spirits that have been waiting to come forth in this day and generation. Their proper channel is through the priesthood, a way has to be provided. But the time has come and they have got to come away."[3] Helen Mar Kimball, one of the Prophet's plural wives, confirmed this teaching: "It was revealed to him [Joseph Smith] that there were thousands of spirits, yet unborn, who were anxiously waiting for the privilege of coming down to take tabernacles of flesh, that their glory might be complete."[4]

Multiplying and replenishing the earth is a way to "raise up seed" to God. It is the only reason mentioned in the Book of Mormon whereby polygamy might be acceptable. The Nephites were given the general commandment: "There shall not any man among you have save it be one wife; and concubines he shall have none."[5] However, the scriptural language three verses later anticipates the possibility that God could command the practice of polygamy in order to "raise up seed" to him: "For if I will, saith the Lord of Hosts, raise up seed unto me, I will command my people; otherwise they shall hearken unto these things."[6] Between 1841, when plural marriage was first introduced in Nauvoo, and 1890, when the practice was revoked, thousands of children were born to polygamous wives, fulfilling the commandment to multiply and replenish the earth.

Many revelations came to the Prophet as he pondered great mysteries. The revelation on celestial marriage, now section 132, was given in response to Joseph's inquiry "to know and understand wherein . . . the Lord, justified . . . Abraham, Isaac, and Jacob, as also Moses, David and Solomon . . . as touching the principle and doctrine of their having many wives and concubines."[7] Abraham was promised that his posterity would be numerous and his descendants would receive the gospel and bear the priesthood.[8] Unfortunately, his wife Sarah was barren. How then was this promise to be fulfilled? It was the custom and civil *law* of the times to allow men to marry polygamously should their first wives be barren. We learn in Doctrine and Covenants 132:34 that "God commanded Abraham, and Sarah gave Hagar to Abraham to wife. And why did she do it? Because this was the *law*; and from Hagar sprang many people. This, therefore, was fulfilling, among other things, the promises." Apparently, the Lord gave his divine sanction for other Old Testament patriarchs such as Isaac, Jacob, Moses, David, and Solomon to marry polygamously under the civil law as well.[9] The Bible gives few details regarding the dynamics of their polygamous relationships, which makes it difficult, if not impossible, to compare it to plural marriage in Joseph Smith's day. However, the fact that these men were polygamists and were highly favored of the Lord intimates that polygamy itself is not inherently sinful when it is practiced through the proper authority and sanction of the Lord. It is never condemned in scripture as are the practices of adultery, homosexual behavior, and fornication.

To Provide a Customized Trial for the Saints of That Time and Place

Another reason given for the establishment of plural marriage is that it brought customized trials that provided special opportunities for spiritual growth to practicing Saints. In an 1831 revelation, Joseph Smith taught the value of tribulations: "Ye cannot behold with your natural eyes, for the present time, the design of your God concerning those things which shall come hereafter, and the glory which shall follow after much tribulation. For after much tribulation come the blessings. Wherefore the day cometh that ye shall be crowned with much glory; the hour is not yet, but is nigh at hand."[10]

Though the Saints suffered many trials and much tribulation, the trial of practicing polygamy was arguably one of the most formidable and enduring. Apostle John Taylor questioned, "Where did this commandment come from in relation to polygamy?" And then he answered: "It . . . came from God. It was a revelation given unto Joseph Smith from God, and was made binding upon His servants. When this system was first introduced among this people, it was one of the greatest crosses that ever was taken up by any set of men since the world stood."[11]

Throughout religious history, God's followers have, at times, received special commandments. For example, Adam was given the law of animal sacrifice, and the Israelites were given the law of Moses. Plural marriage from the 1840s to 1890 may have been such a commandment. Customized mandates like these bring specific blessings to those who obey, but only at the time when they are commanded.

As Part of the "Restitution of All Things" Prophesied in Acts 3:19–21

In Acts 3:21, we are taught that the Savior would not be received in heaven "until the times of restitution of all things, which God hath spoken by the mouth of all his holy prophets since the world began." Regarding this restitution, Joseph Smith was told, "I am the Lord thy God. . . . I have conferred upon you the keys and power of the priesthood, wherein *I restore all things.*"[12]

What "things" needed to be restored? The restitution did not include the hundreds of regulations contained in the law of Moses, which was fulfilled through the Atonement of Christ.[13] Instead, the things that needed restoration were the covenants and ordinances of the gospel. The first of these to be restored was baptism through the Aaronic Priesthood, which occurred on May 15, 1829.[14] The second was the oath and covenant of the Melchizedek Priesthood given to Joseph Smith and Oliver Cowdery by Peter, James, and John shortly thereafter.[15]

No additional authorities with their associated ordinances or covenants were restored until the Kirtland Temple was dedicated on April 3, 1836. On that date, Joseph and Oliver dropped the curtains in the temple, prayed, and Jesus Christ appeared and accepted the temple as his "House of the Lord."[16] Immediately thereafter, three additional angelic messengers appeared: Moses, Elias, and Elijah, restoring keys and authorities that apparently could not be bestowed without a temple and are used to officiate in temple ordinances.[17]

While the keys restored by John the Baptist and Peter, James, and John allowed for the establishment of an earthly church organization, the keys restored in the Kirtland Temple authorized the sealing of families that continues after death in the celestial kingdom. The framework for building eternal families begins by laying a foundation through an eternal marriage covenant, the sealing of a husband and wife together forever. Section 132:19–20 explains:

> And again, verily I say unto you, if a man marry a wife by my word, which is my law, and by the new and everlasting covenant, and it is sealed unto them by the Holy Spirit of promise, by him who is anointed, unto whom I have appointed this power and the keys of this priesthood . . . [it] shall be of full force when they are out of the

world; and they shall pass by the angels, and the gods, which are set there, to their exaltation and glory in all things, as hath been sealed upon their heads, which glory shall be a fulness and a continuation of the seeds forever and ever. Then shall they be gods, because they have no end; therefore shall they be from everlasting to everlasting, because they continue; then shall they be above all, because all things are subject unto them.[18]

Of all of the teachings, authorities, covenants, and ordinances that Joseph Smith restored, eternal marriage appears to be the zenith because it brings exaltation. Brigham Young explained that eternal marriage "lays the foundation for worlds, for angels, and for the Gods; for intelligent beings to be crowned with glory, immortality, and eternal lives. In fact, it is the thread which runs from the beginning to the end of the holy Gospel of salvation—of the Gospel of the Son of God; it is from eternity to eternity."[19]

So if *eternal* marriage was the primary "thing" that needed to be restored, then why do people say that the restoration of polygamy was part of the "restitution of all things"? It is because plural marriage is an element within the doctrine of eternal marriage that has sometimes been allowed.

Section 132 describes the eternal consequences for men or women who are not sealed in an eternal marriage (either on earth or by proxy in the spirit world) prior to the Resurrection: "Therefore, when they are out of the world they neither marry nor are given in marriage; but are appointed angels in heaven, which angels are ministering servants, to minister for those who are worthy of a far more, and an exceeding, and an eternal weight of glory. For these angels did not abide my law; therefore, they cannot be enlarged, but remain separately and singly, without exaltation, in their saved condition, to all eternity; and from henceforth are not gods, but are angels of God forever and ever."[20] Both monogamous and plural marriages performed with the proper sealing keys can create bonds that could last through eternity.[21]

On May 16, 1843, William Clayton recorded Joseph clarifying that "in the celestial glory there was three heavens or degrees, and in order to obtain the highest a man must enter into this order of the priesthood and if he don't he can't obtain it. He may enter into the other but that is the end of his kingdom."[22] The Prophet also publicly alluded to this principle: "Those who keep no eternal Law in this life or make no eternal contract are single & alone in the eternal world."[23] In other words, every man and every woman must be sealed to an eternal spouse in order to be exalted.

POLYGAMY WAS COMMANDED BETWEEN THE 1840s AND 1890

Though the Prophet likely inquired about the ancient practice of polygamy and learned about the new and everlasting covenant of marriage in 1831,[24] it was not until 1843 that the revelation now known as D&C 132 was dictated, which addresses these subjects. In the revelation, the Lord reveals that those who do not abide the new and everlasting covenant of marriage will be damned.[25] In this context, damnation refers to lack of progression after death. The revelation explains that the new and everlasting covenant of marriage is *eternal* marriage, which brings exaltation to worthy couples who are sealed by proper authority.

Section 132 does not command the practice of plural marriage, and no presiding Church leader from Joseph Smith to the present has proclaimed through any revelation or official declaration that all exalted beings will be required to practice polygamy. Joseph told close associates that the commandment originated with an angel who appeared to him three times between 1834 and 1842, mandating the practice.[26] In Kirtland, Ohio, Joseph Smith confided in Church member Lyman Sherman that "the ancient order of plural marriage was again to be practiced by the Church."[27] Later, in Nauvoo, Joseph A. Kelting recalled the Prophet explaining the principle: "He then began a defense of the doctrine by referring to the Old Testament. . . . He then informed me that he had received a revelation from God which taught the correctness of the doctrine of a plurality of wives, and commanding him to obey it."[28]

The Practice of Plural Marriage among the Early Saints

After a brief experiment with plural marriage in Kirtland,[29] Joseph abandoned the practice until the Saints had settled in Nauvoo. The Prophet was married to Louisa Beaman in 1841,[30] and the following year Joseph slowly began authorizing plural marriages among members of the Quorum of the Twelve. The practice was kept secret because of fear of persecution from nonmembers and prosecution for possible violation of Illinois state law.

This was a great challenge for these first polygamists, and many looked forward to moving to the West, where they would be able to openly practice this new marital dynamic. At the time of the Prophet's death on June 27, 1844, twenty-nine men besides Joseph had married a total of fifty plural wives.[31] But it was only after crossing the Mississippi River during their arduous, thousand-mile trek to the Great Basin that these polygamous Saints felt free to begin speaking openly about their relationships.[32]

By 1851, with the Saints firmly ensconced in the Utah Territory, polygamy was no longer a secret among the Saints or the rest of the country. Sensational headlines graced the covers of newspapers from New York to San Francisco decrying the practice and especially commenting on the reported number of wives of Brigham Young, Utah territorial governor and President of the Church.[33] In an August 1852 conference of elders, Apostle Orson

Pratt formally explained the teachings of the Prophet Joseph Smith on the matter, added some additional justifications for the practice, presented the revelation dictated in 1843 to the congregation, and announced that all worthy Latter-day Saint men were now encouraged to marry plurally.[34]

The Trial of the Practice of Polygamy

Those who practiced polygamy during the early decades after it was authorized reported varying experiences. Eliza Partridge, married twice polygamously, declared, "Nothing but a firm desire to keep the commandments of the Lord could have induced a girl to marry in that way. I thought my trials were very severe in this line."[35] Some women who practiced polygamy seemed to have found it a blessing in some aspects. Lucy Walker, one of Joseph's plural wives, recalled the value of plural marriage in teaching character strengths: "I will say [that polygamy] is a grand school. You learn self control, self denial; it brings out the nobler traits of our fallen natures, and teaches us to study and subdue self, while we become acquainted with the peculiar characteristics of each other. There is a grand opportunity to improve ourselves, and the lessons learned in a few years, are worth the experience of a lifetime, for this reason, that you are better prepared to make a home happy."[36]

Polygamy on earth does not seem fair to most observers. It generally expands a man's emotional and sexual opportunities as a husband as it simultaneously diminishes a woman's emotional and sexual opportunities as a wife. Many of our concerns today regarding polygamy are not all that different from those felt by nineteenth-century Latter-day Saints. Helen Mar Kimball remembered, "The Prophet said that the practice of this principle would be the hardest trial the Saints would ever have to test their faith."[37] This statement seems to apply today as much as it did in Nauvoo. Some of the early polygamists were blessed with spiritual experiences as they struggled to gain a testimony of the principle. Reading their stories may aid in understanding their choices to marry into plural unions.[38]

Despite these challenges, neither Joseph Smith nor any other presiding leader gave a reason for the requirement of the practice. In 1892, when asked why the principle of plural marriage was adopted, Apostle Lorenzo Snow simply responded, "I can't tell for I didn't do it."[39] Future Apostle James Talmage stated that "the sole and sufficient reason which led the church to promulgate the doctrine was that the Lord had by revelation taught it and had commanded its acceptance in the present dispensation."[40]

Monogamy Once Again Becomes the Standard in the Church

In 1890, newly passed federal laws threatened the very existence of the Church and greatly impeded the Church's ability to do missionary work and to perform vicarious temple ordinances. Despite this enduring persecution, however, the vast majority of Latter-day Saint polygamists were willing to continue practicing plural marriage, if that was the Lord's requirement. But in September of that year, Wilford Woodruff, who held the sealing keys needed to authorize all valid eternal marriages, declared that the commandment to practice plural marriage had been revoked and was no longer binding upon the Latter-day Saints. Thereafter, the practice of monogamy was the Latter-day Saint standard.

Between 1890 and 1904, a few secret plural marriages were authorized by the Church President each year. Most were performed outside of the United States, but not all. These sealings were eventually discovered by the media, bringing embarrassment to the Church. In April of 1904, Joseph F. Smith, then President of the Church and holder of all priesthood keys, refused to authorize any new plural ceremonies. Since that time, all attempts to practice polygamy have been without authorization, are considered sinful,[41] and are not considered "valid, neither of force when they are out of the world."[42] This is the status of all earthly polygamous marriages entered into by men and women today because they are not performed through authorized priesthood keys.

James Talmage once noted that "plural marriage was an incident, never an essential."[43] There is no ordinance or covenant or ceremony of plural marriage. At the time these marriages were permitted, they were simply a repetition of the eternal marriage rite. Current Church dialogue centers on eternal marriage, the union of one man to one woman for time and eternity,[44] which *is* an ordinance, a covenant, and a ceremony. Monogamous marriage is "the Lord's standing law on marriage."[45] Members can rejoice in modern-day revelation that declares marriage "between a man and a woman is ordained of God" and lays the basis for exaltation and eternal families.[46]

Additional Resources

The Church of Jesus Christ of Latter-day Saints. "Plural Marriage in the Church of Jesus Christ of Latter-day Saints." https://www.lds.org/topics/plural-marriage-in-the-church-of-jesus-christ-of-latter-day-saints.

Hales, Brian C. *Joseph Smith's Polygamy: History and Theology*, 3 vols. Salt Lake City: Greg Kofford Books, 2013.

Hales, Brian C., and Laura H. Hales. *Joseph Smith's Polygamy: Toward a Better Understanding*. Salt Lake City: Greg Kofford Books, 2015.

Hales, Laura Harris. "Joseph Smith's Polygamy: Toward a Better Understanding." Presentation at FairMormon Conference, August 7, 2015. http://www.fairmormon.org/perspectives/fair-conferences/2015-fairmormon-conference/joseph-smiths-polygamy-toward-a-better-understanding.

Joseph Smith's Polygamy. http://JosephSmithsPolygamy.org.

About the Author

Brian C. Hales is the author of seven books dealing with Mormon polygamy. He has presented at numerous meetings and symposia and published articles in *The Journal of Mormon History*, *Mormon Historical Studies*, and *Dialogue*, as well as the *Persistence of Polygamy* series. He also maintains the websites MormonPolygamyDocuments.org and JosephSmithsPolygamy.org. Brian works as an anesthesiologist and has served as the president of both the Utah Medical Association and the medical staff at the Davis Hospital and Medical Center in Layton, Utah. Brian is married to Laura Harris Hales and is the father to four children.

Laura Harris Hales is a freelance copy editor, author, and mother of five avid truth seekers. She received a bachelor's degree in international relations from Brigham Young University and a master's degree in professional writing from New England College. She has also worked as both a paralegal and as an adjunct professor of English. With her husband, Brian C. Hales, she coauthored *Joseph Smith's Polygamy: Toward a Better Understanding* and maintains the website JosephSmithsPolygamy.org.

Notes

1. Erastus Snow, St. George Utah Stake [Conference], General Minutes, Sunday, June 17, 1883, 2 pm, LR 7836 11, reel 1, Church History Library (hereafter CHL).

2. D&C 132:63.

3. Charles Lambert, "Autobiography," CHL; quoted in Danel W. Bachman, "The Authorship of the Manuscript of Doctrine and Covenants Section 132," in *Sidney B. Sperry Symposium: A Sesquicentennial Look at Church History*, January 26, 1980 (Provo, UT: BYU Religious Instruction, 1980), 43, n. 44.

4. Helen Mar Kimball Smith Whitney, *Why We Practice Plural Marriage* (Salt Lake City: Juvenile Instructor Office, 1882), 7.

5. Jacob 2:27.

6. Jacob 2:30.

7. D&C 132:1; emphasis added.

8. See Abraham 2:9, 3:14; Genesis 17:5–6.

9. D&C 132:1.

10. D&C 58:3–4.

11. John Taylor, in *Journal of Discourses* (London: Latter-day Saints' Book Depot, 1854–56), 11:221.

12. D&C 132:40, 45; emphasis added.

13. See 3 Nephi 9:17.

14. D&C 13:1.

15. D&C 27:12.

16. D&C 110:1–7.

17. D&C 110:11–16.

18. D&C 132:19–20.

19. Brigham Young, in *Journal of Discourses*, 2:90 (October 6, 1854).

20. D&C 132:16–17.

21. "Plural Marriage in The Church of Jesus Christ of Latter-day Saints," The Church of Jesus Christ of Latter-day Saints, www.lds.org/topics/plural-marriage-in-the-church-of-jesus-christ-of-latter-day-saints, paragraph 6; See also Doctrine and Covenants 132:7; 131:2–3.

22. George D. Smith, ed., *An Intimate Chronicle: The Journals of William Clayton* (Salt Lake City: Signature Books, 1995), 102; see also D&C 131:1–4.

23. Andrew F. Ehat and Lyndon W. Cook, eds., *The Words of Joseph Smith* (Provo, UT: Grandin Book, 1991), 357; 232 (Franklin D. Richards reporting, July 16, 1843). See also Lorenzo Snow, "Discourse," *Millennial Star* 61, no. 35 (May 8, 1899): 547–48.

24. D&C 132, preface.

25. D&C 132:4–6.

26. Brian C. Hales, "Encouraging Joseph Smith to Practice Plural Marriage: The Accounts of the Angel with a Drawn Sword," *Mormon Historical Studies* 11, no. 2 (Fall 2010): 69–70.

27. Quoted by Benjamin F. Johnson in Dean R. Zimmerman, *I Knew the Prophets: An Analysis of the Letter of Benjamin F. Johnson to George F. Gibbs* (Bountiful, UT: Horizon, 1976), 37–38.

28. Joseph A. Kelting, "Statement," Joseph Smith Affidavits, MS 3423, folder 2, images 11–16a, CHL.

29. Brian C. Hales and Laura H. Hales, *Joseph Smith's Polygamy: Toward a Better Understanding* (Salt Lake City: Greg Kofford Books, 2015), chap. 6.

30. Joseph F. Smith Affidavit Books, 4 vols., MS 3423, CHL, 1:3.

31. Brian C. Hales, *Joseph Smith's Polygamy: History*, 2 vols. (Salt Lake City: Greg Kofford Books, 2013), 2:165.

32. Hales and Hales, *Toward a Better Understanding*, 125.

33. Parley P. Pratt, "'Mormonism!' 'Plurality of Wives!' An Especial Chapter, for the Especial Edification of Certain Inquisitive News Editors, Etc.," San Francisco, July 13, 1852, https://ia600801.us.archive.org/28/items/mormonismplurali00smit/mormonismplurali00smit.pdf.

34. Orson Pratt, *Deseret News*—Extra, September 14, 1852, 14–18.

35. Eliza Maria Partridge Lyman, "Life and Journal of Eliza Maria Partridge Lyman," n.p., pp. 7–8 in the holograph.

36. Lucy Walker, statement, quoted in Lyman Omer Littlefield, *Reminiscences of Latter-day Saints: Giving an Account of Much Individual Suffering Endured for Religious Conscience* (Logan, UT: Utah Journal Co., 1888), 50–51.

37. Richard Neitzel Holzapfel and Jeni Brobery Holzapfel, eds., *A Woman's View: Helen Mar Whitney's Reminiscences of Early Church History* (Provo, UT: Religious Studies Center, 1997), 140.

38. See Brian C. Hales, "Testimonies of Nauvoo Polygamists," Joseph Smith's Polygamy, http://josephsmithspolygamy.org/home-3/stories-of-faith-nauvoo-polygamists/.

39. Lorenzo Snow, deposition, Temple Lot Transcript, Respondent's Testimony, Part 3, p. 121, questions 200–201.

40. James Talmage, "Items on Polygamy—Omitted from the Published Book," undated, written for inclusion but not published in the *Articles of Faith*, James E. Talmage Papers, Archives and Manuscripts, Harold B. Lee Library, Brigham Young University, Provo, UT.

41. D&C 132:38.

42. D&C 132:18.

43. James E. Talmage, *Articles of Faith* (Salt Lake City: Deseret News, 1899), 458.

44. The Church of Jesus Christ of Latter-day Saints, "Lesson 19: The Doctrine of Eternal Marriage and Family," *Foundations of the Restoration Teacher Manual* (Salt Lake City: The Church of Jesus Christ of Latter-day Saints, 2015), 84–88, https://www.lds.org/bc/content/ldsorg/manual/institute/Foundations_of_the_Restoration.v2_eng.pdf.

45. The Church of Jesus Christ of Latter-day Saints, "Plural Marriage in The Church of Jesus Christ of Latter-day Saints," https://www.lds.org/topics/plural-marriage-in-the-church-of-jesus-christ-of-latter-day-saints.

46. The First Presidency and Council of the Twelve Apostles of The Church of Jesus Christ of Latter-day Saints, "The Family: A Proclamation to the World," https://www.lds.org/topics/family-proclamation.

11

Joseph Smith's Practice of Plural Marriage

Brian C. Hales

*I*N THE REVELATION ON ETERNAL MARRIAGE, SECTION 132 OF THE *Doctrine and Covenants*, several doctrinal reasons are given for the authorized practice of polygamy at times specified by the Lord. The Prophet Joseph Smith reported an angel appeared to him in 1834, directing him to practice plural marriage and introduce it among the Saints. However, the monogamous tradition of Church members and nonmembers created a huge obstacle to the open practice of that commandment. Further challenges came as Joseph implemented the principle in Nauvoo. The thin historical record complicates reconstructing a true picture of those first plural marriages in the Church. Nevertheless, a review of the Prophet's decisions as he introduced and practiced polygamy reveals some strange dynamics at times, but nothing that was morally sinful in light of Joseph's teachings on the matter.

In 1831, just one year after the Church was organized, Joseph Smith concluded that Old Testament patriarchs like Abraham and Jacob did not commit sin by marrying plural wives. Lyman E. Johnson recalled that "Joseph had made known to him as early as 1831 that plural marriage was a correct principle."[1] Whether the Prophet knew then that he would later institute it as a practice within the Church is unknown.

However, the Prophet reported that the directive came three years later in Kirtland, Ohio, when an angel appeared commanding him to personally practice plural marriage. Joseph told plural wife Mary Elizabeth Rollins: "The angel came to me three times between the years of 1834 and 1842 and said I was to obey that principle or he would slay me." In response, Joseph "foresaw the trouble that would follow and sought to turn away from the commandment."[2] Uncharacteristically, he "put it off"[3] and "hesitated and deferred from time to time."[4] Eliza R. Snow described Joseph as "afraid to promulgate it."[5]

Facing the Challenges

The Prophet faced several obstacles as he introduced polygamy, including a Church membership rightfully steeped in a tradition of monogamy. Brigham related, "My brethren know what my feelings were at the time Joseph revealed the doctrine; I was not desirous of shrinking from any duty, nor of failing in the least to do as I was commanded, but it was the first time in my life that I had desired the grave, and I could hardly get over it for a long time. And when I saw a funeral, I felt to envy the corpse its situation, and to regret that I was not in the coffin."[6] He later commented, "I never should have embraced it had it not been a command from the Almighty."[7] John Taylor similarly recalled, "[At] the time when men were commanded to take more wives. It made us all pull pretty long faces sometimes. It was not so easy as one might think. When it was revealed to us it looked like the last end of Mormonism. For a man to ask another woman to marry him required more self-confidence than we had."[8]

The nearly universal reaction among LDS women was similar. Bathsheba B. Smith remembered, "We discussed it [polygamy] . . . that is, us young girls did, for I was a young girl then, and we talked a good deal about it, and some of us did not like it much."[9] When asked in 1859, "Is the system of your Church [plurality of wives] acceptable to the majority of its women?" Brigham Young answered: "They could not be more averse to it than I was when it was first revealed to us as the Divine will. I think they generally accept it, as I do, as the will of God."[10] One non-LDS author concluded, "All evidence tends to support the contention that the majority of the Church membership received the doctrine [of polygamy] with abhorrence. They adopted the practice against their natural inclinations, and out of fear of the hereafter, rather than from motives of lust."[11]

Besides pushback from Church members, state laws allowed for and societal norms supported monogamous marriage. Any deviation from that standard quickly generated suspicions regarding the motivations of the participants. Joseph Smith's nephew, Church President Joseph F. Smith, wrote in 1903: "It is difficult to convince the prejudiced mind that any but base intents and impure desires prompted the practice of plural marriage, but nevertheless it was entered into, God knows, with the highest religious and moral motives."[12] Joseph faced formidable resistance from within and without the Church.

Fanny Alger—Joseph Smith's First Plural Wife

The Prophet entered into his first polygamous marriage with Fanny Alger, a domestic working in the Smith home, while living in Kirtland, Ohio. Joseph did not approach Fanny directly to discuss polygamy. Instead he enlisted the assistance of Levi Hancock, a friend, to serve as an intermediary and officiator. Levi's son Mosiah wrote in 1896: "Father goes to Fanny and said 'Fanny Brother Joseph the Prophet loves you and wishes you for a wife will you be his wife'? 'I will Levi' Said She. Father takes Fanny to Joseph and said 'Brother Joseph I have been successful in my mission.'"[13] Using priesthood authority, "Father gave her to Joseph repeating the Ceremony as Joseph repeated to him."[14] The dating of the ceremony is unknown, but was most likely in late 1835 or early 1836. Eliza R. Snow, who was "well acquainted" with Fanny and living in the Smith home at the time of the discovery of the union, corroborated a plural marriage occurred as she personally wrote Fanny's name on an 1887 list of Joseph Smith's plural wives.[15]

While the historical record is incomplete, it seems that Joseph entered his first plural marriage without informing his legal wife, Emma Hale Smith. Not informing Emma of the polygamous marriage created several problems and heartache for all involved. At some point, either years or weeks after the ceremony, Emma discovered the plural relationship. One second-hand account reports, "She went to the barn and saw him and Fanny in the barn together alone. She looked through a crack and saw the transaction!"[16] What Emma witnessed, whether it was the plural marriage ceremony or an exchange of affection, we are not told.

While Joseph had received numerous angelic visitations including one reportedly commanding polygamy, it is apparent Emma had not. She reacted violently and in order to quell the disturbance, Joseph called for Oliver Cowdery to help calm Emma. Oliver became convinced that the relationship between Fanny and Joseph was illegitimate and could not be persuaded otherwise. He held to that opinion despite Joseph's efforts to convince him.[17]

Emma sent Fanny Alger away after the discovery of the relationship.[18] The displaced Fanny rejoined her family who migrated to Indiana, where she soon married a nonmember and raised a large family.[19] In 1874, she joined the Universalist Church and remained a member of that congregation until her 1889 death. However, Benjamin F. Johnson recorded, "Altho she never left the State [of Indiana] She did not turn from the Church nor from her friendship for the Prophet while She lived."[20]

Sealings to Legally Married Women

Some readers may be surprised to learn that about a third of Joseph Smith's plural sealings were to women who were already civilly married and had legal husbands. Most historians have listed these women as some of the Prophet's time-and-eternity plural wives, fueling assumptions that those females practiced a plurality of husbands—technically called polyandry.[21] Many authors have also asserted that these marriages sound and look like genuine polyandry, so they must have been polyandrous and to say they were anything other than polyandry would be to deny reality. In addition, since traditional marriage usually includes mutual affection, a desire for companionship, and sexuality, observers have likewise speculated that the women experienced these with Joseph and their civil spouses during the same time periods.

However, several problems exist with these assumptions. First, no plain evidence has been found supporting the claims. That is, no unambiguous documentation for genuine polyandry in Nauvoo has been located in the historical record. Writers who say Joseph Smith practiced genuine polyandry are basing their conclusions on opinion, rather than on evidence. Demonstrating the existence of a plurality of husbands could be done relatively easily by quoting a single credible supportive statement, if such existed. One well-documented testimony from a participant or other close observer (of which there were dozens) indicating that a woman had two genuine husbands at the same time would constitute such evidence. Even a passing reference to a polyandrous triangle in a letter, journal, or later recollection would be impressive. Also, a revelation or other theological justification traceable to Joseph Smith authorizing those relations would be very convincing. No evidence of this type has been found. Instead, the historical record reads as if sexual polyandry never occurred and would have been condemned if it had.

A second concern is that the teachings of Joseph Smith and all other Church leaders condemn a plurality of husbands as adultery. Section 132 mentions such relations three times, labelling them "adultery," and in two cases stating the woman involved "would be destroyed." When asked in 1852, "What do you think of a woman having more husbands than one?" Brigham Young answered, "This is not known to the law."[22] Orson Pratt similarly instructed: "God has strictly forbidden, in this Bible, plurality of husbands, and proclaimed against it in his law."[23] On October 8, 1869, Apostle George A. Smith taught that "a plurality of husbands is wrong."[24] First Presidency Counselor Joseph F. Smith wrote in 1889: "Polyandry is wrong, physiologically, morally, and from a scriptural point of order. It is nowhere sanctioned in the Bible, nor by the law of God or nature and has not affinity with 'Mormon' plural marriage."[25] Multiple additional condemnations are found in the historical record contrasting the complete absence of any supportive statements.

A third problem is that Doctrine and Covenants 22:1 states, "All old covenants have I caused to be done away in this thing; and this is a new and an everlasting covenant." This revelation was given shortly after the Church was organized in response to a specific question about baptism, which is a new and everlasting covenant between a person and God. Thirteen years later, Joseph recorded another revelation that refers to eternal marriage as "a new and an everlasting covenant."[26] So if "all old covenants" are "done away" by "a new and everlasting covenant," then a previous legal marriage (an "old" marriage covenant) would be "done away" when a woman is sealed to a new husband in the new and everlasting covenant of marriage. This would create the equivalence of a Church divorce. Thereafter, from a religious standpoint, a woman previously civilly married and subsequently sealed would have only one husband in the eyes of the Church. Going back to her legal husband would be considered adultery because, according to the revelations, that marriage ended with the sealing. These scriptures are important because they show that a plurality of husbands is not doctrinally supported as part of the new and everlasting covenant of marriage. While many details are absent, there is no theological basis for a plurality of husbands in Joseph's teachings.

So what was the nature of Joseph Smith's sealings to legally married women? Available evidence indicates that those sealings were of two types. In the early days of the restoration, eternity-only sealings were sometimes permitted. Such sealings did not begin until the man and woman had died. In other words, the woman was married to one spouse during mortality and a different spouse in eternity. The husbands of a few of the women were not active Latter-day Saints, so they could not be sealed to their wives. Doctrine and Covenants 132:17 teaches plainly that eternal marriage is needed for exaltation, so it is easier to understand why these females were sealed to Joseph. Other men besides the Prophet were also sealed to plural wives for eternity only.

However, several of the women were legally married to men who were devout Church members. The motivations behind these sealings—why the women were not instead eternally married to their civil spouses and why Joseph allowed these sealings—are unknown, although in a couple of situations the legal marriages were unhappy. One possible reason is simply because the women chose to be sealed to Joseph Smith for the next life. Lucy Walker, one of Joseph's plural wives, recalled his counsel regarding eternal sealings: "A woman would have her choice, this was a privilege that could not be denied her."[27] These types of sealings are no longer permitted but were apparently allowed at that time because the women had been previously married to their legal husbands "until death, do you part," rather than for time and eternity.

Perhaps eleven of Joseph Smith's fourteen plural marriages to women with legal husbands were nonsexual, eternity-only unions,[28] possibly two were for time and eternity to women who had experienced the equivalence of a Church divorce from their first spouse, and one was a special situation where the woman married legally a "front" or pretend husband *after* her sealing to Joseph to deflect attention from her relationship with the Prophet.[29]

Understandably, these sealings and relationships seem strange, and questions still exist. Many wonder why the two women who were physically separated from their husbands would not simply obtain a civil divorce before being sealed for time and eternity to Joseph Smith as is now required in the Church. One possible reason is that it was difficult to obtain a divorce on the frontier in the nineteenth century. While a justice of the peace could marry a couple, often the state legislature needed to approve a divorce. Also, women did not possess the legal rights they now have; with a divorce, the women would have risked losing claim to their property and custody of their children. What to us seems rather straightforward was actually more complicated when analyzed in deference to the nineteenth-century legal system. Divorce became much easier in the Utah territory under Brigham Young's leadership and was liberally granted to women, eliminating the appearance of polyandrous relationships.

It is important to note that the participants and others with a detailed knowledge of the relationships were apparently unbothered by the dynamics. None of the women recorded complaints, and their legal husbands left no grievances against the Prophet. There were many officiators and witnesses, none of whom protested, and even apostates in Nauvoo did not leave accusations against Joseph Smith concerning these sealings. Perhaps additional manuscripts will be discovered to further clarify the nature of these unusual unions.

Joseph, Emma, and Plural Marriage

On April 5, 1841, Joseph B. Noble sealed his sister-in-law, Louisa Beaman, to the Prophet.[30] It seems clear that Emma was not informed that Joseph planned to unite in this polygamous union. The sealing to Louisa Beaman was for time and eternity, but during the next ten months, Joseph evidently sought almost exclusively sealings to civilly married women. Eight out of the next nine of Joseph Smith's plural marriage proposals (and possibly eleven out of the next twelve) were to legally married women. The one exception was a marriage to a widow. There is no indication of sexual relations in any of those plural sealings. It is possible that Joseph Smith sought nonsexual, eternity-only sealings in order to fulfil a command while being sensitive to Emma's feelings. But from 1842 forward, Joseph proposed to only three more legally married women and each was a unique situation. Most of the subsequent plural sealings were to unmarried females for time and eternity.

Throughout 1842 Emma was unaware of Joseph Smith's plural marriages. Readers would expect the Prophet to be conflicted over his plural marriages and her non-participation and uninformed state. A plausible assumption explaining the chronology of the Prophet's announcement to Emma is that he waited until she was ready to accept the principle of polygamy before presenting her with the details. In 1892, Apostle Lorenzo Snow recalled:

> The people had the most implicit and perfect confidence in Joseph Smith, and when he gave a revelation, whether it was accepted or not, it didn't make any difference with some, for they had the most perfect confidence in him. . . . [A new revelation] would be binding upon such as knew of it. . . . If that revelation is presented to me, and there is a half a dozen men and women and it is presented to them, it would be a law to them, and be binding upon them, and any other part of the church that had knowledge, — distinct and definite knowledge of it, — but I do not think it would be binding upon any other part of the church other than that which had knowledge of its existence.[31]

In addition, the revelation on celestial marriage explains that once Joseph taught Emma about it, she was obligated to "believe and administer unto him," or else "she shall be destroyed."[32] If she rejected the doctrines, "she then becomes the transgressor."[33] As long as the new principles remained undisclosed, her position before the Lord was unchallenged and temporarily secure. The language in the revelation directed toward Emma may seem overly harsh. It is possible that if Joseph had had the opportunity to edit the revelation before publication, he would have softened those words.[34]

Emma probably accepted the *principle* of plural marriage in the spring of 1843 and gave Joseph four wives in May. However, she immediately struggled with its *practice*. On July 12, at Hyrum Smith's suggestion, the Prophet dictated a revelation,[35] which Hyrum presented to Emma in the hope that she would again accept Joseph's practice of polygamy. Afterwards, he reported that "he had never received a more severe talking to in his life, that Emma was very bitter and full of resentment and anger." Immediately she demanded that Joseph transfer financial resources to sustain her and her children should anything happen to Joseph or to their marriage. She apparently also required Joseph to obtain her permission before marrying any additional plural wives (and, indeed, he was sealed to only two women after that date).

Joseph and Emma's marriage resembled, outwardly at least, that of other monogamists in Nauvoo. Even close neighbors were unaware of his plural wives. Mary Ralph recalled in 1883: "I lived in Nauvoo, Illinois, close to the house of Joseph Smith, just across the road, some time. . . . I was well acquainted with the two Partridge girls and the two Walker girls and their two brothers, William and Lorin Walker; they were orphans, and all lived in the family of Joseph Smith; but I never knew they were any of them his wives."[36]

Looking back at Joseph Smith's choices in dealing with the introduction of plural marriage to Emma, it is possible that his actions were less than perfect. The revelation on celestial marriage admonishes Emma saying "forgive my servant Joseph his trespasses."[37] Apparently he had trespassed against Emma. Perhaps as the Prophet dealt with the crosscurrents of polygamy and his own marriage, other approaches would have been better.

Emma's experience with plural marriage was extremely difficult. But despite her struggles and stumbles, she remained true to Joseph. Reportedly when one of his plural wives complained about Emma's behavior, he turned to her and said, "If you desire my love, you must never speak evil of Emma."[38] Immediately after the martyrdom, family friend John P. Greene saw Emma "weeping and wailing bitterly, in a loud and unrestrained voice, her face covered with her hands." He remarked, "This affliction would be to her a crown of life." She quickly replied, "My husband was my crown."[39]

Young Wives

Much attention has been given to the fact that ten of Joseph Smith's plural wives were teenagers: Helen Mar Kimball (fourteen), Nancy M. Winchester (fourteen?), Flora Ann Woodworth (sixteen), Sarah Ann Whitney (seventeen), Sarah Lawrence (seventeen), Lucy Walker (seventeen), Fanny Alger (nineteen?), Emily Dow Partridge (nineteen), Maria Lawrence (nineteen), and Malissa Lott (nineteen). While these ages may seem young to observers in the twenty-first century, none would have been considered scandalous in the 1840s, although the two fourteen-year-olds (Helen Mar Kimball and Nancy M. Winchester) may have been eyebrow-raising. Author Kimball Young explained, "By present standards [1954] a bride of 17 or 18 years is considered rather unusual but under pioneer conditions there was nothing atypical about this."[40] For example, William Clark (of the Lewis and Clark expedition) wed sixteen-year-old Julia Hancock in 1808. Jesse Hale, brother to Emma, married Mary McKune when she was fifteen and he was twenty-three.[41] Martin Harris, one of the Three Witnesses of the Book of Mormon, married his wife, Lucy, when she was only fifteen.[42] In fact, Illinois governor Thomas Ford, the state official who forced the Prophet to appear at Carthage where he was eventually murdered, married Frances Hambaugh in 1828; she was fifteen and he was twenty-eight.[43]

Though Joseph married two young teenagers, there is no evidence of sexuality with either of them. Little information is recorded regarding Joseph's relationship with Nancy Winchester except that it occurred. Heber C. Kimball requested that Joseph be sealed to his daughter, to which Helen agreed.[44] There is no historical data supporting the conclusion that the Prophet initiated that process or actively sought the plural union. Several observations support the view that his sealing to Helen Mar Kimball was never consummated, though it was likely for time and eternity. In 1892, depositions seeking to discover if Joseph Smith practiced polygamy were sought in litigation between the RLDS Church and the Church of Christ. Helen Mar Kimball was not called to testify, even though she lived close to the courthouse and had written two books defending plural marriage. Instead, three wives who lived in more distant areas were summoned and all affirmed sexual relations with the Prophet in their plural marriages to him. A likely reason Helen was not called is that she could not give the required testimony of experiencing sexuality in her sealing to the Prophet.

Although we have no firsthand accounts outlining the Prophet's counsel on marriages to women in their teens, a pattern starting in Nauvoo that carried over into Utah taught that polygamous husbands should allow young wives to physically mature before beginning a family with them. Eugene E. Campbell described Brigham's later instructions. To one man at Fort Supply, Young explained, "I don't object to your taking sisters named in your letter to wife if they are not too young and their parents and your president and all connected are satisfied, but I do not want children to be married to men before an age which their mothers can generally best determine."[45] Writing to another man in Spanish Fork, he said, "Go ahead and marry them, but leave the children to grow."[46] To Louis Robinson, head of the Church at Fort Bridger, Young advised, "Take good women, but let the children grow, then they will be able to bear children after a few years without injury."[47]

A Difficult Practice to Live

Joseph Smith established the divisive principle of plural marriage among the Nauvoo Saints in the early 1840s. The opposition from within and without the Church turned out to be substantial, sometimes requiring creative measures that seem unorthodox today. It may be useful to view the Prophet's behavior as his contemporaries did. According to available evidence, none of the possible thirty-five plural wives sealed to Joseph Smith ever accused him of abuse or deception—even the seven who left the Church. The remaining twenty-eight remained true to a belief in the Prophet's mission throughout their lives. Had any of Joseph's polygamous wives eventually decided that he had tricked them, their subsequent scorn might have easily motivated them to expose him through the pages of the many anti-Mormon presses located across the expanding United States.

"I Never Told You I Was Perfect"

Just weeks before his martyrdom, the Prophet acknowledged: "I never told you I was perfect."[48] He also explained: "a prophet was a prophet only when he was acting as such,"[49] declaring he "was but a man, and [people] must not expect me to be perfect."[50] He once lamented: "Altho' I do wrong, I do not the wrongs that I am charg'd with doing—the wrong that I do is thro' the frailty of human nature like other men. No man lives without fault."[51]

Observers today can review the Prophet's life and actions and expect him to have sincerely striven to keep the commandments[52] but should not expect to see perfection. The Lord allowed Joseph to face challenges, telling him "all these things shall give thee experience, and shall be for thy good."[53] The early practice of polygamy unfolded against legal and social opposition that made it visibly messy and complicated. Looking at Joseph's actions retrospectively, it may appear that the intensity of some challenges he encountered might have been diminished if he had acted differently, but without additional historical details, we may never really know what occurred all those years ago in a frontier town on the banks of the Mississippi.

Additional Resources

The Church of Jesus Christ of Latter-day Saints. "Plural Marriage in Kirtland and Nauvoo." https://www.lds.org/topics/plural-marriage-in-kirtland-and-nauvoo.

Bringhurst, Newell G. and Craig L. Foster, eds., *The Persistence of Polygamy*, 3 vols. Independence, MO: John Whitmer Books, 2010–2015.

Hales, Brian C. "Joseph Smith's Personal Polygamy." *Journal of Mormon History* 38, no. 2 (Spring 2012): 163–228.

Hales, Brian C. *Joseph Smith's Polygamy: History and Theology*, 3 vols. Salt Lake City: Greg Kofford Books, 2013.

Hales, Brian C. and Laura H. Hales. *Joseph Smith's Polygamy: Toward a Better Understanding*. Salt Lake City: Greg Kofford Books, 2015.

Joseph Smith's Polygamy. http://JosephSmithsPolygamy.org.

About the Author

Brian C. Hales is the author of seven books dealing with Mormon polygamy. He has presented at numerous meetings and symposia and published articles in *The Journal of Mormon History*, *Mormon Historical Studies*, and *Dialogue*, as well as the *Persistence of Polygamy* series. He also maintains the websites MormonPolygamyDocuments.org and JosephSmithsPolygamy.org. Brian works as an anesthesiologist and has served as the president of both the Utah Medical Association and the Medical Staff at the Davis Hospital and Medical Center in Layton, Utah. Brian is married to Laura Harris Hales and is the father to four children.

Notes

1. Recalled by his mission companion, Orson Pratt, "Report of Elders Orson Pratt and Joseph F. Smith," *Millennial Star* 40 (December 16, 1878): 788.

2. Lorenzo Snow, quoted by Eliza R. Snow in *Biography and Family Record of Lorenzo Snow* (Salt Lake City: Deseret News, 1884), 69–70.

3. Benjamin F. Johnson, *My Life's Review* (repr.; Mesa, AZ: 21st Century Printing, 1992), 95–96; see also Zina Huntington, quoted in "Joseph, the Prophet, His Life and Mission as Viewed by Intimate Acquaintances," *Salt Lake Herald Church and Farm Supplement*, January 12, 1895, 212.

4. Lorenzo Snow, quoted in *Biography and Family Record of Lorenzo Snow*, 69–70.

5. Eliza R. Snow, quoted in "Two Prophets' Widows, A Visit to the Relicts of Joseph Smith and Brigham Young," in *St. Louis Globe-Democrat*, St. Louis, Missouri, August 18, 1887, 6.

6. Brigham Young, in *Journal of Discourses*, 3:266 (July 14, 1855).

7. Elden J. Watson, *Brigham Young Addresses, 1865–1869, A Chronological Compilation of Known Addresses of the Prophet Brigham Young* (Salt Lake City: Elden J. Watson, 1982), 5:170 (August 5, 1869).

8. John Taylor, Report of the Dedication of the Kaysville Relief Society House, November 12, 1876, *Woman's Exponent* 5, no. 19 (March 1, 1877): 148.

9. Bathsheba Smith, deposition, Temple Lot Transcript, Respondent's testimony, part 3, 292, question 21.

10. Horace Greeley, *An Overland Journey from New York to San Francisco in the Summer of 1859* (New York: H. H. Bancroft & Co., 1860; repr., New York: Ballantine Books, 1963), 138.

11. Harry M. Beardsley, *Joseph Smith and His Mormon Empire* (New York: Houghton Mifflin, 1931), 299.

12. Joseph F. Smith, "The 'Mormonism' of To-day," *The Arena* 29, no. 5 (May 1903): 450.

13. Levi Ward Hancock, autobiography with additions in 1896 by Mosiah Hancock, MS 570, microfilm, 63, CHL; cited portion written by Mosiah.

14. Hancock, autobiography, 63.

15. Andrew Jenson, First List of Plural Wives, MS 17956, box 49, folder 16, doc. 1, Andrew Jenson Papers, CHL.

16. William McLellin, letter to Joseph Smith III, July 1872, Community of Christ Archives.

17. Oliver Cowdery, letter to Warren A. Cowdery, January 21, 1838, letterbook, Huntington Library, San Marino, California.

18. McLellin, letter to Joseph Smith III, July 1872.

19. Eliza R. Snow, MS 17956, box 49, folder 16, doc. 10, Andrew Jenson Papers, CHL.

20. Dean R. Zimmerman, *I Knew the Prophets: An Analysis of the Letter of Benjamin F. Johnson to George F. Gibbs* (Bountiful, UT: Horizon, 1976), 39.

21. See Brian C. Hales, *Joseph Smith's Polygamy: History and Theology*, 3 vols. (Salt Lake City, Utah: Greg Kofford Books, 2013), 1:277–474, for the most detailed description of the women and the relationships.

22. Brigham Young, in *Journal of Discourses*, 1:361 (August 1, 1852).

23. Orson Pratt, in *Journal of Discourses*, 18:55–56 (July 11, 1875).

24. George Albert Smith, in *Journal of Discourses*, 13:41 (October 8, 1869).

25. Joseph F. Smith, letter to Zenos H. Gurley, June 19, 1889, CHL.

26. D&C 132:4.

27. Lucy Walker Kimball, "A Brief Biographical Sketch of the Life and Labors of Lucy Walker Kimball Smith," CHL; quoted in Lyman Omer Littlefield, *Reminiscences of Latter-day Saints: Giving an Account of Much Individual Suffering Endured for Religious Conscience* (Logan: Utah Journal Co., 1888), 46.

28. "Plural Marriage in Kirtland and Nauvoo," The Church of Jesus Christ of Latter-day Saints, https://www.lds.org/topics/plural-marriage-in-kirtland-and-nauvoo, paragraph 17.

29. Joseph C. Kingsbury, "History of Joseph C. Kingsbury," in Ronald and Ilene Kingsbury Collection, MS 522, box 3, folder 2, 13, J. W. Marriott Library, University of Utah.

30. Joseph B. Noble, affidavit, Joseph F. Smith Affidavit Book 1:38, 4:38, CHL; Joseph B. Noble, Temple Lot Case, Respondent's testimony, Part 3, 396, 426–27, questions, 52–53, 681–704.

31. Lorenzo Snow, deposition, Temple Lot Transcript, Respondent's testimony, part 3, 126, questions 284–297.

32. See D&C 132:64.

33. See D&C 132:65.

34. See Joseph F. Smith, in *Journal of Discourses*, 20:29 (July 7, 1878); brackets in original; see also Orson Pratt, *Millennial Star* 17 (April 25, 1857): 260.

35. See D&C 132.

36. Ellen E. Dickinson, *New Light on Mormonism* (New York: Funk and Wagnalls, 1885), 218.

37. See D&C 132:56.

38. Lucy M. Wright, "Emma Hale Smith," *Woman's Exponent* 30, no. 8 (December 15, 1901): 59.

39. B. W. Richmond's statement, quoted in "The Prophet's Death!" *Deseret News Weekly*, December 8, 1875, 11.

40. Kimball Young, *Isn't One Wife Enough?* (New York: Henry Holt and Co., 1954), 177.

41. Jesse Hale, FamilySearch, accessed October 16, 2014, https://www.familysearch.org. Jesse Hale was born February 24, 1792, and Mary McKune was born either September 3 or December 3, 1799. The marriage occurred on July 23, 1815.

42. Susan Easton Black and Larry C. Porter, "For the Sum of Three Thousand Dollars," *Journal of Book of Mormon Studies* 14, no. 2 (2005): 4–11.

43. J. F. Snyder, "Governor Ford and His Family," *Journal of the Illinois State Historical Society* 3, no. 2 (July 10, 1910): 46.

44. Helen Mar Kimball Whitney, "Autobiography, 30 March 1881," MS 744, CHL.

45. Eugene E. Campbell, *Establishing Zion: The Mormon Church in the American West 1847–1869* (Salt Lake City: Signature Books, 1988), 198 note 5.

46. Campbell, *Establishing Zion*, 198, n. 5.

47. Campbell, *Establishing Zion*, 198, n. 5.

48. Andrew F. Ehat and Lyndon W. Cook, eds., *The Words of Joseph Smith*, 369 (May 12, 1844 discourse).

49. Andrew H. Hedges, Alex D. Smith, and Richard Lloyd Anderson, eds., *The Joseph Smith Papers, Journals, Volume 2: 1841–April 1843* (Salt Lake City: Church Historian's Press, 2011), 256 (February 7, 1843).

50. Ehat and Cook, eds., *Words of Joseph Smith*, 132 (Saturday Morning, October 29, 1842).

51. Ehat and Cook, eds., *Words of Joseph Smith*, 130.

52. D&C 109:68.

53. D&C 122:7.

12

Freemasonry and the Latter-day Saint Temple Endowment Ceremony

Steven C. Harper

There is perhaps no topic in LDS Church circles that is as misunderstood as the similarities between the ceremonies of Freemasonry and those performed as part of the Latter-day Saint temple endowment. Both involve rituals, but the purposes of the rituals distinguish them from each other. The Latter-day Saint endowment prepares women and men to return to the presence of God. Masonry encourages men to be circumspect and to build relationships with fellow Masons. In the past, one approach taken by many Latter--day Saints has been to account for the clear similarities between the rituals as coming from the same source in antiquity. The facts, however, are more complex, as is often the case. There seems to be a clear chronological tie between Joseph Smith's introduction to Masonry and the revelation of the temple endowment. Determining the relevance of that correlation remains elusive.

Heber C. Kimball longed for an endowment of divine power—something that would give meaning and direction to his life and something that would make sense of the world as it was and relate it to the world to come. When he was about twenty, Heber moved from his native Vermont to western New York and married Vilate Murray in 1822. She bore a daughter in 1823. He bought land and built a fine house, a woodshed, and a barn. He planted an orchard and was living comfortably, at least physically. But tuberculosis stole his mother in 1824, his father a year later, and his brother and sister-in-law another year later—so no house, no matter how well built, nor any amount of property, could make Heber feel endowed with power over death and the way it ended his relationships. Death could take him or Vilate or their daughter at any instant, and Heber sought richer relationships, more meaning, more security, and more power than his hard work alone could offer.[1]

Seeking Meaning in Life

So, though he was already a potter and a blacksmith, Heber also became a Mason—not a bricklaying mason, but a member of the Masonic fraternity. Members of a Masonic lodge hold elaborate meetings in which they retell stories of the ancient origins of masons who were among those Solomon commissioned to build a temple in Jerusalem. These stories both entertain and teach members to be loyal and worthy of each other's trust, as well as God's.[2]

Masons in western New York where Heber lived held their meetings in a tavern room representing Solomon's temple. In their meetings Masons acted out and enlarged the brief biblical account of Hiram of Tyre, a widow's son of the tribe of Naphtali.[3] In the Masonic story, Solomon charges Hiram to build the temple. Hiram refuses to reveal the word of the Master Mason to some of his subordinates and is murdered for his fidelity. Emulating Hiram, Masons ritually advanced by degrees from Entered Apprentice to Fellow Craft to Master Mason, using gestures, secret words, and ritual clothing.

The Masons let Heber enter their lodge as an apprentice.[4] With each meeting, he learned various signs, words, and symbols he promised not to reveal, all of which conveyed that he was building on a solid foundation and adding to it by degrees of light and knowledge through symbolic ritual. As Heber advanced in the order, he metaphorically went deeper into Solomon's temple on a quest for more light, rising to the degree of a fellow and then finally becoming a Master Mason.

But that's as far as the young Heber went with Masonry, for just as he was about to go further, a Mason named William Morgan, who was publishing Masonic secrets in a nearby town, disappeared and was never heard from again. A great outcry against Masonry followed, since many people suspected Masons of capturing and executing Morgan. In the aftermath of his disappearance, the popularity of Freemasonry plummeted in the region, and Heber's own involvement waned. It was a loss to Heber, who had enjoyed the ideals and friendships Masonry provided and the feeling of growth he experienced within the group.[5] The rituals and stories they shared and discussed made Heber and his fellow Masons feel like they were part of something ancient and mysterious.

Masonry

The Masonic fraternity is mysterious, but it has not been proven to be ancient. It apparently started in Europe as a trade guild around 1300, designed to protect its members from usury and the practical problems a mason's family could encounter in case of death or accident. It seems to have developed into an esoteric fraternity by the mid-1700s. The earliest known Masonic document, a poem called the Halliwell or Regius Manuscript, sets forth a history of the guild:

> On this manner, through good wit of geometry,
> Began first the craft of masonry;
> The clerk Euclid on this wise it found,
> This craft of geometry in Egypt land.
>
> In Egypt he taught it full wide,
> In divers lands on every side;
> Many years afterwards, I understand,
> Ere that the craft came into this land.
> This craft came into England, as I you say,
> In time of good King Athelstane's day;
> He made then both hall and even bower,
> And high temples of great honour,
> To disport him in both day and night,
> And to worship his God with all his might.[6]

The poem dates to around 1390 and includes thirty rules that prescribe what it means to belong to the guild—such as honesty, attendance at meetings, rules governing apprenticeships, integrity in business, fraternity with fellow masons, love for God and church, and secret keeping. It is the earliest known version of a founding constitution for a masonic guild—an organization designed to protect masons and their families. This document and later ones like it tell variations of a legendary story of stone masonry originating in Babylon and of its introduction to Egypt by Abraham or others.[7]

The earliest known minutes of a Masonic lodge, the Lodge of Edinburgh, date to July 31, 1599, and, depending on how typical they were, may indicate that masons at that time were still concerned primarily with regulating those who actually practiced the trade of masonry and forming alliances between them. Later minutes show that by the 1630s there were non-masons admitted to lodges in Scotland, and by 1641 non-masons attended lodges in England. Speculative Masons, as these more genteel newcomers came to be known in contrast to actual or Operative Masons, seem to have overtaken masonry in the eighteenth century, transforming it in the process from a trade union into a fraternity, a brotherhood almost exclusively for men.[8]

By 1737, Masons were telling each other a genesis story about how their forebears learned the ancient art of masonry, used it to build Solomon's temple, protected the temple site, reclaimed it from attackers, rebuilt it when it fell, and preserved secret knowledge all along the way. "Our ancestors, the Crusaders," the story goes, "gathered together from all parts of Christendom in the Holy Land." They were holy architects, "warrior princes who designed to enliven, edify, and protect the living Temples of the Most High," who discovered the ancient book inscribed by Solomon, replaced by Zerubbabel at the direction of Cyrus, which was "rediscovered after the relief of Jerusalem," preserving "our maxims and our mysteries" in the Masonic lodges of Europe.[9] Later versions of this tradition specify that Moses had originally learned of the secrets in Egypt. Other Masonic stories tell of Enoch or Melchizedek or Abraham preserving knowledge. According to tradition, the Knights Templar, Christian Crusaders, had preserved those mysteries.

By the mid-1700s, Royal Arch Masonry had developed in Ireland and America, apparently to resolve the tension in the unfinished story of Hiram Abiff, who died without revealing the Master Mason's Word. The Royal Arch ritual reveals to initiates how the word was recovered by "Mason-Knights, working with trowel in one hand and sword and buckler in the other" during construction of the Second Temple. "They came to . . . an underground vault or crypt . . . under the Ninth Arch wherein was discovered a cubical or white stone or metal plate or triangle upon which appeared the ultimate great Masonic secret."[10]

In American Royal Arch chapters there are nine officers, including three who preside over the others. The highest of these three represents the high priest in Jerusalem at the time of Zerubbabel, and past high priests constitute an Order of High Priesthood. Those who receive the Royal Arch degrees pass through a series of veils into the Holy of Holies, space reminiscent of the Israelite tabernacle. The highest degree conferred by a Royal Arch chapter makes its recipient an anointed member of the Holy Order of the High Priesthood based on a ritual history of Melchizedek.[11]

Seeking Purpose through Religion

Heber Kimball wanted the knowledge Enoch, Abraham, and Moses possessed. He wanted to be like Melchizedek. By the time Heber got involved, Masonry had long since spread to the United States and blurred the borders between Masonic history and mythology, making it impossible to determine for sure how much of what they said actually happened and how much of it they embellished somewhere along the way.

After his involvement with Masonry waned in the late 1820s, Heber began seeking peace in revival meetings held by evangelical Protestants. When the preachers invited seekers like Heber to come forward and take a seat as they preached to and prayed for him, he expressed his desire "to seek relief from the bonds of 'Sin and Death.'" But no relief came for a long time.

Late in 1831, Heber and Vilate found some peace in the rituals of baptism and sacrament offered by a Baptist minister. Shortly thereafter they heard rumors circulating in their neighborhood: stories of a new book, a golden Bible, and a young prophet named Joseph Smith. One winter day Heber hitched up his sleigh and drove it over the snow to the home of a friend who had invited preachers of the new book and the young prophet's message to teach that evening.[12]

Heber listened as one of them said "that a holy angel had been commissioned from the heavens, who had committed the Everlasting Gospel and restored the Holy Priesthood unto men as at the beginning." He "called upon all men everywhere to repent and be baptized for the remission of their sins, and receive the gift of the Holy Ghost" and promised that they would find the power they were seeking and the restoration of lost knowledge, covenants, and ordinances. "As soon as I heard them," Heber said of the preachers known as Mormons, "I was convinced they taught the truth, and I was constrained to believe their testimony."[13] Heber and Vilate were baptized again the following spring, this time as Mormons.

They were now followers of the twenty-five-year-old prophet, Joseph Smith, who had not only revealed the Book of Mormon, translating it from anciently inscribed metal plates by the power of God, but also revealed lost teachings of Moses and Enoch and was in the process of recovering and elaborating lost priesthoods held by Aaron, Melchizedek, and Abraham.[14] The Prophet's revelations promised the faithful an endowment of divine power and called for them to gather and build Zion, a holy city to be crowned with a new temple.

Heber and Vilate followed Joseph—first to Kirtland, Ohio, where they settled with a few thousand other converts. After the initial efforts to establish Zion in Missouri were ended by antagonistic settlers, Heber followed Joseph to Missouri to relieve fellow Saints there and to try to regain their promised land. After witnessing Joseph receive a revelation in Missouri that told him to return to Ohio and finish the temple being constructed there, so the Saints could be endowed with power, Heber returned with him. Back in Ohio, Heber was chosen and ordained as one of Twelve Apostles, participated in washing and anointing rituals in the temple, and was sent to England to preach the gospel. He followed Joseph Smith when he moved to Missouri in 1838, then to Illinois, and then again accepted an assignment to return to England with his fellow Apostles in 1840.

Before he left, Heber met with Joseph and others on the site of a small frontier settlement and envisioned a city of God to be named Nauvoo. Joseph soon announced plans for a bigger, better temple to be built there, in which to endow the faithful with more power, and soon he began revealing more ordinances or rituals designed to defeat death and the destructive power it had on relationships. Vilate wrote to Heber in England about these developments, overjoyed at what Joseph revealed.

Nauvoo's First Masonic Lodge

When Heber returned to Nauvoo in 1841, he found a city rising on the site of the tiny settlement he had left, the temple rising stone by stone on the high ground overlooking the flats along the river, and a brick store near the Mississippi River along with the hundreds of other brick buildings in various states of construction. The store was Joseph's, and its second story served as a gathering place for important meetings. Early on the morning of March 15, 1842, Heber and dozens of other men arrived at the store. They welcomed a distinguished visitor, Abraham Jonas, a politician, one of few Jews in the region, and the Grand Master of all Masons in the state. Heber and Nauvoo's other Masons had invited him to come and establish a lodge now that anti-Masonic hostility had faded.[15]

Nauvoo Masons paraded that day from Joseph's store to the grove at the base of the hill below the rising temple. There they met a crowd of thousands, anticipating a gala ceremony culminating in a speech delivered by Abraham Jonas.[16] Heber, Bishop Newel Whitney, Hyrum Smith, and others who were there to hear Jonas had followed similar paths from Freemasonry to some form of Protestant Christianity to the restored gospel taught by Joseph Smith. Joseph had not followed that path. He had not joined Masonry. That night, however, with the room above Joseph's store serving symbolically as Solomon's temple, Jonas let him enter as an apprentice and passed him as a fellow. The next night, he raised him as a Master Mason. Heber and some others who were present noted the events in their journals, but at the time no one, including Joseph, documented why he joined or what he thought about the Masonic stories and rituals, though he undoubtedly thought about them.[17]

Joseph likely pondered the fraternal ceremony as he contemplated how he could prepare his followers for what awaited them in the new temple, how he might best teach them what he learned over time from angels, from translating ancient records by the power of God, and from what he called "time, and experience, and careful and ponderous and solemn thoughts."[18] He had been trying "to get the minds of the saints prepared to receive the things of God," but he found that revealing anything other than what was already customary caused some of his followers to "fly to peaces [sic] like glass," making him wonder "how many will be able to abide a Celestial law & go through & receive their exaltation."[19]

Joseph knew that preparing hearts and minds to receive all that God had in store couldn't be done easily. But he was not one to conclude that it couldn't be done at all. So, as angels had done with him, and he had done with his followers before, he started with what he had and used what the Saints found familiar to lead them to further light and knowledge.[20] As he left his store for the short walk home that evening, perhaps Joseph thought of Masonic ideas and practices as a way to impart knowledge that was suited to the simplest of Saints and rich enough to reward a lifetime's journey toward the "broad expanse" and "deep import" of God's own thought.[21]

On May 3, 1842, Joseph called on a longtime Mason named Lucius Scovill to transform the rooms above the Red Brick Store into a temporary temple. The next day Joseph gathered his brother Hyrum and a few other trusted associates including Heber into the sacred space. There he spent the day endowing them with power—"things spiritual," as he put it, "and to be received only by the spiritual minded."[22] The Prophet started with instructions about the priesthood ordinances he wished to give them that day. They were not simply the same as the ones Heber and others who were there received in the house of the Lord at Kirtland, Ohio, six years earlier. As promised, Joseph had more to reveal: a ritual washing, a symbolic anointing, and lessons of light and knowledge—all the plans and principles anyone needed to regain God's presence and abide there.[23]

Joseph spent the day explaining and serving. The ordinances he revealed were a crucial part of what he wanted to reveal to the Saints, and he wanted to be sure each man he instructed that day understood the endowment. Each of them was a Master Mason. Most had participated in Masonic meetings in the same space, which also represented a temple.[24] As Masons, they learned through ritual how to increase in knowledge and serve their fellow Masons. Through the endowment ceremony, they used rituals as they covenanted with God and learned the laws governing their return to his presence. Joseph picked these men specifically, maybe in part because they were Masons, and began teaching in a way they understood, starting where they were and leading them to more light and knowledge.

Six weeks after he received this priesthood endowment from Joseph Smith, Heber wrote to his fellow Apostle Parley Pratt, who was preaching in England: "We have received some pressious things through the Prophet on the preasthood that would caus your Soul to rejoice. . . . I can not give them to you on paper for they are not to be riten. So you must come and get them for your Self." Heber announced, "We have organized a Lodge here of Masons," adding that Joseph Smith and most of the Apostles were among more than two hundred men who had joined. "Thare is a similarity of preast Hood in masonry," he explained. "Br. Joseph ses masonry was taken from priesthood but has become degenerated. But menny things are perfect."[25]

Similarities in the Two Ceremonies

Modern-day observers may wonder what accounts for the similarities if the temple is part of a restoration of divine ordinances. The question can be perplexing to those who begin with an unfounded assumption. It goes something like this: *If* Joseph Smith restored truth from God, he did it without reference to anything in his environment. But what if that *if* is wrong? What if the divine restoration was not wholly new but like the restoration of an old house, where the restorer keeps all that's useful and charming and replaces or refurbishes all that's broken, weak, or no longer useful? In that case there are more possible explanations for the similarities.

It is often assumed that Masonry caused or led directly to the priesthood endowment. Proving that assumption would require evidence that the timing of the Prophet's exposure to Freemasonry corresponded to his presentation of the endowment, that the similarities in the ceremonies correlate beyond coincidence, and that there is clear evidence of cause and effect.[26]

A Temporal Connection

There is strong evidence of correlation between the timing of Joseph's exposure to Freemasonry and his revelation of the endowment:

1. In December 1841, eighteen Mormon Masons organized the Nauvoo Lodge.
2. Non-Masons Joseph Smith and Sidney Rigdon applied for membership the following day.
3. Illinois Grand Master Abraham Jonas formalized the lodge on March 15, 1842, installed its officers, and initiated Joseph and Sidney as Entered Apprentices in the upper-floor space above Joseph's Nauvoo store. The next day Jonas passed Joseph and Sidney as Fellow Craft and raised them as Master Masons.
4. Two days later Joseph organized the Female Relief Society in the same space. In a subsequent address, Joseph urged the Relief Society women in Masonic terms to "go into close examination of every candidate—that they were going too fast—that the Society should grow up by degrees."[27]
5. On May 3, 1842, Joseph enlisted a Mormon Mason to "fit up" the same space in which the Masons and Relief Society met, "preparatory to giving endowments to a few elders," which Joseph did the following day.[28]
6. He endowed nine men on May 4, 1842, the same number needed to create a Royal Arch Chapter of Masonry. It is not clear what, if anything, Joseph Smith knew of Royal Arch Masonry by 1842.[29] Still, no Mormon Masons from Nauvoo left known accounts of Royal Arch Masonry, amid the several that spoke of becoming Master Masons.[30]
7. Joseph prepared select Mormon women for the priesthood endowment, using the Relief Society as a preparatory group parallel to the Masons. He promised the women in August 1842 that they would see "the blessings of the endowment rolling on."[31] Late in May 1842, three weeks after receiving the priesthood ordinances from Joseph, Newel Whitney addressed the Relief Society about what they could expect, namely "blessings . . . to be confer'd as soon as our hearts are

prepar'd to receive them." In his message any Mason would have heard common themes, and any Mormon, already endowed by Joseph as Newel Whitney was, could hear more.[32]
8. In September 1843 Joseph Smith began initiating select members of the Relief Society (mainly the wives of Masons he had already endowed) into the promised ordinances.[33]

In these ways, correlation between Masonry and Mormonism was obvious to those, like Newel Whitney and Heber Kimball, who knew both. But the question remains whether the similarities suggest more than chronological correlation. Are they accounted for by cause and effect? If so, did primitive temple rituals later to be restored by Joseph Smith get incorporated into Freemasonry? Or did Joseph Smith incorporate elements of Freemasonry into the ordinances he offered? Or, rejecting a possible false dilemma, is the answer some of each? There is no way to know for sure, though some have assumed that they knew.

Proving a Causal Relationship

In 1974, a Latter-day Saint educator declared to the Mormon History Association that the similarities between the endowment ordinances and Masonry are "so apparent and overwhelming that some dependent relationship cannot be denied." He speculated that Masonry provided the "immediate inspiration" for the endowment.[34] The analysis was zealous and superficially compelling, but it wasn't careful.

It requires a logical leap to bridge the evidentiary gap between *similarity*, which was obvious to those who knew both Masonry and the endowment, and *dependence*, which is assumed—not known. Some people reason that Joseph Smith initiated men and women into the endowment ordinances after he was initiated into Freemasonry; therefore, the temple rituals derived from Masonry. One problem in this theory is that Freemasonry itself borrowed much of its ritual and ceremony from elements preserved since antiquity. There is ample similarity and difference not only between Freemasonry and LDS temple ordinances, but in many other ancient and more modern stories and rituals as well. Disentangling the complex relationships between them is not possible and should not be oversimplified.

It is possible to discern differences in the functions (however similar in form) of Masonic and LDS temple ordinances. Masonic rituals use aprons, door-knockings, and unusual handshakes to foster brotherhood. Bonds are made between men, not between people and God. LDS temple ordinances endow believers with power to regain the presence of God as they make and keep covenants with him. The ritual is not the endowment of power itself. It may be that some ritual forms were adapted from Masonic traditions, but the endowment teaches a divine plan of creation, Fall, and redemption through Christ—promising those who covenant to keep God's laws that they will gain power over the effects of the Fall. As Heber Kimball was perfectly positioned to know, the endowment did not simply mimic Masonry.

Avoiding Hasty Conclusions

Just as the relationships between Masonry and Latter-day Saint temple ordinances should not be oversimplified, they should also not be overstated. They were part of what Joseph Smith had at his disposal, not the sum. So perhaps the lesson we should take away is that we need not make it a false choice—either Joseph borrowed or he did not. The Restoration is characterized by both give and take. It seems reasonable, given the way Joseph Smith found inspiration in a Protestant Bible for restoring the distinctive gospel he taught, to be open to the idea that he found meaning in Masonry, too, and similarly adapted it to divine purposes. The restored gospel Joseph taught appealed to people like Heber and Vilate Kimball precisely because it had so much in common and yet more to offer than what they were then experiencing in their associations with various religions or associations like Masonry. It seems that the ordinances Joseph presented functioned similarly—offering Heber (and later Vilate) something recognizable, but enhancing what they already had.

The historical method and the limited evidence simply cannot reveal the exact reasons for the similarities. It can only tell us how witnesses, participants, and observers answered the question and leave us to decide what meaning and value we will give to their views. Beginning with John Bennett, the Prophet's erstwhile friend who turned into a bitter enemy, critics have explained Joseph's temple teachings as piracy. "Joe Smith has violated his obligations as a mason, and has established 'a new order' himself," Bennett claimed as early as July 1842.[35] But Heber Kimball was there, and he did not interpret the similarities as Bennett did. To the contrary, he believed that Joseph restored a pre-Masonic power: the authentic ordinances and divine story. Joseph's secretary, Willard Richards, concurred that "Masonry had its origin in the Priesthood."[36] Benjamin F. Johnson remembered Joseph telling him that Masonry was a degenerated form of temple worship, just as the many religious sects were weakened versions of the fulness of the gospel.[37]

Scholarly Observations

Joseph seems to have used Masonry as a point of departure, a beginning rather than an end in itself. Several scholars of differing degrees of belief in Joseph Smith's teachings have analyzed the evidence and arrived at this conclusion. Michael Homer argued that "the rituals of Freemasonry provided a starting point for the Mormon prophet's revelation of 'true Masonry.'"[38] David Buerger argued that the pattern of resemblances was too great and the content of the endowment too unique to explain simply. "Thus," he concluded, "the temple ceremony cannot be explained as wholesale borrowing from Masonry; neither can it be explained as completely unrelated to Freemasonry."[39] Allen Roberts concluded that "Joseph's Masonry was not a conventional one. He attempted to restore it in much the same way the gospel was restored. That is, he saw Masonry like Christianity, as possessing some important truths which could be beneficially extracted from what was otherwise an apostate institution."[40]

Knowledge and Power Available for Both Men and Women

Joseph Smith's priesthood endowment did not simply parrot the rituals of Freemasonry. One of the differences between the Masonic rituals and the endowment of power was access.[41] The Mormon Masons in and around Nauvoo let in more members than most Masons did, yet even they were exclusive, determined to keep out more than invite in. With the exception of some French groups, there was no place for women in Masonry, yet Joseph endowed Mormon women with the same ordinances he gave to the men.[42] He also told those first few men he endowed that they were only the beginning, that the Lord wanted each of the Saints to receive the same ordinances and make the same covenants "so soon as they are prepared to receive, and a proper place is prepared to communicate them, even to the weakest of the saints; therefore let the saints be diligent in building the Temple."[43]

Samuel Brown concluded that Joseph translated Masonic ideas, making the endowment ordinances "an amplification and reform of Masonry." Joseph mined the Bible for meaning and restored missing plain and precious parts of the gospel. Why not Masonry as well? In this way of reading the evidence, Masonry, like the Bible or an Egyptian papyrus scroll, was like "an artifact that required the attention of a seer, a text in need of translation."[44]

That's how Joseph's followers who knew both Masonry and the priesthood endowment thought of it. Some of them are on record marveling at the way Joseph breathed life into what was old and broken, restored things that had been lost, made plain things that were confusing, and lighted what had been dark.[45] Heber valued what light Masonry held for him, but he found it "degenerated" compared to experiencing Joseph's regenerated version—the endowment of power.[46]

On May 4, 1842, as Joseph offered ordinances to a small group of trusted men who were Masons, they could see that, however similar, Masonry was no substitute for the possession of priesthood power. Joseph wasn't looking back to Solomon's temple. He was building a new one suited to the dispensation of the fulness of times—one in which the Lord would reveal more knowledge and power than he ever had.[47] Heber, at least, saw beyond obvious similarities and valued what he called the precious priesthood knowledge he only got from Joseph. All his adult life he had been looking for transcendent power and promises. On May 4, 1842, he finally got them "through the Prophet."[48]

Additional Resources

Brown, Samuel. *In Heaven as It Is on Earth: Joseph Smith and the Early Mormon Conquest of Death*. Oxford: Oxford University Press, 2012.

Parry, Donald W., ed. *Temples of the Ancient World*. Salt Lake City: Deseret Book, 1994.

Seely, David Rolph, Jeffrey R. Chadwick, and Matthew J. Grey, eds. *Ascending the Mountain of the Lord: Temple, Praise, and Worship in the Old Testament, The 42nd Annual Brigham Young University Sidney B. Sperry Symposium*. Provo, UT: Religious Studies Center; Salt Lake City: Deseret Book, 2013.

About the Author

Steven C. Harper is a historian in the Church History Department of The Church of Jesus Christ of Latter-day Saints. He earned a PhD in early American history from Lehigh University and was on the history and religion faculties at BYU–Hawaii for two years before joining the faculty of the Department of Church History and Doctrine at BYU for ten years. He has worked on The Joseph Smith Papers and as a document editor for BYU Studies and is the author of a book titled *Promised Land* (on colonial Pennsylvania) and of *Making Sense of the Doctrine and Covenants and Joseph Smith's First Vision*. Among other projects, he is currently at work analyzing how Joseph Smith's First Vision has been remembered over time. He is married to Jennifer Sebring, and they have five children.

Notes

1. Jeni Broberg Holzapfel and Richard Neitzel Holzapfel, eds., *A Woman's View: Helen Mar Whitney's Reminiscences of Early Church History* (Provo, UT: Religious Studies Center, 1997), 79–81.

2. Much of the literature about Freemasonry is marred by author bias or is speculative and unsound. Recently, however, good scholarship on the topic has begun to flourish. A sound introduction to Freemasonry is Margaret C. Jacob, *The Origins of Freemasonry: Facts and Fictions* (Philadelphia: University of Pennsylvania Press, 2006). For Freemasonry in its American context, see Steven C. Bullock, *Revolutionary Brotherhood: Freemasonry and the Transformation of the American Social Order, 1730–1840* (Chapel Hill: University of North Carolina Press, 1996). The most thorough study of the relationships between Masonry and Mormonism is

Michael W. Homer, *Joseph's Temples: The Dynamic Relationship between Freemasonry and Mormonism* (Salt Lake City: University of Utah Press, 2014).

3. See 1 Kings 7.

4. Holzapfel and Holzapfel, *A Woman's View*, 79–81. For context, see Stanley B. Kimball, *Heber C. Kimball: Mormon Patriarch and Pioneer* (Urbana: University of Illinois Press, 1981), 12–13.

5. Heber C. Kimball, "Synopsis of the History of Heber Chase Kimball," *Deseret News*, March 31, 1858, 25.

6. Grand Lodge of British Columbia and Yukon, "The Halliwell Manuscript," http://freemasonry.bcy.ca/texts/regius.html.

7. Museum of Freemasonry, "Gothic Constitutions," http://www.masoniclibrary.org.au/index.php?option=com_content&view=article&id=86:gothic-constitutions&catid=23:lecture&Itemid=30.

8. Freemasonry was largely fraternal, though there were some female lodges in eighteenth-century Europe. See Jan A. M. Snoek, *Initiating Women in Freemasonry: The Adoptive Rite* (Leiden, Netherlands: Brill, 2012). Also see Jacob, *Origins of Freemasonry*, 92–129.

9. The Masonic Trowel, http://www.themasonictrowel.com/Articles/Manuscripts/manuscripts/chevalier_ramsay_oration.htm.

10. Henry Wilson Coil, "Royal Arch." In *Coil's Masonic Encyclopedia* (New York: Macoy, 1961).

11. Coil, "Royal Arch." Michael Homer, "'Similarity of Priesthood in Masonry': The Relationship between Freemasonry and Mormonism," *Dialogue: A Journal of Mormon Thought* 27 (1994): 37–38.

12. Kimball, *Heber C. Kimball*, 15–18.

13. Kimball, *Heber C. Kimball*, 15–18.

14. For evidence of Joseph's explanation of these priesthoods and their role in administering powerful rituals or ordinances, see his "Revelation, Kirtland Township, Ohio, 22–23 September 1832" (D&C 84), in Robin Scott Jensen, Robert J. Woodford, and Steven C. Harper, eds., *Manuscript Revelation Books*, facsimile edition, vol. 1 of the Revelations and Translations series of *The Joseph Smith Papers*, ed. Dean C. Jessee, Ronald K. Esplin, and Richard Lyman Bushman (Salt Lake City: Church Historian's Press, 2009), 275–89, http://josephsmithpapers.org/paperSummary/revelation-22-23-september-1832-dc-84.

15. Kenneth W. Godfrey, "Joseph Smith and the Masons," *Journal of the Illinois Historical Society* 65, no. 1 (1971): 83.

16. Andrew H. Hedges, Alex D. Smith, and Richard Lloyd Anderson, eds., "Joseph Smith, Journal, March 15–16, 1842," in *Journals, Volume 2: December 1841–April 1843*, vol. 2 of the Journals series of *The Joseph Smith Papers*, 45 (hereafter *JSP*, J2).

17. "Joseph Smith, Journal, March 15–16, 1842," *JSP*, J2:45.

18. Joseph Smith, "Letter to the Church and Edward Partridge, 20 March 1839," Joseph Smith Papers, http://josephsmithpapers.org/paperSummary/letter-to-the-church-and-edward-partridge-20-march-1839#!/paperSummary/letter-to-the-church-and-edward-partridge-20-march-1839&p=1.

19. Scott G. Kenney, ed., *Wilford Woodruff Journal, 1833–1898, Typescript*, 9 vols. (Salt Lake City: Signature Books, 1983–1985), 2:342 (January 21, 1844).

20. Greg Kearney, "The Message and the Messenger," presentation, 2005 FAIR Conference, http://www.fairmormon.org/perspectives/fair-conferences/2005-fair-conference/2005-the-message-and-the-messenger-latter-day-saints-and-freemasonry.

21. This is based on Greg Kearney's idea that Masonry provided a highly effective teaching tool for the message Joseph had to convey. See Kearney, "The Message and the Messenger." For more on Joseph Smith and Masonic ritual, see Samuel Brown, *In Heaven as It Is on Earth: Joseph Smith and the Early Mormon Conquest of Death* (Oxford: Oxford University Press, 2012), esp. 178–83.

22. "The Higher Ordinances," *Deseret News Semi-Weekly*, February 15, 1884, 2; "Joseph Smith, Journal, 4 May 1842," *JSP*, J2:53–54, see also n. 198.

23. "Joseph Smith, Journal, 4 May 1842," *JSP*, J2:53–54.

24. According to the minute books of the Nauvoo Lodge, George Miller, Hyrum Smith, and Heber Kimball reported on December 30, 1841, that they had already been advanced to the degree of Master Mason in different lodges. Newel Whitney did the same on January 3, 1842. Brigham Young and Willard Richards were raised to the degree of Master Mason on April 9, William Marks on April 22, and William Law on April 27. Nauvoo Masonic Lodge Minute Books, MS 9115 and MS 3436, Church History Library (hereafter CHL). James Adams was raised as a Master Mason long before May 1842. See Kent L. Walgren, "James Adams: Early Springfield Mormon and Freemason," *Journal of the Illinois State Historical Society* 75, no. 2 (1982): 121–36.

25. Heber C. Kimball, letter to Parley P. Pratt, June 17, 1842, MS 897, CHL.

26. David Hackett Fischer, *Historians' Fallacies* (New York: Harper, 1970), 169.

27. Nauvoo Relief Society Minute Book, March 17, 1842, and March 30, 1842, accessed July 11, 2015, http://josephsmithpapers.org/paperSummary/nauvoo-relief-society-minute-book#1.

28. "The Higher Ordinances," *Deseret News Semi-Weekly*, February 15, 1884, 2.

29. Apparently there was a Royal Arch chapter functioning in Springfield, Illinois, by September 1841, to which James Adams, one of those Joseph Smith endowed on May 4, 1842, possibly belonged. Another of the original nine, Newel Whitney, reportedly associated with Royal Arch Masonry earlier, in Ohio. See Michael W. Homer, *Joseph's Temples*, 95; Homer, "'Similarity of Priesthood,'"37–38. As an off shoot of Freemasonry, there have always been fewer Royal Arch chapters than traditional Masonic lodges. Homer, *Joseph's Temples*, 95.

30. Samuel Brown concluded that Royal Arch degrees were not available in Illinois in Joseph's lifetime, but he may have gained knowledge of them from conversations or exposés. See Brown, *In Heaven*, 179. Kent L. Walgren documents Adams's involvement in Masonry in Springfield and Illinois generally, but says nothing of any possible involvement in Royal Arch Masonry. See Kent L. Walgren, "James Adams: Early Springfield Mormon and Freemason," *Journal of the Illinois State Historical Society* 75, no. 2 (Summer 1982): 121–36. D. Michael Quinn located an 1844 document in the Harold B. Lee Library at BYU by Oliver Huntington that, according to Quinn, included "the Masonic cipher of the Royal Arch Degree." D. Michael Quinn, *Early Mormonism and the Magic World View* (Salt Lake City: Signature, 1987), figure 19.

31. "History, 1838–1856, volume D-1 [1 August 1842–1 July 1843]," Joseph Smith Papers, http://josephsmithpapers.org/paperSummary/history-1838-1856-volume-d-1-1-august-1842-1-july-1843?p=284&highlight=the%20blessings%20of%20the%20endowment%20rolling%20on.

32. "Minutes of the Proceedings of the Tenth Meeting of the Society," Nauvoo Relief Society Minute Book, 54, http://josephsmithpapers.org/paperSummary/nauvoo-relief-society-minute-book?p=1&highlight=relief%20society%20minute%20book#!/paperSummary/nauvoo-relief-society-minute-book&p=55.

33. Nauvoo Relief Society Minute Book, August 31, 1842, http://josephsmithpapers.org/paperSummary/nauvoo-relief-society-minute-book?p=79&highlight=endowment%20roll%20on. See also the Editorial Note at the beginning of the Nauvoo Relief Society Minute Book for context relating to the endowment ordinances, accessed July 11, 2015, http://josephsmithpapers.org/paperSummary/nauvoo-relief-society-minute-book?p=87&highlight=endowment%20roll%20on.

34. Homer, "'Similarity of Priesthood,'" 1.

35. "Astounding Disclosures!," *Sangamo Journal*, Springfield, Illinois, July 8, 1842.

36. Willard Richards, letter to Levi Richards, March 7–25, 1842, Richards family papers, MS 1558, CHL. The Mormon Master Mason in charge of Joseph's induction into Masonry reportedly said that Joseph understood the ceremonies better than longtime Masons. Horace Cummings, autobiography, 1, Horace H. Cummings Papers, MS 4285, CHL.

37. Benjamin F. Johnson, *My Life's Review* (Independence, MO: Zion's Printing, 1947), 94–97.

38. Homer, "Similarity of Priesthood," 112.

39. David John Buerger, "The Development of the Mormon Temple Endowment Ceremony," *Dialogue: A Journal of Mormon Thought* 20 (Winter 1987): 33–76.

40. Allen D. Roberts, "Where Are the All-Seeing Eyes," *Sunstone* 10, no. 5 (May 1985): 36–48.

41. 2 Nephi 26:33.

42. Jacob, *Facts and Fictions*, 92–129.

43. "Joseph Smith, Journal, 4 May 1842,'" *JSP*, J2:53–54. See also footnote 198; "History, 1838–1856, volume C–1 [2 November 1838–31 July 1842]," http://josephsmithpapers.org/paperSummary?target=X7188#!/paperSummary/history-1838-1856-volume-c-1-2-november-1838-31-july-1842&p=502.

44. Brown, *In Heaven*, 185.

45. See D&C 124:28, 38; Willard Richards to Levi Richards.

46. Heber C. Kimball to Parley P. Pratt.

47. D&C 124:40–43.

48. Heber C. Kimball to Parley P. Pratt.

13

Race, the Priesthood, and Temples

W. Paul Reeve

The history of the race-based priesthood and temple restrictions within The Church of Jesus Christ of Latter-day Saints is best understood as an evolution away from racially open priesthood and temples toward segregated priesthood and temples and then back again. This evolution is difficult to understand without first understanding the power of white privilege in nineteenth-century American politics, economy, and society and the corresponding effort among the white Protestant majority to deny the blessings of whiteness and therefore social respectability to Mormons. Even though the majority of Mormons were white in the nineteenth century, outsiders persistently suggested that they did not act white or look white and that they were more like other marginalized racial groups—red, black, or yellow—than white. The scientific and medical communities even suggested that Mormon polygamy was spawning a new, degraded race. Within this context, the Church moved unevenly across the course of the nineteenth century toward whiteness, an evolution that came at the expense of fellow black Saints. In 1978 the Church reversed course and returned to its racially universalistic roots.

A racially expansive vision of redemption through Jesus Christ for all of God's children marked the early decades of the Church's existence. One early leader, William Wines Phelps, wrote in 1835 that "all the families of the earth . . . should get redemption . . . in Christ Jesus," regardless of "whether they are descendants of Shem, Ham, or Japheth." Another publication declared that all people were "one in Christ Jesus . . . whether it was in Africa, Asia, or Europe." Apostle Parley P. Pratt similarly professed his intent to preach "to all people, kindred, tongues, and nations without any exception" and included India's and Africa's "sultry plains" in his vision of the global reach of Mormonism.[1]

This universal invitation initially included extending all of the unfolding ordinances of the Restoration to all members. To date there are no known statements made by Joseph Smith Jr. of a racial priesthood or temple restriction. In fact, there is incontrovertible evidence for the ordination of at least two black men, Q. Walker Lewis and Elijah Abel, during the Church's first two decades. However, racial restrictions developed under Brigham Young and were solidified over the course of the last half of the nineteenth century under subsequent leaders.

Brigham Young's rationale for the restriction was taught and preached as doctrine and centered upon the biblical curse and "mark" that God placed upon Cain for killing his brother Abel. Over time, other justifications tied to the premortal existence and the War in Heaven attempted to validate the practice, even though they were never used by Brigham Young. Some leaders also looked to the Book of Abraham and its passages regarding a Pharaoh whose lineage was "cursed . . . as pertaining to the priesthood."[2] Even though Joseph Smith produced the Book of Abraham, he never used it to justify a priesthood restriction, and neither did Brigham Young.[3]

The curse in the Book of Mormon of a "skin of blackness"[4] was never used as a justification for withholding the priesthood or temple ordinances from black Mormons. LDS leaders and followers alike understood the Book of Mormon curse to apply to Native Americans and viewed it as reversible. It was a vision of Indian redemption that placed white Latter-day Saints as agents in that process. In contrast, Brigham Young claimed the biblical curse of Cain was in God's hands only, something humankind could not influence or remove until God commanded it.[5]

Whiteness in American History and Culture

Being white in American history was considered the normal and natural condition of humankind. Anything less than white was viewed as a deterioration from normal, a situation that made such a person unfit for the blessings of democracy. Being white meant being socially respectable; it granted a person greater access to political, economic, and social power. Politicians equated whiteness with citizenship and fitness for self-rule. In 1790, Congress passed a naturalization act that limited citizenship to "free white persons," a decision that had a significant impact on race relations in the nineteenth century. Even Abraham Lincoln, the future "great emancipator," believed that as long as blacks and whites coexisted, "there must be the position of superior and inferior," and he favored the "white race" in the "superior position." After the Civil War, as Southern whites reasserted white superiority, the Supreme Court affirmed their efforts when it ruled that separate-but-equal facilities were constitutional, a decision that legalized the segregation of most facets of American life.[6]

Mormonism's founding decades coincided with a period in which whiteness itself came under question. "Race" at the time was a word loosely used to refer to nationality as much as skin color. People spoke of an "Irish race," for example, and began to create a hierarchy of racial identities, with Anglo-Saxons at the top. A variety of less-white "races" were further down the list. Scots, Teutons, Welch, Latin, Caucasian, Nordic, Celt, Slav, Alpine, Hebrew, Mediterranean, Iberic, and other such identifiers emerged to additionally blur racial categories.[7]

Mormonism was born in this era of splintering whiteness and did not escape its consequences. The Protestant majority in America was never quite certain how or where to situate Mormons within conflicting racial schemes, but they were nonetheless convinced that Mormonism represented a racial decline. Many nineteenth-century social evolutionists believed in the development theory: all societies advanced across three stages of progress, from savagery to barbarism to civilization. As societies advanced, they left behind such practices as polygamy and adherence to authoritarian rule. In the minds of such thinkers, Mormons violated the development theory in practicing polygamy and theocracy, something that no true Anglo-Saxon would do. Mormons thereby represented a fearful racial descent into barbarism and savagry. Within this charged racial context, Mormons struggled to claim whiteness for themselves despite the fact that they were overwhelmingly white.[8] As legal scholar Ariel Gross argues, whiteness in the nineteenth century was measured in distance from blackness, and Mormons spent considerable effort attempting to become securely white at the expense of their own black converts.[9]

Racialization of Mormons

The Saints' troubled sojourns in Ohio, Missouri, and Illinois were fraught with the perception that Mormons were too open and inviting to undesirable people—blacks and Indians in particular. In 1830, the founding year of the Church, Black Pete became the first known African-American to join the faith. Within a year of his conversion, the fact that the Mormons had a black man worshiping with them made news in New York and Pennsylvania.[10] Edward Strutt Abdy, a British official on tour of the United States, noted that Ohio Mormons honoured "the natural equality of mankind, without excepting the native Indians or the African race." Abdy feared, however, that it was an open attitude that may have gone too far for its time and place. He believed that the Mormon stance toward Indians and blacks was at least partially responsible for "the cruel persecution by which they have suffered." In his mind, the Book of Mormon ideal that "all are alike unto God," including "black and white," made it unlikely that the Saints would "remain unmolested in the State of Missouri."[11] Other outsiders tended to agree. They complained that Mormons were far too inclusive in the creation of their religious kingdom. They accepted "all nations and colours," they welcomed "all classes and characters," they included "aliens by birth" and people from "different parts of the world" as members of God's earthly family. Outsiders variously suggested that the Mormons had "opened an asylum for rogues and vagabonds and free blacks," maintained "communion with the Indians," and walked out with "colored women." In short, Mormons were charged with creating racially and economically diverse transnational communities and congregations, a stark contrast to a national culture that favored the segregation and extermination of undesirable racial groups.[12]

Some Latter-day Saints recognized the ways in which outsiders denigrated them and called their whiteness into question. In 1840, Apostle Parley P. Pratt, for example, complained that during the Saints' expulsion from Missouri "most of the papers of the State" described them as "Mormons, in contradistinction to the appellation of citizens, whites, &c., as if we had been some savage tribe, or some colored race of foreigners." John Lowe Butler, another Mormon expelled from Missouri, recalled one Missourian who declared that "he did not consider the 'Mormons' had any more right to vote than the niggers." In Illinois, Apostle Heber C. Kimball acknowledged that Mormons were not "considered suitable to live among 'white folks'" and later declared, "We are not accounted as white people, and we don't want to live among them. I had rather live with the buffalo in the wilderness."[13]

The open announcement of polygamy in 1852 moved the concern among outsiders in a new direction, toward a growing fear of racial contamination. In the minds of outsiders, Mormon polygamy was not just destroying the traditional family—it was destroying the white race. A US Army doctor reported to Congress that polygamy was giving rise to a "new race," filthy, sunken, and degraded. One writer argued that polygamy placed "a mark of Cain" on Mormon women while another said that Mormonism was "as degrading as old-fashioned negro slavery."[14] In general, outsiders conflated Mormons with blacks in a variety of ways. Their views were fluid and inconsistent, yet several themes emerged to suggest that outsiders sometimes viewed Mormons as racially suspect. Such depictions were designed to marginalize Mormons and justify discriminatory policies against them. As some outsiders described it, Mormon polygamy was a system of "white slavery," worse than the black slavery that "existed in the South, and *far more filthy*." Mormon men were sometimes depicted as violent or indolent slave drivers and Mormon women as their "white slaves."[15] In 1882, Alfred Trumble's *The Mysteries of Mormonism*, a sensationalized dime novel, captured this national theme in pictorial form in an illustration simply labeled "wives as slaves" (see figure 1).[16]

More troubling to outsiders was the perception that Mormon polygamy was a system of unbridled interracial sex and marriage. One political cartoon depicted Brigham Young with two black wives and degraded interracial offspring. A parade in Indiana similarly featured a mock version of Brigham Young's family. It included six wives seated in Brigham Young's wagon, "white, black and piebald better-halves," a group of women unmistakably costumed to heighten national fears of race mixing and project them onto Mormons. The *New York Times* reported on two supposed "negro balls" in Salt Lake City where "negro men and women, and Mormon men and women, [were] all dancing on terms of perfect equality." The writer called it "the most disgusting of spectacles." Other cartoons and dime novels portrayed Mormon plural marriages as hotbeds of interracial sex, depictions deliberately designed to heighten American alarm over a perceived violation of racial boundaries and to portray Mormons as facilitators of racial contamination.[17]

Figure 1. "Wives as Slaves," reprinted from Alfred Trumble, *The Mysteries of Mormonism*, New York *Police Gazette*, 1882. Special Collections, Rare Books Division, J. Willard Marriott Library, University of Utah, Salt Lake City, used by permission.

Cartoons sometimes portrayed Mormon polygamous families as interracial, and unabashedly so. In September 1896, during the presidential race between Democrat William Jennings Bryan and Republican William McKinley, *Judge* magazine ran one such cartoon (see figure 2). The illustration was titled "The 16 to 1 Movement in Utah." It used a contentious issue in the campaign that year to make fun of polygamy. Bryan advocated freeing the nation's monetary system from the gold standard by allowing for the coinage of silver at a ratio of sixteen to one. In the *Judge* cartoon, however, sixteen to one took on new meaning in Utah: sixteen women to one man. The polygamist man carried a bag labeled "from Utah" and stood front and center of his sixteen wives, eight on either side. It was not merely the number of women to men, however, that made the cartoon significant. It was the interracial nature of the Mormon family it depicted. The sixteen wives were portrayed in a variety of shapes, sizes, and relative beauty, but it was the first wife holding the man's left arm that was meant to unsettle its audience. She was a black woman boldly at the front of the other wives, a

Figure 2. Zim, "The 16 to 1 Movement in Utah," reprinted from *The Judge*, September 12, 1896, 176. L. Tom Perry Special Collections, Harold B. Lee Library, Brigham Young University, Provo, UT.

visual depiction of the racial corruption that outsiders worried was inherent in Mormon polygamy.[18]

The Priesthood and Temple Restrictions Begin

At the same time that outsiders persistently criticized Mormons as facilitators of racial decline, Mormons moved in fits and starts across the course of the nineteenth century away from blackness toward whiteness. It is a mistake to try to pinpoint a moment, event, person, or line in the sand that divided Mormon history into a clear before and after. Rather, the policies and supporting doctrines that Church leaders developed over the course of the nineteenth century increasingly solidified a rationale and gave rise to an accumulating precedent that each succeeding generation reinforced, so that by the late nineteenth century, LDS leaders were unwilling to violate policies they mistakenly remembered beginning with Joseph Smith. By 1908, Joseph F. Smith solidified the priesthood and temple restrictions in place when he erased Elijah Abel, a black priesthood holder, from collective Mormon memory. The new memory moving forward would be that of a white priesthood in place from the beginning, traceable from the founding prophet back to God, something with which no human could or should interfere.

Although Brigham Young's two speeches to the Utah Territorial legislature in 1852 mark the first recorded articulations of a priesthood restriction by a Mormon prophet-president, it is a mistake to solely attribute the ban to seemingly inherent racism in Brigham Young. His own views evolved between 1847, when he first dealt with racial matters at Winter Quarters, and 1852, when he first publicly articulated a rationale for a priesthood restriction. In 1847, in an interview with William (Warner) McCary, a black Mormon who married Lucy Stanton, a white Mormon, Brigham Young expressed an open position on race. McCary complained to Brigham Young regarding the way he was sometimes treated among the Saints and suggested that his skin color was a factor: "I am not a President, or a leader of the people" McCary lamented, but merely a "common brother," a fact that he said was true "because I am a little shade darker." In response, Brigham Young asserted that "we dont care about the color." He went on to suggest that color did not matter in priesthood ordination: "We have to repent & regain what we have lost," Brigham Young insisted, "we have one of the best Elders, an African in Lowell—a barber," he reported. Brigham Young here referred to Q. Walker Lewis, a barber, abolitionist, and leader in the black community in Lowell, Massachusetts. Apostle William Smith, younger brother to Hyrum and Joseph Smith, had ordained Lewis an elder in 1843 or 1844. Brigham Young was fully aware of Lewis's status as a black man and priesthood holder and favorably referred to that status in his interview with McCary. Brigham Young offered Lewis as evidence that even black men were welcome and eligible for the priesthood in Mormonism.[19]

By December of 1847, however, Brigham Young's perspective had changed. Following his expedition to the Salt Lake Valley that summer, he returned to Winter Quarters. There he learned of McCary's interracial exploits in his absence. McCary had started his own splinter polygamous group predicated upon white women being "sealed" to him in a sexualized ritual. When his exploits were discovered, he and his followers were excommunicated and McCary left the Church, never to return. Young was also greeted with news of the marriage of Enoch Lewis, Q. Walker Lewis's son, to Mary Matilda Webster, a white woman in the Lowell, Massachusetts, branch. In response, Brigham Young spoke forcefully against interracial marriage, even advocating capital punishment as a consequence. Like Joseph Smith before him, Brigham Young opposed racial mixing and made some of his most pointed statements on the subject. Yet none of the surviving minutes from the meetings that Brigham Young held that year raise priesthood as an issue negatively connected to race. It would be five more years before Brigham Young articulated his position on that subject.[20]

Brigham Young most fully elaborated his views in 1852 before an all-Mormon Utah Territorial legislature as it contemplated a law to govern the black slaves that Mormon converts from the South brought with them as they gathered to the Great Basin. In fact, the very universalism of the gospel message in its first two decades created the circumstances for the restriction. Among those gathered to the Great Basin by 1852 were abolitionists and anti-abolitionists, black slaves, white slave masters, and free blacks. In casting a wide net, Mormonism had avoided the splits or schisms that divided the Methodists, Baptists, and Presbyterians over issues of race and slavery during the same period. Mormonism welcomed all comers into the gospel fold, black and white, bond and free. These various people brought their political and racial ideologies with them when they converted to Mormonism, ideas which initially existed independently of their faith. In 1852, however, Brigham Young prepared to order his diverse group of followers according to prevailing racial ideas, white over black and free over bound.[21]

Brigham Young tapped into long-standing biblical interpretations to draw upon Noah's curse of Canaan, but more directly to link a racial priesthood ban to God's purported "mark/curse" upon Cain for killing his brother Abel. "If there never was a prophet or apostle of Jesus Christ spoke it before, I tell you, this people that are commonly called Negroes are the children of old Cain. I know they are, I know they cannot bear rule in the priesthood."[22] In America, as scholar David M. Goldenberg demonstrates, the idea that black people were descendants of Cain dated back to at least 1733 and in Europe to as early as the eleventh century, long before Mormonism's founding in 1830. It was an idea that infused American culture and permeated racialized understandings of who black people were before Mormonism existed. In 1852, Brigham Young drew upon these same centuries-old ideas to both justify Utah Territory's law legalizing "servitude" and to argue for a race-based priesthood curse.[23]

Brigham Young insisted that because Cain killed Abel, all of Cain's posterity would have to wait until all of Abel's posterity received the priesthood. Brigham Young suggested that "the Lord told Cain that he should not receive the blessings of the Priesthood, nor his seed, until the last of the posterity of Abel had received the Priesthood." It was an ambiguous declaration he and other Mormon leaders returned to time and again. It suggested a future period of redemption for blacks but only after the "last" of Abel's posterity received the priesthood. Brigham Young and other leaders failed to clarify what that meant, how one might know when the "last" of Abel's posterity was ordained, or even who Abel's posterity were. In Brigham Young's mind, Cain's murder of Abel was an effort on Cain's part to usurp Abel's place in the covenant chain of priesthood leading back to father Adam.[24]

Brigham Young's position was fraught with inconsistencies and significant departures from aspects of other foundational Mormon principles. The Book of Mormon unambiguously posited that "all are alike unto God," "male and female, black and white, bond and free," and that all were invited to come unto Christ.[25] The Book of Mormon declared a universal salvation, a gospel message for "every nation, kindred, tongue, and people." It rhetorically demanded, "Hath [the Lord] commanded any that they should not partake of his salvation?" and then answered, "Nay." It declared that "all men are privileged the one like unto the other, and none are forbidden."[26] The Lord had established no limits to whom he invited to "partake of his salvation," even as the priesthood and temple restrictions created barriers to the fullness of that "salvation."

Brigham Young was also departing from his own earlier position on Q. Walker Lewis's ordination to the priesthood. And when he suggested that the priesthood was taken from blacks "by their own transgressions," he was further creating a race-based division to cloud black redemption and make each generation after Cain responsible anew for the consequences of Cain's murder of Abel. Although Joseph Smith rejected long-standing Christian notions of original sin to argue that "men will be punished for their own sins and not for Adam's transgression," Brigham Young held millions of blacks responsible for the consequences of Cain's murder, something in which they obviously took no part.

By insinuation, Brigham Young's position removed the role of individual agency in the lives of blacks, a fundamental Mormon tenet. It instead gave Cain's poor exercise of agency immitigable power over millions of his supposed descendants. To make matters worse, Brigham Young's position failed to distinguish exactly what it was that made Cain's murder of Abel worthy of a multigenerational curse when other biblical figures who also committed homicidal acts did not experience the same fate. As Brigham Young argued, it was the fractured human network that resulted from Cain's effort to usurp Abel's place in the great chain of beings that most animated his articulation of a priesthood curse.[27]

Even though Brigham Young and other nineteenth-century leaders relied upon the curse of Cain as the reason for the priesthood and temple restrictions, another explanation gained ground among some Latter-day Saints in the late nineteenth and early twentieth centuries. Because the curse of Cain so directly violated the role of individual agency in the lives of black people, some Mormons turned to the premortal realm to solve the conundrum. In this rationale, black people must have been neutral in the War in Heaven and thus were cursed with black skin and barred from the priesthood. In 1869, Brigham Young rejected the idea outright, but it did not disappear.[28] In 1907, Joseph Fielding Smith, then serving as assistant church historian, argued that the teaching was "not the official position of the Church, merely the opinion of men."[29] In 1944, John A. Widtsoe also argued against neutrality when he said, "All who have been permitted to come upon this earth and take upon themselves bodies, accepted the plan of salvation." Nonetheless, he argued that because black people themselves "did not commit Cain's sin," an explanation for the priesthood restriction had to involve something besides Cain's murder of Abel. "It is very probable," Widtsoe believed, "that in some way, unknown to us, the distinction harks back to the pre-existent state."[30]

By the 1960s, Joseph Fielding Smith slightly altered the idea, from "neutral" to "less valiant" and offered his own explanation. In his *Answers to Gospel Questions*, he claimed that some premortal spirits "were not valiant" in the war in heaven. As a result of "their lack of obedience," black people came to earth "under restrictions," including a denial of the priesthood.[31] The neutral/less valiant justifications grew over time to sometimes overshadow the curse of Cain explanation.

Brigham Young, nonetheless, tied the ban to Cain's murder of Abel and did not stray from that rationale throughout his life. It became the de facto position for the LDS Church, especially as it hardened in practice and preaching across the course of the nineteenth century. Brigham Young also spoke out forcefully against interracial sex and marriage, something that marked him more American than uniquely Mormon. Although his bombast advocated capital punishment, an extreme position even in the nineteenth century, those views were never codified into Utah law but certainly shaped attitudes among Mormons regarding race mixing.[32]

Brigham Young's two speeches to the territorial legislature were never published. Even though black priesthood ordination officially ended under Brigham Young, it was far from a universally understood idea. In 1879, two years after Brigham Young's death, Elijah Abel, the sole remaining black priesthood holder (Lewis had died in 1856) appealed to John Taylor for his remaining temple blessings: to receive the endowment and to be sealed to his wife. Abel had received the washing and anointing ritual in the Kirtland Temple and was baptized as proxy for deceased relatives and friends at Nauvoo but was living in Cincinnati by the time the endowment and sealing rituals were introduced.

It is impossible to know what might have happened if Abel had lived in Nauvoo during the introduction of temple rituals there. Surviving records, however, indicate that the Saints maintained an open racial vision to that date. At Nauvoo the Saints anticipated "people from every land and from every nation, the polished European, the degraded Hottentot, and the shivering Laplander" flowing to that city. They awaited "persons of all languages, and of every tongue, and of every color; who shall with us worship the Lord of Hosts in his holy temple, and offer up their orisons in his sanctuary."[33] By 1879, however, the space for full black participation was no longer as expansive, and Abel's appeal for his temple blessings prompted a further contraction.

John Taylor presided over an investigation into Abel's priesthood, which concluded that Abel was ordained an elder in 1836 and then a member of the Third Quorum of the Seventy that same year. Abel claimed that Joseph Smith himself sanctioned his ordination as an elder and he produced certificates to verify his claims. John Taylor nonetheless concluded that Abel's ordination was something of an exception, which was left to stand because it happened before the Lord had fully made his will known on racial matters through Brigham Young. John Taylor was unwilling to violate the precedent established by Brigham Young, even though that precedent violated the open racial pattern established under Joseph Smith. John Taylor allowed Abel's priesthood to stand but denied him access to the temple. Abel did not waver in his faith, though, and died in 1884 after serving a third mission for the Church. His obituary, published in the *Deseret News*, noted that he passed of "old age and debility, consequent upon exposure while laboring in the ministry in Ohio" and concluded that "he died in full faith of the

Gospel." It also substantiated his priesthood ordinations as an integral part of his identity.³⁴

With Abel dead, Jane Manning James, another faithful black pioneer, took up the cause. She repeatedly appealed for temple privileges, including permission to receive her endowment and asked on one occasion to be sealed to Q. Walker Lewis. She was just as repeatedly denied. The curse of Cain was used to justify her exclusion. Although Church leaders did allow her to perform baptisms for dead relatives and friends and to be "attached" via proxy as a servant to Joseph and Emma Smith, she was barred from further temple access.³⁵

Between the 1879 investigation led by John Taylor and 1908 when Joseph F. Smith solidified the bans, LDS leaders adopted an increasingly conservative stance on black priesthood and temple admission. They responded to incoming inquiries by relying upon distant memories and accumulating historical precedent. Sometimes they attributed the bans to Brigham Young and other times they mistakenly remembered them beginning with Joseph Smith.³⁶ George Q. Cannon also began to refer to the Book of Abraham as a justification for the ban. As finally articulated sometime before early 1907, leaders put a firm "one drop" rule in place: "The descendants of Ham may receive baptism and confirmation but no one known to have in his veins negro blood, (it matters not how remote a degree) can either have the Priesthood in any degree or the blessings of the Temple of God; no matter how otherwise worthy he may be."³⁷

Then in 1908, President Joseph F. Smith solidified this decision when he recalled that Elijah Abel was ordained to the priesthood "in the days of the Prophet Joseph" but suggested that his "ordination was declared null and void by the Prophet himself." Four years earlier, Joseph F. Smith had implied that Abel's ordination was a mistake that "was never corrected," but now he claimed that Mormonism's founder had in fact corrected that mistake although he offered no evidence to substantiate his claim. Joseph F. Smith then recalled that Abel applied for his endowments and asked to be sealed to his wife and children, but "notwithstanding the fact that he was a staunch member of the Church, Presidents Young, Taylor, and Woodruff all denied him the blessings of the House of the Lord." Joseph F. Smith also deliberately curtailed missionary efforts among black people, a decision that ensured a white identity for Mormonism moving forward.³⁸

This new memory became so entrenched among leaders in the twentieth century that by 1949 the First Presidency declared that the restriction was "always" in place: "The attitude of the Church with reference to Negroes remains as it has always stood. It is not a matter of the declaration of a policy but of direct commandment from the Lord." The "doctrine of the Church" on priesthood and race was in place "from the days of its organization," it professed. The First Presidency said nothing of the original black priesthood holders, an indication of how thoroughly reconstructed memory had come to replace verifiable facts.[39]

Even though President David O. McKay pushed for reform on racial matters, he was convinced that it would take a revelation to overturn the ban. Hugh B. Brown, his counselor in the First Presidency, believed otherwise. Brown reasoned that because there was no revelation that began the ban, no revelation was needed to end it. McKay's position held sway, especially as McKay claimed he did not receive a divine mandate to move forward.[40] As early as 1963, however, Apostle Spencer W. Kimball signaled an open attitude for change: "The doctrine or policy has not varied in my memory," Kimball acknowledged, "I know it could. I know the Lord could change his policy and release the ban and forgive the possible error which brought about the deprivation."[41] That forgiveness ultimately came with Kimball at the helm in 1978.[42]

Understanding the Priesthood and Temple Bans

Apostle Bruce R. McConkie, a man responsible for some of the Church's justifications for a racial ban, denounced his own statements within months of the 1978 revelation. He asked an LDS audience at Brigham Young University to "forget everything that I have said, or what President Brigham Young or ... whomsoever has said in days past that is contrary to the present revelation. We spoke with a limited understanding and without the light and knowledge that now has come into the world."[43] It was a statement that suggested that prior teachings on race were devoid of the "light and knowledge" that revelation represents to Latter-day Saints.

Even still, it is a difficult question with which some Saints continue to grapple: How could race-based priesthood and temple restrictions creep into the Church and last for so long? Was Brigham Young speaking for himself in 1852 when he announced the priesthood ban to the territorial legislature or for God? If for himself, why would God permit him to do so? If for God, why implement a restriction that violated scriptural notions of equality? Some have suggested that while the explanations for the bans are invalid, the bans themselves were inspired for purposes known only to God. In an American culture that so thoroughly privileged whiteness, the priesthood and temple restrictions brought Mormonism into conformity with the national mainstream. In this explanation, Brigham Young's and later leaders' implementation of the restrictions over time were bound by surrounding cultural norms, a violation of which may have produced significant disdain and additional turmoil for the nineteenth-century Church. This interpretation is problematic because if God or his prophets were somehow bound by cultural norms, the introduction of polygamy into an American society that so thoroughly abhorred it would have never taken place.

Others view the priesthood and temple restrictions as perhaps a trial for both white and black Latter-day Saints, or a way in which they were forced to confront the prejudices of their day, be it the 1850s or the 1950s. In this version, race becomes a calling, not a curse. Perhaps it was and is a test that forces Latter-day Saints to search their hearts to see if they might summon the courage and strength to rise above differences and embrace commonalities centered upon the worship of Jesus Christ. Could white Latter-day Saints transcend cultural norms and the privileges of being white in America, both before and after 1978, to welcome black people into the gospel fold, into the priesthood, into the temple, and into their hearts? Could black Latter-day Saints embrace a gospel message, both before and after 1978, that views them as children of God but that historically was burdened with teachings that they were cursed, less valiant, or neutral children of that same God? If God stands at the helm of his Church and directs his kingdom, what were his purposes and how does one square them with scriptural messages of universal salvation?

Ezra Taft Benson, speaking as an Apostle in 1975, offered an overarching principle that is broadly applicable to the historical development of the priesthood and temple bans. Benson was not speaking specifically about race, but his guiding philosophy might be useful in approaching the issue.

> If you see some individuals in the Church doing things that disturb you, or you feel the Church is not doing things the way you think they could or should be done, the following principles might be helpful: God has to work through mortals of varying degrees of spiritual progress. Sometimes he temporarily grants to men their unwise requests in order that they might learn from their own sad experiences. Some refer to this as the "Samuel principle." The children of Israel wanted a king like all the other nations. The prophet Samuel was displeased and prayed to the Lord about it. The Lord responded by saying, Samuel, "they have not rejected thee, but they have rejected me, that I should not reign over them." The Lord told Samuel to warn the people of the consequences if they had a king. Samuel gave them the warning. But they still insisted on their king. So God gave them a king and let them suffer. They learned the hard way. God wanted it to be otherwise, but within certain bounds he grants unto men according to their desires.[44]

President Benson's Samuel principle suggests a viable way of looking at the race question in the LDS Church, but first let us consider other examples. This concept applies to the lost 116 manuscript pages of the Book of Mormon as well. God let Joseph Smith give those pages to Martin Harris and then let him learn from "his own sad experience." The Lord called Joseph Smith to repentance in D&C 3:6–7: "And behold, how oft you have transgressed the commandments and the laws of God, and have gone on in the persuasions of men. For, behold, you should not have feared man more than God."

Even the Prophet is susceptible to "the persuasions of men." Later, Joseph Smith organized the Kirtland Safety Society Anti-Banking Institution. He and other leaders did so after being denied a bank charter by the state of Ohio. They inserted the prefix "anti" before the word "banking" and opened the doors for business. Many Saints at the time believed the Prophet gave them assurances of the bank's success. Instead, the bank failed within a few months. Some Mormons lost their money and their faith. It was a factor in the disillusionment of many Saints, so much so that by June of 1837, Heber C. Kimball claimed that not twenty men in Kirtland believed Joseph Smith was a prophet. Parley and Orson Pratt, David Patten, Frederick G. Williams, Warren Parrish, David Whitmer, and Lyman Johnson all dissented. Why did God not stop Joseph Smith from founding the bank? God knew it would fail before it was founded. Why not simply tell Joseph Smith not to start the bank and save the Church from all of the turmoil that followed?[45]

Again, it seems that God let Joseph Smith and the Saints learn from their sad experiences. Perhaps the same principle is applicable to the development of the priesthood and temple bans. Were Church leaders susceptible to the "persuasions of men"? Did they borrow from then current political and "scientific" ideas about race that dominated nineteenth-century American thought? In what ways did the racialization of Mormons at the hands of outsiders have an impact upon events on the inside?

While I don't believe that God instigated the priesthood and temple restrictions, I do believe he let them happen, just as he let the children of Israel have a king, let Joseph Smith give Martin Harris the lost 116 pages, and let Joseph Smith open an "anti-banking institution." As President Benson said, "Sometimes [God] temporarily grants to men their unwise requests in order that they might learn from their own sad experiences."[46] In the end it makes me wonder what we are to learn from our racial history, and have we learned it? It should force us to stare the myth of a micromanager God squarely in the face and allow ample room for women and men with divine callings to fall short of the divine. My work as a historian has habituated me to messy history, something I expect just as much of religious people reaching toward heaven as I do of American history in general. As the American Historical Association puts it, "Multiple, conflicting perspectives are among the truths of history."[47]

As a twenty-first-century Latter-day Saint, I am not bound by Mormon leaders' past teachings on race any more than I am bound as an American by Thomas Jefferson's views on race. Past LDS leaders only speak for me on matters of race as far as they point me toward a universal redemption through Christ. For all of the emphasis that outsiders place upon a perceived blind obedience to authority among Mormons, they fail to give equal weight to the democratizing impact of personal revelation, a central tenet of the faith from its beginnings. Even Brigham Young, sometimes depicted as an extreme authoritarian, counseled Mormons to avoid blind faith: "Let every man and woman know by the whispering of the spirit of God to themselves whether their leaders are walking in the path the Lord dictates or not. This has been my exhortation continually."[48]

While one may indeed find Latter-day Saints today who hold racists views, they do so in direct violation of Church standards, specifically a 2006 call to repentance by Church President Gordon B. Hinckley: "How can any man holding the Melchizedek Priesthood arrogantly assume that he is eligible for the priesthood whereas another who lives a righteous life but whose skin is of a different color is ineligible?" Speaking to the men of the Church, he further admonished, "Brethren, there is no basis for racial hatred among the priesthood of this Church. If any within the sound of my voice is inclined to indulge in this, then let him go before the Lord and ask for forgiveness and be no more involved in such."[49]

The 1978 Official Declaration is the only revelation in the LDS canon on priesthood and race. It returned the Church to its universalistic roots and reintegrated its priesthood and temples. It confirmed the biblical standard that God is "no respecter of persons"[50] and the Book of Mormon principle that "all are alike unto God."[51] The LDS Church in the twenty-first century no longer teaches that black skin is a curse, that black people are descendants of Cain or Ham, that blacks were less valiant or neutral or rejected the priesthood in the premortal existence, that mixed-race marriages are a sin or culturally undesirable, that blacks are inferior in any way to whites, or that the priesthood and temple restrictions were revelations from God. It does however emphatically endorse the admonition of President Gordon B. Hinckley, "Let us all recognize that each of us is a son or daughter of our Father in Heaven, who loves all of His children."[52]

Additional Resources

The Church of Jesus Christ of Latter-day Saints. "Race and the Priesthood." https://www.lds.org/topics/race-and-the-priesthood.

Bringhurst, Newell G. and Darron T. Smith, eds. *Black and Mormon*. Urbana: University of Illinois Press, 2004.

Bringhurst, Newell G. and Matthew L. Harris. *The Mormon Church and African Americans: A Documentary History*. Urbana: University of Illinois Press, 2015.

Bush, Lester E., Jr. "Mormonism's Negro Doctrine: An Historical Overview." *Dialogue* 8, no. 1 (Spring 1973): 11–68.

———. "Writing 'Mormonism's Negro Doctrine: An Historical Overview' (1973): Context and Reflections, 1998." *Journal of Mormon History* 25, no. 1 (Spring 1999): 229–71.

———, and Armand L. Mauss. *Neither White nor Black: Mormon Scholars Confront the Race Issue in a Universal Church*. Midvale, UT: Signature Books, 1984.

Kimball, Edward L. "Spencer W. Kimball and the Revelation on Priesthood." *BYU Studies* 47, no. 2 (2008), 4–78.

Mauss, Armand. *All Abraham's Children: Changing Mormon Conceptions of Race and Lineage*. Urbana and Chicago: University of Illinois Press, 2003.

Reeve, W. Paul. *Religion of a Different Color: Race and the Mormon Struggle for Whiteness*. New York: Oxford University Press, 2015.

About the Author

W. Paul Reeve is the director of Graduate Studies in the History Department at the University of Utah, where he teaches courses on Utah history, Mormon history, and the history of the western United States. His most recent book is *Religion of a Different Color: Race and the Mormon Struggle for Whiteness*, published by Oxford University Press. He is also the author of *Making Space on the Western Frontier: Mormons, Miners, and Southern Paiutes* and coeditor with Ardis E. Parshall of *Mormonism: A Historical Encyclopedia*. With Michael Van Wagenen, he coedited *Between Pulpit and Pew: The Supernatural World in Mormon History and Folklore*.

Notes

1. "The Gospel, No. 5," *Latter Day Saints' Messenger and Advocate*, Kirtland, Ohio, February 1835; "The Ancient Order of Things," *Latter Day Saints' Messenger and Advocate*, September 1835; Parley P. Pratt, *A Voice of Warning and Instruction to All People, Containing a Declaration of the Faith and Doctrine of the Church of the Latter Day Saints, Commonly Called Mormons* (New York: W. Sandford, 1837), 140; Parley P. Pratt, *The Millennium and Other Poems: To Which Is Annexed a Treatise on the Regeneration and Eternal Duration of Matter* (New York: W. Molineux, 1840), 58.

2. Abraham 1:26.

3. For explanations on the Book of Abraham and race, see Alma Allred, "The Traditions of Their Fathers: Myth versus Reality in LDS Scriptural Writings," in *Black and Mormon*, ed. Newell G. Bringhurst and Darron T. Smith (Urbana: University of Illinois Press, 2004), 34–49; Richard Lyman Bushman, *Joseph Smith: Rough Stone Rolling* (New York: Alfred A. Knopf, 2005), 285–89; Hugh Nibley and Michael Rhodes, *One Eternal Round* (Salt Lake City: Deseret Book; Provo, UT: FARMS, 2010), 162; Hugh Nibley, *Abraham in Egypt*, ed. Gary P. Gillum (Provo, UT: FARMS; Salt Lake City: Deseret Book, 2000), 360–61, 428, 528.

4. 2 Nephi 5:21.

5. For a thorough exploration of these events, see W. Paul Reeve, *Religion of a Different Color: Race and the Mormon Struggle for Whiteness* (New York: Oxford University Press, 2015), chaps. 4–7 and conclusion.

6. "An Act to Establish an Uniform Rule of Naturalization," 1st Cong., March 26, 1790, Sess. II, chap. 3, 1 stat 103; *Congressional Globe*, 30th Cong., 1st Sess. (Washington, DC: Blair and Rives, 1848*)*, 53–56, 96–100; *Political Debates Between Hon. Abraham Lincoln and Hon. Stephen A. Douglas, in the Celebrated Campaign of 1858, in Illinois* (Columbus, OH: Follett, Foster and Company, 1860), 136; Scott v. Sandford, 60 U.S. 393 (1857), 407.

7. Matthew Frye Jacobsen, *Whiteness of a Different Color: European Immigrants and the Alchemy of Race* (Cambridge, MA: Harvard University Press, 1998), 37–38, 41; Matthew Frye Jacobson, *Barbarian Virtues: The United States Encounters Foreign Peoples at Home and Abroad, 1876–1917* (New York: Hill and Wang, 2000), 140–49; Nell Irvin Painter, *The History of White People* (2010; repr., New York: W. W. Norton & Company, 2011), 132–50.

8. David R. Roediger, *Working Toward Whiteness: How America's Immigrants Became White* (New York: Basic Books, 2005), 12; Reeve, *Religion of a Different Color*, introduction and chap. 1.

9. Patricia J. Williams, *The Alchemy of Race and Rights* (Cambridge, MA: Harvard University Press, 1991); Patricia J. Williams, *Seeing a Color-Blind Future: The Paradox of Race* (New York: Noonday Press, 1997); Ariela J. Gross, *What Blood Won't Tell: A History of Race on Trial in America* (Cambridge, MA: Harvard University Press, 2008), 138–39; Reeve, *Religion of a Different Color*, chaps. 4–7.

10. "Fanaticism," *Albany Evening Journal* (Albany, NY), February 16, 1831, 3; "Mormonites," *The Sun* (Philadelphia, PA), August 18, 1831, 1; "Mormonism," *Boston Recorder*, October 10, 1832, 161; Mark Lyman Staker, *Hearken, O Ye People: The Historical Setting of Joseph Smith's Ohio Revelations* (Salt Lake City: Greg Kofford Books, 2009), 64–65.

11. E. S. Abdy, *Journal of a Residence and Tour in the United States of North America, From April, 1833, to October, 1834*, 3 vols. (London: John Murray, 1835), 1:324–25; 3:40–42, 54–59.

12. Simon G. Whitten (La Harpe, Illinois), to Mary B. Whitten (Parsonsfield, Maine), June 22, 1844, Mormon File, HM 31520, box 13, Huntington Library, San Marino, CA; Captain Frederick Marryat, *Monsieur Violet: His Travels and Adventures among the Snake Indians and Wild Tribes of the Great Western Prairies* (London: Thomas Hodgson, 1849), 275; "To His Excellency, Daniel Dunklin, Governor of the State of Missouri," *Evening and the Morning Star* (Kirtland, OH), December 1833, 114; To the Citizens of Howard County, October 7, 1838, in *Document Containing the Correspondence, Orders, &C. in Relation to the Disturbances with the Mormons; and the Evidence Given Before the Hon. Austin A. King* (Fayette, MO: Office of the Boon's Lick Democrat, 1841), 40; Abraham Owen Smoot, diary, May 28, 1836, MSS 896, vol. 1, L. Tom Perry Special Collections, Harold B. Lee Library, Brigham Young University, Provo, UT. I am indebted to Jonathan Stapley for this reference.

13. Parley P. Pratt, *Late Persecution of the Church of Jesus Christ of Latter-day Saints. Ten Thousand American Citizens Robbed, Plundered, and Banished; Others Imprisoned, and Others Martyred for their Religion. With a Sketch of their Rise, Progress and Doctrine* (New York: J. W. Harrison, 1840), 59; William G. Hartley, *My Best for the Kingdom: History and Autobiography of John Lowe Butler, a Mormon Frontiersman* (Salt Lake City: Aspen Books, 1993), 389; "Speech Delivered by Heber C. Kimball," *Times and Seasons*, July 15, 1845, 969–71; "Conference Minutes," *Times and Seasons*, November 1, 1845, 1012.

14. Reeve, *Religion of a Different Color*, chap. 1; US Senate, "Statistical Report on the Sickness and Morality in the Army of the United States, compiled from the Records of the Surgeon

General's Office; Embracing a Period of Five Years from January 1, 1855, to January, 1860," Senate Executive Document 52, 36th Congress, 1st session, 301–2; Jennie Anderson Froiseth, ed., *The Women of Mormonism; or the Story of Polygamy as Told by the Victims Themselves* (Chicago: A. G. Nettleton & Co., 1881), iv, 25; "The Old Mormons Likely to Give Way," *Chicago Daily Tribune*, March 10, 1873, 7.

15. William Jarman, *U. S. A. Uncle Sam's Abscess, or Hell Upon Earth for U. S. Uncle Sam* (Exeter, England: H. Leduc's Steam Printing Works, 1884), 6; emphasis in original.

16. Alfred Trumble, *The Mysteries of Mormonism* (New York: Police Gazette, 1882).

17. Reeve, *Religion of a Different Color*, chap. 6; *Frank Leslie's Budget of Fun* (New York, NY), January 1872, 16; "Immense Meeting in Indianapolis," *New York Times*, July 21, 1856, 2; "Later From Utah," *New York Times*, February 7, 1859, 1.

18. Zim, "The 16 to 1 Movement in Utah," *The Judge*, September 12, 1896, 176; Reeve, *Religion of a Different Color*, chap. 6.

19. Reeve, *Religion of a Different Color*, chaps. 4 and 5; Church Historian's Office, General Church Minutes, 1839–1877, CR 100 318, box 1, folder 52, March 26, 1847, Church History Library (hereafter CHL); spelling standardized.

20. Reeve, *Religion of a Different Color*, 128–39; William W. Major (Elk Horn), to Brigham Young, June 16, 1847, Brigham Young Collection, CR1234/1, box 21, folder 8, reel 30, CHL; Nelson W. Whipple, autobiography and journal, microfilm, manuscript, MS 9995, 30–31, CHL; General Church Minutes, CR100–318, box 1, folder 59, 3 December 1847, 6–7, CHL; William I. Appleby, autobiography and journal, MS 1401, folder 1, May 19, 1847, 170–71; December 3, 1847, 203–4, CHL; William I. Appleby, Batavia, New York, letter to Brigham Young, June 2, 1847, Brigham Young Collection, CR1234/1, box 21, folder 5, reel 30, CHL.

21. Reeve, *Religion of a Different Color*, 122–23, chap. 5.

22. Brigham Young, February 5, 1852, a speech before a Joint Session of the Territorial Legislature, Papers of George D. Watt, MS 4534, box 1, folder 3, CHL, transcribed by LaJean Purcell Carruth; Richard S. Van Wagoner, *The Complete Discourses of Brigham Young* (Salt Lake City: Smith-Pettit Foundation, 2009), 1:468–72.

23. David M. Goldenberg, *The Curse of Ham: Race and Slavery in Early Judaism, Christianity, and Islam* (Princeton, NJ: Princeton University Press, 2003), 178–82; see for example, David Walker, *Walker's Appeal, in Four Articles; Together with a Preamble, to the Coloured Citizens of the World, but in Particular, and Very Expressly, to Those of the United States of America, Written in Boston, State of Massachusetts, September 28, 1829* (Boston: David Walker, 1830), 68.

24. Young, February 5, 1852; Reeve, *Religion of a Different Color*, 145–46, 152–61.

25. 2 Nephi 26:33.

26. 2 Nephi 26:13, 26–28.

27. Reeve, *Religion of a Different Color*, 155–57; "Church History," *Times and Seasons*, March 1, 1842; Royal Skousen, *The Book of Mormon: The Earliest Text* (New Haven, CT: Yale University Press, 2009), 137.

28. Scott G. Kenney, ed., *Wilford Woodruff's Journal* (Midvale, UT: Signature Books, 1984), 6:511 (December 25, 1869). For Orson Pratt and B. H. Roberts's use of the idea, see "The Pre-Existence of Man," *The Seer*, Washington, DC, April 1853; B. H. Roberts, "To the Youth of Israel," *Contributor*, May 1885.

29. Joseph F. Smith, Jr., letter to Alfred M. Nelson, January 13, 1907, microfilm, MS 14591, CHL.

30. John A. Widtsoe, "Were Negroes Neutrals in Heaven?" *Improvement Era*, June 1944, 385.

31. Joseph Fielding Smith, *Answers to Gospel Questions*, 5 vols. (Salt Lake City: Deseret Book, 1966), 5:163–64.

32. Reeve, *Religion of a Different Color*, 158–59; Young, February 5, 1852.

33. Reeve, *Religion of a Different Color*, 195–201; Dean C. Jessee, Mark Ashurst-McGee, and Richard L. Jensen, eds., *Journals, Volume 1: 1832–1839*, vol. 1 of the Journals series of *The Joseph Smith Papers*, ed. Dean C. Jessee, Ronald K. Esplin, and Richard Lyman Bushman (Salt Lake City: Church Historian's Press, 2008), 152; "Report from the Presidency," *Times and Seasons*, October 1840, 188.

34. Reeve, *Religion of a Different Color*, 195–200; L. John Nuttall, diary, vol. 1 (Dec. 1876–Mar. 1884), typescript, 290–93, L. Tom Perry Collection; Council Meeting, June 4, 1879, Lester E. Bush Papers, MS 685, box 10, folder 3, Special Collections, J. Willard Marriott Library, University of Utah, Salt Lake City, Utah; "Deaths," *Deseret News*, December 31, 1884, 800.

35. Reeve, *Religion of a Different Color*, 200–210.

36. George A. Smith Family Papers, MS 36, box 78, folder 7; December 15, 1897; March 11, 1900; August 18, 1900; January 2, 1902; and August 16, 1908, Manuscripts Division, Special Collections, J. Willard Marriott Library.

37. George A. Smith Family Papers, extract from George F. Richards record of decisions by the Council of the First Presidency and the Twelve Apostles (no date given, but the next decision in order is dated 8 February 1907), J. Willard Marriott Library.

38. Reeve, *Religion of a Different Color,* 208–10; George A. Smith Family Papers, Council Minutes, August 26, 1908, J. Willard Marriott Library; for the "never corrected" instance, see David McKay, Huntsville, UT, letter to John R. Winder, Salt Lake City, March 14, 1904, Joseph F. Smith, Stake Correspondence, CR 1/191, box 12, folder 17, CHL.

39. Reeve, *Religion of a Different Color, 255–56;* First Presidency Statement, August 17, 1949, in Lester E. Bush Jr. and Armand L. Mauss, eds., *Neither White nor Black: Mormon Scholars Confront the Race Issue in a Universal Church* (Midvale, UT: Signature Books, 1984), 221.

40. Edward L. Kimball, "Spencer W. Kimball and the Revelation on Priesthood," *BYU Studies* 47, no. 2 (2008): 21–22, 27; Gregory A. Prince and William Robert Wright, *David O. McKay and the Rise of Modern Mormonism* (Salt Lake City: University of Utah Press, 2005), chap. 4; D. Michael Quinn, *The Mormon Hierarchy: Extensions of Power* (Salt Lake City: Signature Books, 1997), 13–14; Matthew L. Harris, "Mormonism's Problematic Racial Past and the Evolution of the Divine-Curse Doctrine," *The John Whitmer Historical Association Journal* 33 (Spring/Summer 2013), 106–7; Reeve, *Religion of a Different Color*, 259–60.

41. Edward L. Kimball, ed., *The Teachings of Spencer W. Kimball: Twelfth President of The Church of Jesus Christ of Latter-day Saints* (Salt Lake City: Bookcraft, 1982), 448–49.

42. Kimball, "Spencer W. Kimball and the Revelation on Priesthood."

43. Bruce R. McConkie, "All Are Alike unto God," August 18, 1978, Second Annual Church Educational System Religious Educators' Symposium, Brigham Young University, Provo, UT.

44. Ezra Taft Benson, "Jesus Christ—Gifts and Expectations," *New Era*, May 1975, 16. See also 1 Samuel 8.

45. Larry T. Wimmer, "Kirtland Economy," in *Encyclopedia of Mormonism,* ed. Daniel H. Ludlow (New York: Macmillan, 1992), 792–93; Staker, *Hearken, O Ye People*, 391–548.

46. Ezra Taft Benson, "Jesus Christ—Gifts and Expectations," *New Era*, May 1975, 16.

47. American Historical Association, "Statement on Standards of Professional Conduct," http://www.historians.org/pubs/Free/ProfessionalStandards.cfm.

48. Brigham Young, "Remarks," *Deseret News*, February 12, 1862, 257.
49. Gordon B. Hinckley, "The Need for Greater Kindness," *Ensign*, May 2006, 58–61.
50. Acts 10:34.
51. 2 Nephi 26:33.
52. Hinckley, "The Need for Greater Kindness," 58.

14

Finding Lehi in America through DNA Analysis

Ugo A. Perego

The Book of Mormon begins with Lehi and his family leaving Jerusalem, making their way through the desert, crossing the sea, and eventually arriving somewhere in the Americas. Among those who are familiar with this narrative, there are some that have assumed the continent was uninhabited at their arrival. If this were true, then all Native Americans should be descendants from Book of Mormon peoples. However, is this an accurate assumption? A closer reading of the scriptures and recent scientific discoveries have shown that this interpretation could be too narrow. Genetic studies have been able to successfully describe broad population trends, and DNA collected from Native Americans revealed their origins in ancient Asia. These results do not necessarily mean that Lehi and his family never existed but only that whatever small genetic contribution they made to the whole indigenous population of the Americas has not been, or cannot be, identified by modern science. A DNA approach cannot prove or disprove the historical authenticity of the Book of Mormon or address the genetics of those who traveled with Lehi to the "promised land."[1] Those who declare otherwise disregard the complexities and constraints of DNA research in population studies.

Have you ever wondered what Lehi, Mulek, and the brother of Jared encountered when their ships landed on the shores of America? Likely they each encountered different things since they arrived at different times and at different locations. The majority of the Book of Mormon covers a period of approximately one thousand years, from 600 BC to AD 400, but most of the details of the text focus on spiritual matters rather than historical ones, so we are left to guess what and who greeted these emigrants. Additionally, the Book of Mormon portrays itself as a summary taken from other records, which contained a more complete history of the whereabouts of the people described within its pages. Studies of archaeology, linguistics, genetics, and anthropology can offer clues, but little has been discovered that can be tied specifically to the history of this group of colonizers. In regard to information gleaned from DNA studies of modern Native Americans, much of the research would seem to contradict the narrative of the Book of Mormon. Closer examination of the findings, however, reveals that while science can partially answer the question of what the Book of Mormon peoples would have found upon their arrival on the continent, it cannot address their genetic legacy.

THE EMPTY CONTINENT THEORY

Most early Latter-day Saints assumed that the Jaredites, Mulekites, and Lehites were the first to settle the Americas. The original Book of Mormon text, however, does not claim that the peoples mentioned in its narrative were either the predominant or the exclusive inhabitants of the lands they occupied. It provides only subtle and short references to possible cultural contacts between the peoples it describes and others who may have lived nearby.

Over time, this view that the American continent was empty at the time of the arrival of the Book of Mormon peoples has been perpetuated among some members of the Church. In more recent times and with the advance of DNA technology, it has also been assumed that Book of Mormon migrants should have carried the most typical genetic signatures found in the modern Middle East, implying that all Native Americans today should have a similar genetic makeup to their Israelite forefathers. If these two hypotheses were true, it would make sense to think that DNA should be able to *prove* the Book of Mormon to be a factual account. But this is not the case. In fact, to be able to successfully employ DNA research to demonstrate the truthfulness of the Book of Mormon, these additional conditions would also be required:

1. None of the Jaredites described in the Book of Mormon would have survived;
2. Mulek and his group, founders of the city Zarahemla, would meet the same genetic composition criteria as Lehi's group; and
3. Middle Easterners today, specifically those identifying themselves as Jews, carry the same DNA as their Israelite ancestors who lived in the same geographic region (Jerusalem) where Lehi lived 2,600 years ago.

Unfortunately, none of these circumstances can be verified by the text of the Book of Mormon. The summary made by Mormon on the plates does not talk explicitly about others, but it also does not say that no one else was in the Americas. In fact, cultural and demographic clues in its text hint at the presence of other groups.

Some incorrectly insist that the Church has taught for years that the American continent was uninhabited until the arrival of Book of Mormon people and that only recently this position has changed. This is incorrect. The Church has never expressed an official opinion with regard to either Book of Mormon geography or population dynamics.[2] This, of course, does not mean that members, leaders, and scholars have not shared their personal opinions one way or the other, including several instances in which the concept of an already inhabited continent was shared even before scientists began to bring forth the DNA evidence.[3] At the April 1929 general conference, President Anthony W. Ivins of the First Presidency cautioned: "We must be careful in the conclusions that we reach. The Book of Mormon . . . does not tell us that there was no one here before them. It does not tell us that people did not come after."[4]

The argument about the Church's supposed change of position on the issue seems to stem from the introduction added in 1981 at the beginning of the Book of Mormon, which read that "after thousands of years, all were destroyed except the Lamanites, and they are the *principal* ancestors of the American Indians" (emphasis added). Although the term "principal" already presupposes the existence of other ancestors, this was recently changed. The current edition of the Book of Mormon now reads: "All were destroyed except the Lamanites, and they are *among* the ancestors of the American Indians" (emphasis added).

This change does not drastically affect the concept of heritage and ancestry of modern Native Americans in relation to ancient Lamanites because of the change in the meaning of the term *Lamanite* as used in the latter part of the Nephite history. In 4 Nephi, the writer explains that following the visitation of the Savior to the Americas, the formerly warring people became united, without genetic or ethnic distinction among them: "There were no robbers, nor murderers, *neither were there Lamanites*, nor any manner of -ites; but they were in one, the children of Christ, and heirs to the kingdom of God."[5]

The record continues by stating that eventually there "were a small part of the people who had revolted from the church and *taken upon them the name of Lamanites; therefore there began to be Lamanites* again in the land."[6] It is very likely that this choice of designation was social or religious rather than genealogical in nature, based on the character of the Lamanites prior to Christ's visit. In fact, 4 Nephi 1:36–39 reports that, in a similar fashion, others decided to use the term "Nephites" again to distinguish themselves as "true believers of Christ," restating that those that "rejected the gospel were called Lamanites" and were "taught to hate the children of God, even as the

Lamanites were taught to hate the children of Nephi from the beginning."[7] Here the use of the word "even" underscores the practice of choosing a name that had a specific social meaning in the past.

Another reference to ancestry is recorded toward the end of the Nephite civilization. Mormon twice declares his ancestry: as a genealogical descendant of Nephi[8] and a "pure descendant" of Lehi,[9] possibly implying the existence of outside populations contributing to the ethnicity of the people of the Book of Mormon in Mormon's day.[10] Because the term "Lamanite" lost its genetic meaning in the latter part of the Book of Mormon narrative, attempts to define original Lamanite ancestry would be nearly impossible, as the modern remnant of this ancient population would have to include both true descendants of Lehi's original party as well as others already inhabiting the land.

DNA as a Genealogical Tool

The early 1990s marked the beginning of the DNA era in the study of human diversity and the clarification of the genetic relationships and origins of different world populations. With newly developed technology, scientists were able to analyze segments of female-inherited DNA found in organelles called mitochondria and to identify small but important genetic differences that could uniquely be linked to specific populations. Mitochondria are structures within cells that convert energy from food into a form that cells can use. This DNA, called mitochondrial DNA or mtDNA, is separate and in addition to the larger amount of genetic material found within the cell's nucleus in structures known as chromosomes (called nuclear DNA). Nuclear DNA has also been employed in more recent years in the study of population migrations. One particular chromosome found only in males is inherited exclusively along the father-to-son line and it is called the Y chromosome (Ycs for short). The remaining non-gender-related chromosomes constitute the majority of a person's DNA and may reveal distinct insights into human history and expansions. Therefore, when talking about DNA studies, one essential component is to be aware of the existence of these three different genetic approaches following separate inheritance patterns, with their own strengths, differences, and limitations.

Dating through the use of mtDNA and Y chromosomes is concerned mostly with the divergence between two lineages sharing a common ancestor. It reveals only how far back in time the split took place, not where the split occurred or the geographic locations of these lineages today. At the present time, thanks to the complete sequencing of large numbers of mtDNA genomes, scientists performing research of worldwide populations are dissecting individual mtDNA lineages to discover important details missed in the past. Though mtDNA can reveal much about genetic background, it is not fail proof.

Before discussing the DNA markers in Native Americans, it may be helpful to consider how relying on genetic information alone can lead to incorrect conclusions. To demonstrate these principles, I will use my personal family history. I was born in Italy into a multi-generational Italian family and consider myself full-blooded Italian. As a geneticist, I have studied my genetic markers, or scientific genealogy, very closely. From this approach, I have learned that my autosomal DNA makeup is nearly one hundred percent European,[11] but surprisingly my paternal line (found on my Y chromosome) is typically shared with individuals from Asia, North America, and Oceania. The frequency of this particular genetic lineage in the Mediterranean Basin is close to zero. A plausible explanation for the introduction of Asian-like DNA in my paternal family line could be the invasions of barbaric groups in Europe (all the way to Northern Italy) between the fifth and seventh century. There is no family tradition or genealogical record to confirm this information, only speculation based on history and the available DNA in my particular family.

The reason this is important is that if I were to relocate to Asia today, and someone were to find my skeleton and extract my DNA two thousand years from now, based on the Y chromosome data alone, they would believe that I was indigenous to Asia and not a migrant from Europe. This error would be made because I had an ancestor of Asian origins whose Y chromosome markers persisted for many generations but whose autosomal DNA failed to survive in my current genetic makeup. As my personal DNA illustrates, and based on the inheritance properties of autosomal DNA, if a single individual or a relatively small number of people from Asia would mix with a large pool of Southern Europeans, their autosomal DNA would likely disappear over time.[12]

Origins of Native Americans

With regard to mtDNA studies, the first analyzed samples came from Native American populations. The data showed that nearly all the mtDNAs could be clustered into one of four groups, which were initially labeled A, B, C, and D, and later groupings identified in other populations proceeded alphabetically with alphanumerical subsets.[13]

These earlier studies utilized a small section of the mitochondrial genome, often limited to just a few hundred DNA bases. Genetic studies are conducted on both modern and ancient samples, but the latter are more difficult to collect and the DNA could be damaged. The benefit of working with ancient samples would be to glance directly into the history of Native American populations rather than trying to reconstruct them from the DNA that has randomly survived to the present time. Three significant findings were published during the 1990s based on mtDNA diversity that help us understand Native American origins:

1. The highest level of mtDNA variation was observed in sub-Saharan African groups, indicating that all humans shared a common female ancestor from Africa and that human colonization of the planet started from there. The existence of a common maternal ancestor from Africa for all mtDNA lineages does not mean that she was the only female alive at that time, but merely the lucky one in perpetuating her genetic lineage.
2. Four distinct lineages named A, B, C, and D were observed in the Americas as well as in modern Asian populations, supporting the theory that the ancient maternal ancestors of Native Americans were of Asian origins, surviving the last Ice Age on the continent-sized land bridge called Beringia that once connected northeast Siberia to Alaska.[14]
3. A fifth lineage was observed in Native American populations from the Great Lakes area and in a few other North American groups. This new mtDNA was labeled X because it was different from the previously known Native American mtDNA lineages. It was also observed in many modern European, African, and Middle Eastern populations,[15] as well as in a small region of Central Asia.[16]

Arriving on the Continent

The first and major genetic clue to the ancestry of Native Americans is the presence of mtDNA lineages labeled A, B, C, and D on both sides of the Bering Strait, which once connected Siberia to Alaska. This is in agreement with data from different disciplines and has helped scientists conclude that thousands of years ago, a relatively small group of hunter-gatherers made their way across East/North Asia all the way to Beringia where they were eventually trapped because of the worsening of the climate conditions.[17]

During the following millennia, they probably survived by living in a manner similar to modern-day Arctic natives. Population growth was probably halted because of scarcity of resources. They were physically separated from their source population, gradually developing their own unique linguistic, cultural, and genetic characteristics.[18] Eventually, the climate began to improve again, and the large glaciers on each side of Beringia started to withdraw.

Following this glacial era, temperatures increased and sea levels began to rise again, gradually submerging Beringia and most of the world's coastlines. At that time, at least one and perhaps two entryways became available to the ancestors of American natives moving eastward into a pristine and empty American continent.[19] Lack of competition for resources allowed a quick spread southward. Populations began to grow, and by the time the Europeans arrived after Columbus's discovery of the Americas in 1492, at least 20 million people lived in the Americas.[20]

Distinct mtDNA Develops

Starting within the isolated Beringian enclave and later on the separate American double-continent, the ancestor of modern Native Americans did not have meaningful contact with their Asian "cousins." This is when genetic divergence occured as well as the gradual but significant introduction of random DNA dissimilarities; these resulted in a uniquely distinct Native American gene pool. It is also commonly accepted that if a non-Native American mtDNA lineage is observed in the Americas, even in tribal groups considered deeply indigenous, the atypical DNA was introduced more recently, after the discovery of the New World by Europeans.

Although this may be accurate in most instances, it is not a verifiable assumption. The variant in the DNA could just as likely have been introduced in another manner. This is a critical and often overlooked limitation in using DNA to try to isolate a migration by a small group to the Americas in the recent past. Simply stated, if the proper testable circumstances are missing, the estimates to calculate rare genetic contributions, such as the one that would have been represented by Lehi's group, are not sufficiently sensitive and accurate.

A Native American in Iceland

At the present time, scientists performing research on worldwide populations are dissecting individual mtDNA lineages to discover important details missed in the past. This microgeographic approach is revealing a number of peculiar situations that, for the most part, are still not fully explained. For example, a majority of people living in Iceland today are just a small representation of the people that lived there only three hundred years ago.[21] Most interesting to this discussion is that mtDNA associated with Native Americans has been identified in relatively small quantities in Iceland.[22]

The natural question is, how did the distinct subset of Native American DNA end up in Iceland? The most accepted hypothesis is that Vikings took a Native American female, or females, with this distinct genetic marker with them when they left the Western Hemisphere; this genetic legacy persists today in the Icelandic population. Interestingly, although this distinct DNA marker originated in the New World, it has not been found in the Americas. Either the genetic marker failed to perpetuate, it was eliminated with the genocide following the European invasion, or it is extremely rare and has yet to be located on American soil. It is possible that scientists would be unaware that the sublineage existed if it was not located in Iceland. In simple terms, the example of the Native American mtDNA genome found in Iceland but not in America indicates that it is not unreasonable that genetic types once found in the Americas are no longer present.

Lehi's DNA

Many have wondered why no DNA associated with Middle Easterners has been identified in Native American groups. Finding such DNA could be powerful scientific evidence supporting the validity of the Book of Mormon. There are several factors that limit scientists' ability to accomplish this task. One major problem identifying Lehi's DNA is that we don't know what it looked like. The small group that left Jerusalem to embark on a journey to a new land was not selected based on their genetic uniqueness or because they represented the typical genetic signature found in their homeland. These people were unaware of their genetic profile, and so are we. This fact alone seriously compromises any effort to bring forth DNA as evidence that these people existed or that the Book of Mormon is the religious and historical record it claims to be.

With DNA studies, it is possible to determine a genetic lineage that could approximate a typical ancestor living in Jerusalem during approximately 600 BC, but we have no way of determining if Lehi carried typical ancient Israelite mtDNA. In addition, virtually any individual DNA profile can be found in any population, although at varying levels. From a genetic viewpoint, anyone from any region of the Old World could have carried practically any mtDNA lineage to the Americas during the post-Columbus conquest era. The problem with not knowing the DNA of Lehi and his group is categorized as the absence of specific information, meaning it would be impossible to recognize their DNA even if it survived evolutionary forces and cultural isolation because we don't know what we are looking for.

Population genetic studies are based on statistical evidence, so they are weak when evaluating rare occurrences in the sampled population. If we were trying either to detect or measure the amount of genetic contribution from Book of Mormon peoples to the current indigenous population, the hypothesis to be tested would not be how much Middle Eastern DNA is observed in native populations but rather how much DNA from Lehi or other Book of Mormon peoples survived to our day. In other words, how many lineages could be confidently assigned to them?

Unfortunately, no matter how large or small they eventually became as a people in the American continent, Lehi's family still was a very small initial group with extremely limited genetic variation that would not constitute a large enough sample of their native population to ensure that their genetics would be properly represented in the New World.

Intermingling DNA

Even if Lehi and the members of his family carried the most representative modern Middle Eastern genetic profiles, the only way these Middle Eastern markers would have survived past the first few generations in the American continent would be in the unlikely event that Lehi's descendants were successful in maintaining an isolated population with limited mixing with the hosting population.

The abridged history contained in the Book of Mormon gives only a few sporadic details about the whereabouts of its people with regard to potential interactions with other groups. For instance, Nephi set out to build a temple when his adult male relatives would have numbered less than five, which would be insufficient to build such a structure.[23] After twenty-five years in the land, there were great wars between the Nephites and Lamanites.[24] How could armies be mustered from such a small number of initial emigrants? Additionally, several times in the Book of Mormon the Lamanites are said to have been far more numerous than the Nephites.[25] This observation seems inconsistent with the early Nephite descriptions of them as savage hunters, who normally require much more land per person than farmers require.[26] So where did all these extra Lamanites come from? One possible answer is from indigenous settlers of Asiatic ancestry.[27]

From these passages, it is not unreasonable to assume there was some intermingling. The initial group of emigrants accompanying Lehi consisted of his family, Ishmael's widow and her children, and Zoram—the servant of Laban—which would have been about thirty to forty individuals. Henry C. Harpending, distinguished professor of anthropology at the University of Utah, commented on how this type of scenario would have affected the persistence of their DNA in the Americas. He was asked, "If a group of, say, fifty Phoenicians (men and women) arrived in the Americas some 2,600 years ago and intermarried with indigenous people, and assuming their descendants fared as well as the larger population through the vicissitudes of disease, famine, and war, would you expect to find genetic evidence of their Phoenician ancestors in the current Native American population? In addition, would their descendants be presumed to have an equal or unequal number of Middle Eastern as Native American haplotypes?" Professor Harpending's reply was, "I doubt that we would pick up [evidence of the Phoenicians] today at all, but it does depend on how they intermixed once they were here. If they intermixed freely and widely, and if there were several millions of people here in the New World, then the only trace would be an occasional strange stray haplotype. Even if we found such a haplotype we would probably assume it was the result of post-Columbian admixture."[28]

The natural process of DNA markers disappearing in populations over time is called "genetic drift." The concept of genetic drift is partly based on the inheritance properties of DNA. With regard to markers received from one parent only (Y chromosome and mitochondrial DNA), inheritance is contingent on the gender of offspring. If a couple has only girls, none of them (and therefore no posterity) will receive the father's Y chromosome. If a couple has only boys, they will all receive the mother's mitochondrial DNA, but none of the grandchildren will inherit it.

Over just a few generations, potentially all of a couple's genetic material will be diluted and lost, as they will represent an ever-smaller percentage of the ancestors contributing to the DNA of a single descendant. Simply stated, as with the previously-mentioned example of my autosomal DNA, there is a considerable difference between being genealogically related and having a genetic inheritance. In fact, it is estimated that at the tenth generation level, and given an equal chance to propagate their autosomal DNA, people would carry only DNA representing approximately 12 percent of their total possible 1,024 ancestors.[29] This phenomenon can be observed in as few as a couple of generations at a family level, but the effects of genetic drift at the population level are even more visible. Depending on the population size and the variety of DNA present in that population, over a time measured in generations, some of that variation will inevitably be lost due to chance.

From a numerical point of view, the arrival of Lehi and his group on the continent would be comparable to a grain of salt in a sandbox. Though the salt is in the sandbox, it would be nearly impossible to detect or distinguish from the grains of sand. This analogy does not extend perfectly to DNA and inheritance at the population level, but it does illustrate the difficulty in finding DNA remnants from a small population assimilated into a large one. Although the group of Old World migrants was small (a grain of salt), the DNA may or may not have survived to the present time due to social and evolutionary variables. If it disappeared, it would be as if someone removed the grain of salt from the sandbox such that it seemed never to have been there in the first place. Of course, this would be heavily dependent on the level of isolation the Book of Mormon party experienced—something not clearly stated and therefore not testable.

Lack of DNA Evidence Proves Nothing

By the time Christopher Columbus discovered the Americas in 1492, perhaps as many as one hundred million inhabitants could have populated the entire double-continent.[30] The clash with European settlers—followed by disease, slavery, and warfare—resulted in a population decline of tremendous proportions. In the unlikely scenario that the descendants of the few migrants described in the Book of Mormon were able to transmit a modest genetic signature to future generations, the devastating conquest by Europeans in the 16th and 17th centuries has created a situation in which even the most experienced researchers admit the limited knowledge available to properly infer the complete history of American colonization prior to that time.

This would not be the only event affecting the lack of Old World DNA found among Native Americans. The Book of Mormon itself describes at great length two additional major events that, presuming historical accuracy, would have had a tremendous impact on the survival of any genetic lineages carried to the Americas by any of its original groups.

The first event took place after the biblical account of the crucifixion of Jesus Christ in Jerusalem. Only one of the Gospels of the New Testament briefly mentions the geological events experienced in the Holy Land following the death of Christ.[31] Far greater destructive natural forces were witnessed in the Western hemisphere as recorded in 3 Nephi 8, with entire cities being destroyed and the geographical landscape becoming greatly changed. The extent of destruction over the whole American continent is not known, as the writer in the Book of Mormon was likely writing about his immediate vicinity. However, since this debate concerns the genetics of Book of Mormon people, it is not unreasonable to think that such devastation and loss of life would also have had a great effect on the survival and transmission of any Old World genetic lineages to future generations.

In addition to the natural destruction described in the Book of Mormon at the time of the death of Jesus Christ in the Holy Land, there is the targeted elimination of people referred to as Nephites through massive warfare starting in the fourth century AD. It is a difficult task to estimate the level of genetic intermingling experienced by the descendants of those that came from Jerusalem around 600 BC, but from the population growth described occasionally in the Book of Mormon, it could be that the Lamanites were more consistently absorbed with locals than the Nephites.[32]

Currently Unanswerable Questions

Genetic testing has been used over the last twenty years to establish informative genealogical links among world populations and to track migration patterns over millennia. However, as a tool for discerning where, how, and if the peoples of the Book of Mormon inhabited the American continents, it is of limited utility because of the lack of important data. In order to use genetic testing to establish or refute the existence of Old World ancestors, scientists will need to answer the following questions:

1. What did the DNA of the Book of Mormon people look like?
2. What was the typical DNA found in the population of Jerusalem in 600 BC?
3. Can Lehite DNA from 600 BC be clearly differentiated from that of Europeans arriving after 1492?
4. Are the current estimates used in assessing the timing of ancient genetic events adequate to discern pre- from post-Columbian DNA to the New World?
5. To what extent did the people of Lehi intermingle with local natives?
6. How long were the people of Lehi an isolated population after their arrival in America?

Currently, there are too many unpredictable variables in order to use DNA effectively as a tool to test conclusively for the existence of Book of Mormon people. Geneticists can state that the DNA of Book of Mormon people has either disappeared or has not been detected through time, following very basic and widely accepted population genetics principles. However, they cannot honestly deny that such people never existed simply based on the lack of genetic evidence.

We need to be wary about any statement against or in favor of the historical accuracy of the Book of Mormon based on DNA and take the time to understand the difference between scientific data and claims people make about it. Scientists in general are extremely cautious to make statements based on the available data that point to a single conclusion and leave no room for an alternative explanation. As with other religious texts and topics, science is often an inadequate tool to corroborate spiritual or historical truths. Perhaps as technology improves and more DNA studies are conducted, we will learn more about the genetic origins of Native Americans, including possible genetic links between the Old and the New World.

Additional Resources

The Church of Jesus Christ of Latter-day Saints. "Book of Mormon and DNA Studies." https://www.lds.org/topics/book-of-mormon-and-dna-studies.

Meldrum, D. Jeffrey and Trent D. Stephens, "Who Are the Children of Lehi?" *Journal of Book of Mormon Studies* 12, no. 1 (2003): 38–51.

Perego, Ugo A. "Book of Mormon Genetics: A Reappraisal." Presentation at FairMormon Conference, August 2, 2012. http://www.fairmormon.org/perspectives/publications/the-book-of-mormon-and-the-origin-of-native-americans-from-a-maternally-inherited-dna-standpoint.

Perego, Ugo A. "The Book of Mormon and the Origin of Native Americans from a Maternally Inherited DNA Standpoint." In *No Weapon Shall Prosper: New Light on Sensitive Issues*, edited by Robert Millet, 171–216. Provo, UT: Religious Studies Center, 2011.

Sorenson, John L. and Matthew Roper. "Before DNA." *Journal of Book of Mormon Studies* 12, no. 1 (2003): 6–23, 113–15.

Stewart, David. "DNA and the Book of Mormon." Presentation at FairMormon Conference, August 4, 2003. http://www.fairmormon.org/perspectives/publications/dna-and-the-book-of-mormon-stewart.

About the Author

Ugo A. Perego has a PhD in genetics and biomolecular studies from the University of Pavia in Italy, where he studied under the mentorship of Professor Antonio Torroni, who was part of the team of scientists to first identify genetic diversity among Native American populations in the early 1990s. Dr. Perego was a senior researcher for the Sorenson Molecular Genealogy Foundation for twelve years, where he contributed to the building of one of the world's largest repositories of combined genealogical and genetic data. He has published and presented extensively on DNA and its application in populations, forensic, ancestry, historical, and genealogical studies. He currently resides in Italy, where he is the director of the Rome Institute campus and is a visiting scientist at the University of Perugia.

Notes

1. 1 Nephi 18:23.

2. Carrie A. Moore, "Debate Renewed with Change in the Book of Mormon Introduction," *Deseret Morning News*, November 8, 2007, http://www.deseretnews.com/article/695226008/Debate-renewed-with-change-in-Book-of-Mormon-introduction.html?pg=all.

3. John L. Sorenson, "When Lehi's Party Arrived in the Land, Did They Find Others There?" *Journal of Book of Mormon Studies* 1 (1992): 1–34; John L. Sorenson and Matthew Roper, "Before DNA," *Journal of Book of Mormon Studies* 12, no. 1 (2003): 4–23.

4. Anthony W. Ivins, in Conference Report, April 1929, 15–16.

5. 4 Nephi 1:17; emphasis added.

6. 4 Nephi 1:20; emphasis added.

7. 2 Nephi 5 is compelling. In verse 6, Nephi spells out who goes with him, referring to others not on the boat, and in verses 6 and 9, he goes on to say that those who are called Nephites are those who "believed in the warnings and revelations of God"—a religious designation.

8. Mormon 1:5.

9. 3 Nephi 5:20.

10. Note that Mormon may have been distinguishing himself as a descendant of Lehi rather than a descendant of the Mulekites. Of course, the presence of Mulekites and the lack of "-ite" designations for them at this time of the narrative already shows that there is an oversimplification of the genealogy and naming.

11. These figures come from a commercial ancestral DNA test based on more than 500,000 SNPs. 23andMe: The Largest Ancestry Service in the World, https://www.23andme.com.

12. The Coop Lab: Population and Evolutionary Genetics, UC Davis, "How Many Genetic Ancestors Do I Have?," http://gcbias.org/2013/11/11/how-does-your-number-of-genetic-ancestors-grow-back-over-time/.

13. Antonio Torroni et al., "Asian Affinities and Continental Radiation of the Four Founding Native American mtDNAs," *American Journal of Human Genetics* 53 (1993): 560–90.

14. Mannis van Oven and Manfred Keyser, "Updated Comprehensive Phylogenetic Tree of Global Human Mitochondrial DNA Variation," *Human Mutations* 30 (2009): E386–94, http://www.phylotree.org.

15. Peter Forster et al., "Origin and Evolution of Native American mtDNA Variation: A Reappraisal," *American Journal of Human Genetics* 59 (1996): 935–45.

16. Maere Reidla et al., "Origin and Diffusion of mtDNA Haplogroup X," *American Journal of Human Genetics* 73 (2003): 1178–90.

17. Jennifer A. Raff and Deborah A. Bolnick, "Palaeogenomics: Genetic Roots of the First Americans," *Nature* 506 (2014): 162–63.

18. Erika Tamm et al., "Beringian Standstill and Spread of Native American Founders," *PLOS ONE* 9 (2007): 829.

19. Ugo A. Perego et al., "Distinctive Paleo-Indian Migration Routes from Beringia Marked by Two Rare mtDNA Haplogroups," *Current Biology* 19 (2009): 1–8.

20. Michael H. Crawford, *The Origins of Native Americans: Evidence from Anthropological Genetics* (Cambridge: Cambridge University Press, 1998), 4.

21. Agnar Helgason et al., "A Population-Wide Coalescent Analysis of Icelandic Matrilineal and Patrilineal Genealogists. Evidence for a Faster Evolution Rate of mtDNA Lineages than Y Chromosomes," *American Journal of Human Genetics* 75 (2003): 1370–88.

22. Sigríður Sunna Ebenesersdóttir et al., "A New Subclade of mtDNA Haplogroups C1 Found in Icelanders: Evidence of Pre-Columbian Contact?" *American Journal of Physical Anthropology* 144 (2011): 92–99.

23. John L. Sorenson and Matthew Roper, "Before DNA," *Journal of Book of Mormon Studies* 12, no. 1 (2003): 14.

24. See 2 Nephi 5:34.

25. See Jarom 1:6; Mosiah 25:3; Helaman 4:25.

26. See Enos 1:20; Jarom 1:6.

27. Note that this approach is not unusual as many colonizers, including Europeans after 1492 employed local natives as allies against other native groups in their conquering efforts.

28. Henry C. Harpending, "What Happens Genetically when a Small Population is Introduced into a Larger One?" Signature Books: Publisher of Mormon and Western Americana, http://signaturebooks.com/2010/06/dna-and-the-book-of-mormon.

29. "Autosomal DNA Statistics," International Society of Genetic Genealogy, http://www.isogg.org/wiki/Autosomal_DNA_statistics.

30. Alan Taylor, *American Colonies: The Settling of North America* (New York: Penguin Books, 2002), 40.

31. Matthew 27:51.

32. James E. Smith, "How Many Nephites?: The Book of Mormon at the Bar of Demography," in *Book of Mormon Authorship Revisited: The Evidence of Ancient Origins*, ed. Noel B. Reynolds (Provo, UT: FARMS, 1997), chap. 10.

15

Latter-day Saint Women in the Twenty-First Century

Neylan McBaine

The Church of Jesus Christ of Latter-day Saints today practices a gendered division of labor, meaning that administrative functions in the Church are largely separated by what men can do and what women can do. Gendered division of labor is becoming more and more unusual in current American institutions, and some members both old and young struggle to understand why the Church maintains administrative divisions. The doctrinal foundation for the division—the fact that only men hold the priesthood and women do not—has been challenged in recent years, and dialogue about women's roles has been tense at times. This essay aims to summarize what our leaders are currently teaching about this gendered division of labor and how members can best align practices to support this doctrine.

Sam Gordon is a football sensation. The eleven-year-old has been the subject of a Super Bowl commercial, has been featured on the front of a cereal box, and has appeared on national television. There's also Sam's autobiography (written with the help of a ghostwriter), Sam's YouTube channel, and Sam's recent press conference with the governor of Utah. Why all the attention? Well, Sam has one of the best rushing and touchdown records for any eleven-year-old football player, but it also has a lot to do with the fact that Sam Gordon is a girl.

Sam is short for Samantha, and Sam has been dominating her local youth football leagues for three years now. Sam also happens to be a Mormon girl, and the ghostwriter of her book is her family's home teacher. Here is a girl—a Mormon girl—who is receiving the highest accolades a child of her age can receive because she is breaking into boys' territory.

She reflects an instinct among Americans, and, as her fame is demonstrating, among Mormons, to celebrate crossing over the gender divide. We want girls to have a fighting chance in whatever they attempt. We crave parity. We look for it in our governments and in our boardrooms. We push for girls to pursue careers in technology, math, and science because we know these disciplines will be strengthened by the impact of strong, intelligent women.

Realities like these of the twenty-first century American culture can create tension when contrasted with the gendered division of labor that characterizes many practices in the Church. For many American LDS youth, institutional gender division is introduced to them through the framework of Church administration and doctrine. The idea that women could and *should* break into male-only spheres, the way Sam Gordon is doing with football, has often not even been considered. How do we navigate between aspiring to gender parity in our external institutions and interactions and supporting the gendered division of labor inherent in our current divinely mandated Church structure?

Gender Roles

For much of the twentieth century, the Church's division of labor was in harmony with mainstream American culture: men and women typically occupied separate spheres, with the man in the workplace and the woman at home. That cultural dynamic was comfortably mirrored in Church structure, where men were responsible for public administration and women for private nurturing. That public/private division, however, is no longer the norm in our broader culture, and our youth are growing up without that formerly idealized division of gender roles. What our youth see and celebrate is that women around the world are benefitting from the explosion of rights and protections now given them by governments, institutions, and family culture. The strong cultural force driving toward the potential of women to gain education, fulfill their personal ambitions, earn money for their families, and have a public voice in all settings has undeniably resulted in a better quality of life for women worldwide.

It is not coincidental that this explosion of women's voices and opportunities has corresponded with the Restoration of the gospel of Jesus Christ in the last days. The founding of the Relief Society corresponded with a trend toward the improvement of women's lives globally. Apostle Orson F. Whitney noted that the "lifting of the women of Zion ... was the beginning of a work for the elevation of womankind throughout the world. ... The spirit of women's work [is] ... one of those sunbursts of light that proclaim the dawning of a new dispensation."[1] What we are experiencing now in the liberation of women from historical strictures is "one of those sunbursts of light" delivered by the Restoration.

But the Church doesn't appear to be facilitating the institutional opportunities that in our secular culture have resulted in so many open doors for our grandmothers, our mothers, and now us. Instead, the vast majority of leadership opportunities, of administration responsibilities, and of ecclesiastical oversight are the sole domain of men in the Church. On the one hand, the Restoration allowed the world to consider equal opportunities for women as for men, but on the other, in our own Church men and women's opportunities to contribute are by divine mandate largely separated by gender. How are we to balance these two realities?

THE DEFINITION OF EQUALITY

There are several key considerations that allow us to hold these two realities congruently and celebrate each for its goodness, rather than be distracted by seeming contradictions. First, the definition of equality recognized by earthly institutions seems not to be the same definition the Lord uses to describe the practices of his kingdom. In short, the Church does not practice equality in the same way schools, workplaces, and government organizations do. In our daily lives, the concept of equality is seen through the lens of a mathematical paradigm, where "equal" means the same, or 50/50, or where something offered to one person is also offered to another. In the Lord's kingdom, though, scriptures and Apostles teach that all factors do not need to be the same in order for two things, or two people, to be considered of equal worth or value in the Lord's eyes. "Equal worth," "equal value," and "equal opportunity" to return to live with our Heavenly Parents are the phrases used by leaders to represent the way God sees us, and they are careful to stress that these do not mean that opportunities, expectations, and responsibilities will be the same for each person.

Elder M. Russell Ballard is particularly focused on separating the concept of doctrinal equality from its earthly, mathematical lens. In *Counseling with our Councils*, he has suggested an analogy to help us understand that men and women can contribute differently, but their offerings are received by the Lord with the same degree of acceptance, approval, and love. He stated:

> Perhaps we might look at the respective contributions of men and women in this way: You have no doubt visited the ophthalmologist for an eye exam. In the process of determining a patient's correct vision, the doctor will typically test the patient's eyesight by asking him or her to look through a variety of settings on a machine, some of which are blurry.... Only when he can determine the exact prescription for both eyes can a patient's vision be corrected precisely.
>
> In much the same way, men and women express themselves differently and tend to have different skills, talents, and points of view. When either viewpoint is taken in isolation, the resulting image may

be blurry, one-dimensional, or otherwise distorted. It is only when both perspectives come together that the picture is balanced and complete. Men and women are equally valuable in the ongoing work of the gospel kingdom.[2]

Elder Ballard restated this message in his talk at BYU Education Week in 2013: "Our Church doctrine places women equal to and yet different from men. God does not regard either gender as better or more important than the other."[3] In examples such as this, we see our leaders attempting to create through metaphor an image of what "equal to and yet different from" could actually look like. Creating a functional model in Church governance of what this actually looks like still remains a challenge for which we have little worldly precedence, but our leaders have made our mission clear.

Gender Roles and the Priesthood

A second consideration is the truth that men and women actually have much more in common than Church rhetoric typically admits. Often Church rhetoric serves to underscore the differences between men and women: the emphasis on eternal gender identity and the separate gendered responsibilities outlined in "The Family: A Proclamation to the World" lead us to a hyperawareness of the divine differences to the point that we can lose sight of both the commonality and interdependence of men and women. Even while Elder Ballard stresses that men and women have differences, his metaphor of two eyes working together implicitly suggests that those two eyes are much more alike than they are different. Similarly, while we may discuss different divine natures of men and women, we should not let those conversations distract us from the fact that we are not only all children of God but also that we all have access to priesthood power. In fact, we are both part of Church organizations structured similarly to each other up to the highest levels of Church governance.

Discussion of gender roles inevitably leads to the assertion that men "hold the priesthood" and therefore *are* the priesthood. However, more nuanced and emphatic language from recent leaders has encouraged members to look more carefully at the intragendered nature of priesthood power. Scholar Valerie Hudson Cassler has called this recent shift a "new and higher level of discussion" and "a firmer foundation for our people."[4] One potent example of this higher level of discussion was articulated by Elder Dallin H. Oaks. He emphasized the commonality of priesthood power when he stated:

> We are not accustomed to speaking of women having the authority of the priesthood in their Church callings, but what other authority can it be? When a woman—young or old—is set apart to preach the

gospel as a full-time missionary, she is given priesthood authority to perform a priesthood function. The same is true when a woman is set apart to function as an officer or teacher in a Church organization under the direction of one who holds the keys of the priesthood. Whoever functions in an office or calling received from one who holds priesthood keys exercises priesthood authority in performing her or his assigned duties.[5]

Elder Ballard adds more to this higher discussion: "When men and women go to the temple, they are both endowed with the same power, which by definition is priesthood power. . . . The endowment is literally a gift of power. All who enter the house of the Lord officiate in the ordinances of the priesthood. This applies to men and women alike." Having established that endowed women hold priesthood power, Elder Ballard builds on the idea that there are two great works in the Lord's kingdom: building a family and building the Church. "It takes a man and a woman to create a family, and it takes men and women to carry out the work of the Lord in the Church." And finally, these two works require complete interdependence: "Just as a woman cannot conceive a child without a man, so a man cannot fully exercise the power of the priesthood to establish an eternal family without a woman. . . . In the eternal perspective, both the procreative power and the priesthood power are shared by husband and wife."[6]

In *Women and the Priesthood*, Sheri Dew adds to the discussion by being careful to distinguish between priesthood power, priesthood authority, and priesthood keys—not all of which are exclusively male. "Both men and women would have full access to this [heavenly] power, though in *different ways*."[7] She continues, "The manner in which He authorizes the distribution of *His* authority and power throughout the earth is through priesthood keys."[8] She further goes on to state, "I believe that the moment we learn to unleash the full influence of converted, covenant-keeping women, the kingdom of God will change overnight."[9]

If the Priesthood with a capital *P* includes both male and female priesthood authority, as these apostolic statements suggest, how is that doctrine currently reflected in our Church practices and structure? The truth is that we see today a shadow of what it could be, but we are still somewhat blinded by the persistent and pervasive disconnect that leads some members to believe that women's participation in building the kingdom should be limited to being counselors and influencers rather than decision makers and leaders. We have important but limited female influence in the decision-making councils of the Church. Each organization led by women in the Church, for instance, has a full presidency and a general board, and these structures are echoed down to the very lowliest ward and branch. But we are far from having those groups work as co-presidencies, as "equal to but different from" the male governing bodies. The object of reevaluating female government would not be to give women more work; indeed, women's work in the Church is abundant. The potential lies in making that female government more public, more authoritative, and more focused on causes and people that women themselves have independent stewardship over. This is our challenge.

It can be argued that this model isn't a new one, but would, rather, be a harkening back to the original intention of the Relief Society. In the early decades of its history, the Relief Society functioned as an autonomous organization, administratively and financially independent of the male hierarchy. As a result of this radical independence in an era before women's emancipation or suffrage, Latter-day Saint women ran their own magazine, their own cooperative store, their own granary, and their own hospital and led their own social causes. The result was a feeling of driven productivity and impact that lasted, according to personal accounts,[10] until about the 1970s when the *Relief Society Magazine* was phased out, manuals were no longer written by the Relief Society board, and Relief Society finances were folded into the general Church ledgers. Despite dedicated work and countless hours in Church meetings today, many women long for the autonomy and mission-driven focus that characterized female government in the nineteenth and early twentieth centuries. While this earlier model still doesn't overtly address how male and female priesthood could function, it offers a hopeful precedent for reflecting doctrine more accurately in our practice.

CHANGING THE PERCEPTION OF THE ROLE OF WOMEN

There are ample signs that our leadership is working out what co-leadership might look like in a functional, comprehensive way. Over the past several years, we've seen small but significant changes in the way women are seen, heard, and included at the very highest levels. The change in age for missionaries signaled a desire to have young women embrace their ecclesiastical authority more completely; the addition of the female general officers' portraits in the Conference Center and the general conference *Ensign* suggested these women should be considered by the Church membership to be global leaders and not just figureheads. The change of the general women's meeting to the general women's session, now the first session of general conference, evidenced a desire to shore up the "equal to but different from" model in every way, even in semantics and structure.

With awareness of and willingness to support co-leadership becoming more apparent at the general Church level, it is the responsibility of the membership to assume that same awareness and willingness on the local level. The question for us is what can we do in our wards and stakes to demonstrate a similar commitment to co-leadership by emphasizing the equality, commonality, and interdependence of men and women just as much as we do their differences? There are several ways each of us on the local level can help adapt our practices to be more consistent with this vision of co-leadership. As members and local leaders study *Handbook of Instruction 2*, the guide available to all members of the Church that outlines how the local Church should be run, we can seek for opportunities to expand our current practices, excavate previously untapped sources of female input, and look for places where we can put women front and center in our meetings.

Is there more we can do to acquaint the ward members with the Young Women as well as they are acquainted with the Young Men through the passing of the sacrament, handling of the testimony microphone, and home teaching? Are there ways we can put our Relief Society, Young Women, and Primary presidencies front and center, respected as the ecclesiastical and administrative authorities they have been set apart to be, when having ward or stake conference? Can we quote women or use female examples in every talk or lesson we give to demonstrate women's wisdom and closeness to God? Through these small changes, we can demonstrate to our youth that we don't just pay lip service to the equality of women in our doctrine; we actually align our practices to that doctrine by recognizing in our worship, learning, and government the unique but divine power that resides in each woman.

For some women, taking on this process of evaluation and adjustment can represent a seismic shift in their own sense of identity and self. Understandably, it is proving uncomfortable for some women to critically examine their willing participation in the organization and acknowledge that their daughters and granddaughters and even peers might not find the same fulfillment in certain practices or attitudes. Many women in the Church do feel heard and loved by male leaders, and these feelings of acceptance and community make women's structural inequity seem to them to be irrelevant, or worse, a distraction from eternal truths. Because addressing women's changing relationship with the Church and the world around them can be fundamentally threatening to a Mormon woman's treasured identity, some of the fiercest battles about these shifts happen among Mormon women themselves, either in public, on social media, or in local or private interchanges where women explore the boundaries of their influence and governance against the pushback of other women, even when male leaders encourage greater female impact.

It is a hard thing to examine our own community and have the humility to seek for greater wisdom. But it is essential that we continue to ask ourselves and our Father in Heaven for insight and knowledge regarding women. If we better align our practice with our doctrine, then a young woman like Sam Gordon would discover that she doesn't have to share the man's world of spiritual kingdom building to lead and contribute. She will realize she has all the tools she needs as a daughter of God not only to return to live with him but also to lead the Church in our midst here on earth in a different but equal way to her male counterpart. She will believe gender roles are different but equal not because anyone tells her they are, but because she will be supported in her efforts, see the fruits of her work, and know for herself. For Sam and for all of our youth, we must stretch ourselves to see opportunities we have not yet explored and be committed to modeling not the *same* leadership but co-leadership between men and women at every level of Church governance.

Additional Resources

Dew, Sheri. *Women and the Priesthood: What One Mormon Woman Believes.* Salt Lake City: Deseret Book, 2013.

McBaine, Neylan. *Women at Church: Magnifying LDS Women's Local Impact.* Salt Lake City: Greg Kofford Books, 2014.

Mormon Women Project. http://www.mormonwomen.com.

Oaks, Dallin H. "The Keys and Authority of the Priesthood." *Ensign*, May 2014, 49–52.

Oscarson, Bonnie L. "Sisterhood: Oh, How We Need Each Other." *Ensign*, May 2014, 119–21.

Uchtdorf, Dieter F. "Four Titles." *Ensign*, May 2013, 60–62.

Women at Church. http://www.womenatchurch.com.

About the Author

Neylan McBaine is the founder and editor in chief of the Mormon Women Project, a continuously expanding digital library of interviews with LDS women from around the world found at www.mormonwomen.com. Founded in 2010, the Mormon Women Project has published nearly three hundred interviews with women in twenty-two countries. As a writer, Neylan has been published in *Newsweek*, the *Washington Post*, and *Dialogue*. Neylan is a native New Yorker, lifelong Mormon, graduate of Yale University, and mother of three literarily named daughters.

Notes

1. Orson F. Whitney, "Woman's Work and Mormonism," *Young Woman's Journal* 17, no. 7 (July 1906), 295–96, http://cdm15999.contentdm.oclc.org/cdm/compoundobject/collection/YWJ/id/12943/rec/17.

2. M. Russell Ballard, *Counseling with Our Councils* (Salt Lake City: Deseret Book, 2012), 102–3.

3. M. Russell Ballard, "Let Us Think Straight," Brigham Young University Campus Education Week devotional, August 20, 2013, 6, available at http://speeches.byu.edu/?act=viewitem&id=2133.

4. Valerie Hudson Cassler, "Zion in Her Beauty Rises: Current Discourse on Women and the Priesthood by Ballard, Dew and Oaks," *SquareTwo* 7, no. 1 (Spring 2014), http://squaretwo.org/Sq2ArticleHudsonMcBaine.html.

5. Dallin H. Oaks, "The Keys and Authority of the Priesthood," *Ensign*, May 2014, 51.

6. Ballard, "Let Us Think Straight," 4.

7. Sheri L. Dew, *Women and the Priesthood* (Salt Lake City: Deseret Book, 2014), 74; emphasis added.

8. Dew, *Women and the Priesthood*, 81; emphasis added.

9. Dew, *Women and the Priesthood*, 163.

10. Helen Claire Sievers, "What Women in the Church Have Lost in My Lifetime," *Exponent II* 33, no. 3 (Winter 2014): 18–22.

16

Homosexuality and the Gospel

Ty Mansfield

Sexuality is a complex and deeply personal aspect of the human experience, and issues related to same-sex attraction are increasingly at the heart of cultural debates and discussions surrounding The Church of Jesus Christ of Latter-day Saints and its doctrines and political positions. Because sexuality and relationships strike at the heart of questions of identity and life purpose, discussion of them can stir up strong emotions and passionate agendas. These agendas run the gamut from more personal ones like clinging to problematic beliefs and identities out of a drive for meaning or self-preservation, to a social or political agenda rooted in beliefs about social rights or social goods, or to a religious agenda in which there is a battle for souls and salvation. Much of the controversy is rooted in oversimplifying or distorting the nature of the dynamics at play, and problematic assumptions are too often simply accepted without serious thought. Once we can understand how these attitudes have harmed our understanding, then we can then move to a better place to understand the Church's teachings.

The Complexity of Human Sexuality

Sexuality is complex, multidimensional, and influenced in its development by a host of different factors—genetic, hormonal, psychological, emotional, social, and cultural, just to name a few. Because of that complexity, there is potential for a great diversity of experience from person to person. Also because of that complexity, it may be important to define what sexuality is; the term is often used differently by different people in different contexts. It may also be important to have a more textured and nuanced understanding of sexuality in order to fully appreciate Church teachings on sexuality and what it means to live the law of chastity.

Just as *personality* is the "ality" of our *person*, sexuality is the "ality" of our *sex*—not only the *act* of sex or of the nature of sexual or companionate desire but also all that makes us unique as men and women, masculine and feminine, including the godly purposes of that gendered and complimentary uniqueness. In addition to the relational aspect of sexuality we may more commonly think about, there are also deeply spiritual aspects of sexuality, so we have to be careful not to inappropriately reduce sexuality simply to erotic or romantic behavior—particularly when we talk with youth and seek to influence their attitudes, beliefs, and behaviors around sex and sexuality. In their book *Soul Virgins: Redefining Single Sexuality*, Christian therapists Doug Rosenau and Michael Todd Wilson talk about how our sexuality is ultimately the driving force in our quest for intimacy in *all* of our relationships, including with God, with both men and women, and within ourselves, as much as it might be with a potential spouse.

When we categorize people simply as "gay," "straight," or "bisexual," it assumes that sexuality is one-dimensional and exists upon a single linear continuum of erotic or romantic attraction. It is not and does not. Entertaining this idea frames and perpetuates false ideas around sexuality that have a tendency to reduce and politicize sexuality in ways that induce our culture into a sort of unthinking sentimentality about love, sex, intimate relationships, and societal goods. Therefore, in order to discuss the complexities of sexuality, including nonbiological factors shaping sexual desire, or the malleability or fluidity of sexuality, we need to set aside political correctness and social labels.

That said, potential distortion isn't limited to popular cultural labels and categories. Even the way we talk about "same-sex attraction"—the historically preferred term in the Church cultural vernacular—can be fraught with limitations and problems because there are many different kinds and qualities of attraction: sexual, romantic, aesthetic, affectional, emotional, and even spiritual. It can be especially problematic when we talk about "same-sex attraction" only in terms of a "trial" or "weakness" or "challenge" that should be "overcome." To the contrary, some qualities of attraction are good and even godly, and we should *embrace* and *cultivate* them in our lives. For example, the desire for closeness and belonging with others of the same sex is something all people feel to varying degrees. LDS author and speaker Brad Wilcox wrote:

> Some have felt relieved as they learn that homo-emotional needs are real and acceptable. The word *intimacy* is often associated with sexual acts, but it doesn't need to be. Non-sexual intimacy is essential to our growth and development at all ages of our lives. We all need to love and be loved by both women and men. Meeting that need

in healthy ways is one of the foundations of happiness as well as mental and emotional wellness. Often the feelings and attractions we have toward others are evidence of a deep need within us. Once recognized, it is up to us to fill that need in ways that are in harmony with God's plan for our lives and relationships. Similarly, hunger lets your body know of a need for food, but we must choose to meet that need with a healthy and nutritious diet rather than potato chips and French fries.[1]

This even extends to appropriate, non-sexual/non-romantic physical affection. When Charles W. Dahlquist II, Dean R. Burgess, and Michael A. Neider were released as the Young Men General Presidency during the Saturday session of the April 2009 general conference, they were holding hands as the camera panned on them.[2] It was clear they had a very close and special relationship to each other. Is it wrong for men to hold hands? Is holding hands "gay"? Is the *attraction* and *intimacy* and *bond* they may feel with one another something they should overcome since they are of the same sex? To the contrary, I can imagine God smiling upon pure expressions of love, intimacy, and affection between those of the same sex.

There are certainly qualities of attraction or desire that we need to appropriately channel, such as erotic or romantic attraction, but scripture teaches us that our aim should be to "bridle" our passions—not to eradicate them— "that [we] may be filled with love."[3] And Church leaders have been more careful to nuance their teachings so members understand more clearly that to feel sexual or romantic *attractions* is never a *sin*, even when toward the same sex, but rather that they're part of the broad range of human experience we're called to *channel* and *transcend* if we're to become divine. Only lustful thoughts or behaviors (regardless of the sex they're directed toward) or sexual expression outside the bounds the Lord has set are considered sinful.

A Four-Tiered Approach to Understanding Sexuality

As stated earlier, when it comes to how we commonly think about sexuality, defining "same-sex attraction" or what it means for some to identify as "being gay" is fraught with limitations. In order to better understand some of the nuances and layers of sexuality that often get conflated, it is helpful to think of sexuality as composed of a loose, four-tiered framework[4] that includes (1) attraction and desire, (2) persistent patterns of attraction or orientation, (3) behavior, and (4) identity.

Attraction and Desire
Similar to sexuality as a whole, the qualitative experiences we have of attraction and desire are complex, multidimensional phenomena. We are attracted

to, or desire, different things for different reasons—hobbies, life philosophies, professions, jobs, friendships, or romantic partners. Some desires may be rooted in personal gifts, such as having a remarkably mature capacity for empathy and sensitivity to others' feelings and needs, while other desires may be rooted in wounds or weaknesses, such as an addiction to pornography that has conditioned an individual to objectify and lust after certain fragmented traits in others. In human relationships alone, romantic or platonic, there are multiple feelings, emotions, and impulses. It is important to differentiate between these feelings, yet they are frequently lumped together—attraction, desire, love, euphoria, lust, emotional attachment, meaning, and so forth.

Humans are capable of a wide range of tastes, affinities, attractions, and impulses. Culture, emotional maturity, capacity for intimate relationships, and sense of self or identity have as much or more of an influence on how those attractions develop as do genes or biology. For example, some African cultures see heavy women as more sexually preferable to thin women because of a cultural attribution of meaning around wealth and social status attached to weight. Similarly, in some Chinese cultures, muscled, tanned bodies are seen as much *less* erotic or desirable than nonmuscled, pasty-skinned bodies because of social values and attributions around wealth and status—being a farmer as opposed to a white-collar worker. However, in American culture, the opposite tends to be true.

Beyond these more external aspects or objects of desire, there's an entirely distinct quality of attraction and desire we can experience through emotional and spiritual vulnerability and bonding. Even where there may be no immediate attraction to external features or qualities, deep emotional intimacy can actually serve as a wellspring or fertile growing space for romantic and sexual desire. One therapist remarked on how we should not be afraid of experiencing deep feelings for others simply because there's potential for development of sexual feelings, but rather we should find and walk the line of integrity:

> We have such rich and deep connections with people, with one another, truly deep loving intimacy. So how to keep that door open, how to keep that heartfelt life there, but not be seduced by the power and attraction of that intimacy? Because it is in that deep intimacy, of course, that sexual attraction and energy can arise and emerge. So how to maintain an integrity in that intimacy, and be true to our feelings of love for one another, and not fall into that well of sexual misconduct? . . . I have many boundaries and ethics that I apply in those situations, particularly through my psychotherapy training.[5]

This can even become confusing or concerning when it occurs between individuals of the same sex who have no inclination to homoerotic attraction or behavior. Writing about men in particular, Sam Keen, a former editor of *Psychology Today*, noted in his book *Fire in the Belly: On Being a Man*: "'Normal' American men are homophobic, afraid of close friendships with other men. The moment we begin to feel warmly toward another man, the 'homosexual' panic button gets pressed. It makes us nervous to see French or Italian men strolling down the street arm in arm. . . . From a cross-cultural perspective, it is we who are odd; close male friendship is the norm in most societies and is usually considered a more important source of intimacy than romantic relationships."[6] Some men have questioned their sexuality simply because they developed a deep emotional love for another man. It seems our culture often has difficulty distinguishing deep love and intimacy from sexual or romantic desire.

We don't fully understand the complexity of what shapes sexual desire and how the nature and objects of sexual desire change over a life span—or even over the course of single relationships. Sonja Lyubomirsky, a professor of psychology at the University of California, Riverside, noted that the stage of relationship development that researchers call "passionate love," a state of intense longing, desire, and attraction, typically has a "short shelf life." It's a stage of love that research shows lasts an average of two years, after which it generally morphs into "companionate love," a less impassioned blend of deep affection and connection.[7]

No single theory accounts for the complexity of how sexuality develops and is expressed across a wide range of human experiences. Where we often get into difficulty in our efforts to identify or understand the what, why, and how of sexual desire is when we try to attribute the root of that desire to a single factor. The popular cultural myths that either people are "born gay" or they chose to be homosexual are both oversimplifications and cannot explain much, if anything, about the development of sexuality and sexual desire.

It's interesting that popular culture seems to be so sure about something that science and experienced researchers are not. The American Psychological Association's official pamphlet addressing sexual orientation concedes this point, noting that ultimately, "There is no consensus among scientists about the exact reasons that an individual develops a heterosexual, bisexual, gay, or lesbian orientation. Although much research has examined the possible genetic, hormonal, developmental, social, and cultural influences on sexual orientation, no findings have emerged that permit scientists to conclude that sexual orientation is determined by any particular factor or factors. Many think that nature and nurture both play complex roles."[8]

Lisa Diamond, a University of Utah researcher, noted that because sexual fluidity is a general feature of human sexuality, we have to acknowledge that sexual categories or identity constructs are mental shortcuts that may be helpful in making quick judgments, but which can be problematic in that they also reflect or lead to biases. She noted, "We're not in fact cutting nature at its joints; we're . . . imposing some joints on a very messy phenomenon. . . . We have to be careful about presuming that [these sexual categories] are natural phenomenon."[9]

Sexual Orientation: Persistent Patterns of Attraction

Given that we feel different kinds of attraction toward different people for different reasons, and given that various attractions or even patterns of attraction may either change over time or remain more stable, the idea of "sexual orientation" refers to those patterns of attraction that tend to be persistent. Dr. Diamond proposes a model for romantic love and sexual desire that is based on an assumption that "the evolved processes underlying sexual desire and affectional bonding are functionally independent," given that the components of sexual attraction and emotional connection in a relationship "do not always agree."[10] Finding someone sexually desirable does not always mean one will be romantically bonded to them or vice versa. It's also important to note that sometimes an attraction we *interpret* as sexual may, in reality, be more emotional or intellectual in nature.

Furthermore, the dominant paradigm in our culture is that the *sex* or *gender* we are attracted to is the chief organizing principle of our "sexual orientation," but it is far from the only possible one. We could just as easily label sexual orientation around shape, size, race, personal values, ethnic traits, emotional bond, religious belief, social class, or economic status. There may even be greater persistence in some of these variables than the variable of gender preference. We are the ones, as a culture, who have drawn the conceptual lines. They are not inherent. Anyone who is opposite-sex oriented knows that they are not attracted to all or even most people of the opposite sex, and those who are same-sex oriented know they are not attracted to all or even most people of the same sex. The mere fact that someone is male or female is insufficient to make them sexually or romantically desirable. Therefore, some other factor or cluster of factors is more decisive than mere gender when it comes to physical attraction. So why are we attracted to the few of either sex we *are* attracted to, and how might that inform us regarding our "orientation"?

Again, a variety of individual factors and experiences have influenced and shaped the nature of sexuality, sexual desire, and our personal sexual identity. The concept of sexual orientation, particularly as it's been narrowly and exclusively defined by gender, is limited and not very explanatory. This realization can help individuals more effectively explore the congruence and resolution they seek between their sexuality and their personal value systems.

Sexual Behavior and Relationships

It is vital to understand that the choices we make with regard to sexual behavior and relationships arise from personal values and beliefs. Some would say that "homosexuality is not a lifestyle choice," but anything that can be categorized in terms of "lifestyle" involves some significant measure of personal choice. For Latter-day Saints, "lifestyle" is the factor most easily moderated by exercise of agency. Absolutely fundamental to LDS theology is the concept that we are moral agents who co-create our world as eternal intelligences *who act rather than are acted upon*. While we do not always choose our circumstances, we *do* choose our response to those circumstances. As noted by Elder Dallin H. Oaks in his 1995 *Ensign* article addressing same-sex attraction:

> Some kinds of feelings seem to be inborn. Others are traceable to mortal experiences. Still other feelings seem to be acquired from a complex interaction of "nature and nurture." All of us have some feelings we did not choose, but the gospel of Jesus Christ teaches us that we still have the power to resist and reform our feelings (as needed) and to assure that they do not lead us to entertain inappropriate thoughts or to engage in sinful behavior. . . .
>
> Different persons have different physical characteristics and different susceptibilities to the various physical and emotional pressures we may encounter in our childhood and adult environments. We did not choose these personal susceptibilities either, but we do choose and will be accountable for the attitudes, priorities, behavior, and "lifestyle" we engraft upon them.[11]

Given the diversity of experience, and the varied persistence of that experience, for whom might homosexual behavior become a sin and for whom is it simply unfair, as some would characterize, to be required to live the standards guiding sexual behavior and relationship as articulated by Church leaders?

While the laws and commandments and covenants are the same for each of us, the weight of each of those laws and covenants will press upon each of us very differently. For example, restrictions found in the Word of Wisdom may be a temptation for some but not for others. Similarly, some may find paying tithing difficult while others do not. Even with same-sex attraction, some people manage it quite well despite the possible belief they'll never get married to someone of the opposite sex in this life, but others feel that it is simply too much of a load to bear and too unreasonable for the Church to require them to sacrifice their desires.

There also seems to be this assumed idea that because a feeling or impulse or desire is "natural," it must also therefore be good or morally acceptable. "Natural" does not necessarily equate to good or desirable. The only thing that "natural" means is that feelings, desires, and impulses naturally manifest themselves within a given set of circumstances. Regardless of whether something shows up naturally, it may still require the exercise of inherent agency to channel, control, manage, bridle, or *educate*. Psychiatrist M. Scott Peck stated in his book *The Road Less Traveled*: "The tendency to avoid challenge is so omnipresent in human beings that it can properly be considered a characteristic of human nature. But calling it natural does not mean it is essential or beneficial or unchangeable behavior. It is also natural to ... never brush our teeth. Yet we teach ourselves to do the unnatural until the unnatural becomes itself second nature. Indeed, all self-discipline might be defined as teaching ourselves to do the unnatural."[12]

Even the natural desires and affections we have that are essentially good are still vulnerable to all of the distortions inherent to life in a fallen, mortal world and, as President John Taylor taught, "want sanctifying." He stated, "We have a great many principles innate in our natures that are correct, but ... like everything else, [they have] to be sanctified. An unlawful gratification of these feelings and sympathies is wrong in the sight of God, and leads down to death, while a proper exercise of our functions leads to life, happiness, and exaltation in this world and the world to come. And so it is in regard to a thousand other things."[13]

Christian biblical scholar N.T. Wright has similarly observed:

> We have lived for too long in a world, and tragically even in a church ... where the wills and affections of human beings are regarded as sacrosanct as they stand, where God is required to command what we already love and to promise what we already desire. The implicit religion of many people today is simply to discover who they really are and then try to live it out—which is, as many have discovered, a recipe for chaotic, disjointed, and dysfunctional humanness. The logic of cross and resurrection, of the new creation which gives shape to all truly Christian living, points in a different direction. And one of the central names for that direction is joy: the joy of relationships healed as well as enhanced, the joy of belonging to the new creation, of finding not what we already had but what God was longing to give us.[14]

Several prophets have taught that we are "gods in embryo," and in Mormon theology the work of Godhood is a work of creation and order—of organizing intelligences[15] or of bringing order to disordered or chaotic elements in the universe to form new worlds. The call of authentic, imaginative, and generative spirituality is to identify opportunities to actively engage in this creative work of godhood every day, whether through managing emotions, ordering distorted thought patterns, bridling passions, educating desires, growing souls or organizing families. Godhood isn't about seeking to live according to what is natural but to take natural element and shape it, organize it, build it, channel it, bridle it, and nurture it toward something transcendent—whether that be the element of our bodies or the element of the cosmos.

Identity

"Being gay" is not a scientific idea, but rather a cultural and philosophical one, addressing the subjective concept of *identity*. Our sense of identity is something we negotiate with our environment, which can include our biological environment. From an LDS perspective, the essential spiritual person within us exists independent of our mortal biology, so even our biology, or our body, is part of our "environment" and something that we relate to and negotiate our identity with, rather than something that inherently or essentially defines us. Also, while there have likely always been homoerotic attraction, desire, behavior, and even relationships among humans, the narratives through which sexuality is understood and incorporated into one's sense of self and identity is subjective and culturally influenced. The "gay" person or personality as we might conceptualize it today didn't exist prior to the mid-twentieth century.

In an LDS context, people often express concern about words that are used—whether they be "same-sex attraction," which some feel denies the realities of the "gay" experience, or "gay," "lesbian," or "LGBT," which some feel speaks more to specific belief systems and lifestyle choices contrary to the gospel. What's important to understand, however, is that identity isn't just about the words we use but the paradigms and worldviews and perceptions of or beliefs about the self and selfhood through which we interpret and integrate our various experiences into a sense of personal identity, sexual or otherwise. And identity is highly fluid and subject to modification with change in personal values or sociocultural contexts.

The terms "gay," "lesbian," and "bisexual" aren't uniformly understood or experienced in the same way by everyone who may use or adopt those terms, so it's the way those terms or labels are incorporated into selfhood that accounts for identity. One person might describe himself or herself as "gay" simply as convenient shorthand for the mouthful of "son or daughter of God who happens to experience romantic, sexual, or other attractions toward persons of the same sex for causes unknown and perhaps for only the short duration of mortality," while another person describes himself or herself as "gay" as a sort of eternal identity and state of being, believing they were gay or same-sex oriented in the premortal world and that they will again be so in the eternal world.

An important philosophical thread in the overall experience of identity is the experience of "selfhood"—what it means to have a self, and what it means to "be true to" that self. The question of what it means to be true to ourselves is a philosophical rather than a scientific one. In her book *Multiplicity: The New Science of Personality, Identity, and the Self*, award-winning science and medical writer Rita Carter explores the plurality of "selves" who live in each one of us and how each of those varied and sometimes conflicting senses of self inform various aspects of our identity(ies). This sense seems to be universal. In the movie *The Incredibles*, there's a scene in which IncrediBoy says to Mr. Incredible, "You always, always say, 'Be true to yourself,' but you never say which part of yourself to be true to!"[16]

However one chooses to self-identify here in a fallen, temporal world limited by human culture and human language, I firmly believe that, like Daniel's interpretation of Nebuchadnezzar's dream in which all social and political systems were swallowed up in the gospel stone that rolled forth to consume the nations, so will the spiritual ideals and identities of the kingdom of God and the celestial nature swallow up all of our social identity constructs that blur eternal identity.[17] The more deeply we understand and feel spiritually connected to eternal realities and our eternal identity, the less meaningful any proximate, mortal identities or labels will feel to us.

Chastity, Consecration, and Spirituality

With a more nuanced understanding of sexuality as background, how should we best understand and approach sexuality through the lens of Latter-day Saint theology? LDS scholar Hugh Nibley stated:

> [The] words of the prophets cannot be held to the tentative and defective tests that men have devised for them. Science, philosophy, and common sense all have a right to their day in court. But the last word does not lie with them. Every time men in their wisdom have come forth with the last word, other words have promptly followed. The last word is a testimony of the gospel that comes only by direct revelation. Our Father in heaven speaks it, and if it were in perfect agreement with the science of today, it would surely be out of line with the science of tomorrow. Let us not, therefore, seek to hold God to the learned opinions of the moment when he speaks the language of eternity.[18]

While science, philosophy, and common sense can enhance our understanding of sexuality and gender as part of the broad spectrum of our human experience, the last word does not lie with them. Regardless of what scientific inquiry will reveal over time about the origin and developmental nuances of sexuality—and it's still far from conclusive—it will never be sufficient to frame the eternal lenses through which we harness and channel our human passions and guide our life choices. Our choices as Latter-day Saints are guided by the values and beliefs informed by the "language of eternity," and we learn through the Spirit and through the inspired teachings of divinely commissioned prophets and apostles.

One of those values and beliefs is the law of chastity. Many Latter-day Saints are prone to think of chastity as an individual virtue—and even at times, perhaps, as one that is only applicable while single—the law of chastity being a list of do's and don'ts one adheres to until married. But I would like to propose here a more expansive view of what we have traditionally called the law of chastity because I believe we too often become legalistic and behavioristic in our thinking around chastity, which can actually serve to cripple spiritual growth.

The words "chaste" and "chastity" share their root with the terms "chasten" or "chastise." While people are typically not prone to think fondly of the idea of being chastened or chastised, the term *chaste* simply means "to be pure," and *chastening* or *chastisement* mean "to make pure." Psychiatrist Elizabeth Kubler-Ross stated that "the most beautiful people we have known are those who have known defeat, known suffering, known struggle, known loss, and have found their way out of the depths. These persons have an appreciation, a sensitivity, and an understanding of life that fills them with compassion, gentleness, and a deep loving concern. Beautiful people do not just happen."[19] Similarly, Elder Orson F. Whitney stated, "No pain that we suffer, no trial that we experience is wasted. It ministers to our education, to the development of such qualities as patience, faith, fortitude and humility. All that we suffer and all that we endure, especially when we endure it patiently, builds up our characters, purifies our hearts, expands our souls, and makes us more tender and charitable, more worthy to be called the children of God."[20] All of our life experiences have the capacity, if we consecrate them to the Lord, to make us more pure—or more chaste. The essence of chastity is something we *become*, not something we *do*.

The idea of chastening is most frequently expressed in modern-day scripture in the context of building Zion, with the Lord stating that the Saints were not ready, were not pure enough, to build Zion in Jackson County, Missouri—that they must be "chastened for a season"[21] until they could abide "by the law of the celestial kingdom."[22] At the heart of their lack of preparation was their unwillingness to fully live the law of consecration: to give everything they had and everything they were to the building of Zion. As a people, we cannot turn our efforts toward building Zion without a deep sense of humility, seeing ourselves and our lives as an important but small part of a much larger purpose and work, and being mindful and caring of the needs of the people and world around us. The Saints were told that they needed to be chastened because they "d[id] not impart of their substance, as becometh saints, to the poor and afflicted among them."[23]

The principles of chastity and consecration are intimately interwoven in the concept of creating Zion. The willingness to surrender all that we have and all that we are to the building up of Zion, including our sexuality, is key to the process of developing purity and holiness of heart that are the defining virtues of Zion. We cannot become truly pure in heart without recognizing that all that we are is intimately interconnected with all life.

In an essay titled "Chastity and the Environment," Suzanne Evertson Lundquist, BYU associate professor of English, describes how through interactions with Latin and Native American cultures and myths she was able to see more clearly that chastity is not just an individual virtue—or even a virtue between consenting, loving adults—but a social virtue. "*The principles of chastity govern all relationships—relationships* with self, with community, with the earth, and with deity."[24] Chastity affects entire families, communities, nations, and the world as a whole. The connection between reproduction and the cyclic nature of life, death, and creation show that the law of chastity maintains a delicate harmony. When we adopt incorrect and harmful attitudes about sex or family relationships, we disrupt the balance and cause effects that will ripple throughout time and space unless we repent and bring our attitudes, beliefs, and behaviors back into harmony with divine principle. In essence, the law of chastity is not even how we express *sexuality*, but *relationality*. Sexuality is only one subset of relationality. To consecrate our sexuality is to employ it only toward the divine ends for which it—and we—were created.

To think that the process of righteousness or perfection happens solely on an individual level is erroneous. Christ told the story of the rich young ruler who came to him saying he'd kept the commandments from birth and wondered what he lacked. The Savior, wanting to teach him that holiness isn't about behavioral or ritual conformity but rather about caring for and becoming ministers of grace and healing to others, commanded him to sell all and give to the poor.[25] But consecration isn't just about giving up temporal possessions. Elder Jeffrey R. Holland taught, "We must be willing to place all that we have—not just our possessions (they may be the easiest things of all to give up), but also our ambition and pride and stubbornness and vanity—we must place it all on the altar of God, kneel there in silent submission, and willingly walk away."[26]

In his talk "Spiritual Ecology," Elder Neal A. Maxwell stated, "We worry about pollution and rightfully so, but a home in which there is not adequate love pollutes society just as surely as we pollute the air and streams around us, and people further 'down stream' pay a price."[27] Immorality is social pollution—but morality doesn't just govern personal behavior. The principles of morality and chastity govern how we treat and express love towards one another, including those whose current lifestyle choices are not in harmony with gospel law—for a family to disown or reject a child because of behavior they don't approve of would also be considered immoral and unchaste. These principles also call us to social advocacy for harmony and order regarding sex and family relationships. It is principles of chastity that petition us in "The Family: A Proclamation to the World" to "promote those measures designed to maintain and strengthen the family as the fundamental unit of society."[28] It can be difficult to sensitively navigate the tensions between expressing unconditional love toward others whose life choices are out of harmony with gospel law and advocating for the social harmony and order that the spirit of Zion invites us into. In a conference address, Elder Holland said, "So if love is to be our watchword, as it must be, then by the word of Him who is love personified, we must forsake transgression and any hint of advocacy for it in others. Jesus clearly understood what many in our modern culture seem to forget: that there is a crucial difference between the commandment to forgive sin (which He had an infinite capacity to do) and the warning against condoning it (which He never ever did even once)."[29]

In sum, the law of chastity is intimately interwoven with the law of consecration and a broader view of human society, and we can employ our sexuality or promote sexuality for either the good or ill of the world at large. Sexuality and chastity are *social* virtues that we consecrate toward ends of divine sociality, not merely premarital or marital behavioral codes.

THE CHANGING CONVERSATION

Over the course of the last few years, there has been a remarkable shift in the conversation about homosexuality in LDS culture, and I believe we'll continue to see some additional shifts. While core doctrines of the Church with regard to the appropriate bounds of sexual expression have not and will not change, there has been a clarifying and nuancing of Church teaching. For example, prophets and apostles are clear to teach that sexual attraction or temptation is not a sin, only inappropriate indulgence in thought or behavior is sinful. There has also been a notable shift in our cultural and relational attitudes. We're becoming much more open and compassionate and loving in our relationships with others wherever they may be in their journey of faith, even as we continue to embrace our own faith in the Savior and the doctrines of the restored gospel.

Around this topic, where there is still so much we do not understand, many look at how past practices of the Church have changed over time, such as cessation of polygamy and the ordination of all worthy males to the priesthood, as hopeful signs that additional understanding of this issue and changed practices will be forthcoming. But both of these analogies are misguided. Perhaps a more useful parallel to review is a comparison to the Church's changing attitude towards Darwinian evolution. Instead of denouncing evolution as counter to a belief that God is the Creator, leaders have taken the position that the purpose of scripture and of the revelation of God through prophets is to tell us *why* man was created, not to tell us *how* man was created.

People can believe what they want about *how* sexuality develops and in what ways it may or may not change over the lifespan, but when it comes to the role sexuality plays in the eternal plan and how we fulfill the measure of our creation here, our choices must be guided by the *why* of our doctrine and our covenants, not by any particular biological, psychological, or social theory currently in vogue. Elder Holland wrote: "As for why you feel as you do, I can't answer that question. A number of factors may be involved, and they can be as different as people are different. Some things, including the cause of your feelings, we may never know in this life."[30]

So what does that mean, exactly, in terms of practical, everyday living? I believe it means we *pray* and we *practice*. It means we have to pray both to understand what true love and intimacy really is, and then we have to seek it and nurture and grow it in our lives and relationships. As Brad Wilcox has so eloquently and memorably stated, we are not here on earth to *earn* heaven—we're here to *learn* heaven.[31] As noted earlier, while there may be feelings of sexual or other attraction that we're called to *channel* and *transcend* if we're to become divine, there are other qualities of attraction that are good and godly and that we should *embrace* and *cultivate* in our lives.

While we will continue to learn much about the human dynamics associated with homosexual attraction and the myriad potential factors influencing its development through the scientific disciplines, God's living prophets have spoken clearly and with divine authority regarding the order and appropriate bounds of sexual expression. Proverbs reads, "When there is no prophetic vision the people cast off restraint, but the one who keeps the law, blessed is he!"[32] The gift and blessing of the gospel, both for us and for those we have the opportunity to share it with, is that it invites us into an expansive and transcendent way of being and an expression of our sexuality that not only invites us into deeper love and intimacy and connectedness with *everyone* around us but also reassures us that any potential conflicts in our feelings will be resolved into their proper place in the world to come if, while on our mortal journey here on earth, we pursue that higher, celestial love in chastity and self-restraint.

Additional Resources

Campbell, Laurie. *Reborn That Way: The True Story of One Woman, One Faith, and Countless Miracles*. Salt Lake City: North Star Harbinger, 2013.

Cohen, Richard. *Gay Children, Straight Parents: A Plan for Family Healing*. Downers Grove, IL: IVP Books, 2007.

Dahle, Dennis et al., eds. *Understanding Same-Sex Attraction: Where to Turn and How to Help*. Brigham City, UT: Brigham Distributing, 2009.

Girgis, Sherif, and Ryan T Anderson, and Robert P George. *What Is Marriage? Man and Woman: A Defense*. Jackson, TN: Encounter Books, 2012.

Godfrey, Floyd, Janette K. Gibbons, Daniel Garner, and Arthur Goldberg. *A Young Man's Journey: Healing for Young Men with Unwanted Homosexual Feelings*. Seattle, WA: CreateSpace, 2012.

Hallman, Janelle. *The Heart of Female Same-Sex Attraction: A Comprehensive Counseling Resource*. Downers Grove, IL: IVP Books, 2008.

Hill, Wesley. *Spiritual Friendship: Finding Love in the Church as a Celibate Gay Christian*. Grand Rapids, MI: Brazos Press, 2015.

Holland, Jeffrey R. "Helping Those Who Struggle with Same-Gender Attraction." *Ensign*, October 2007, https://www.lds.org/ensign/2007/10/helping-those-wh-struggle-with-same-gender-attraction.

"Love One Another: A Discussion on Same-Sex Attraction." www.mormonsandgays.org.

Mansfield, Ty, ed. *Voices of Hope: Latter-day Saint Perspectives on Same Gender Attraction—An Anthology of Gospel Teachings and Personal Essays*. Salt Lake City: Deseret Book, 2011.

Matis, Fred, Marilyn Matis, and Ty Mansfield. *In Quiet Desperation: Understanding the Challenge of Same-Gender Attraction*. Salt Lake City: Deseret Book, 2004.

North Star International. http://www.NorthStarLDS.org.

Oaks, Dallin H. "Same-Gender Attraction." *Ensign*, October 2005. https://www.lds.org/ensign/1995/10/same-gender-attraction.

Voices of Hope Project. http://www.LDSVoicesofHope.org.

Williams Paris, Jenell. *The End of Sexual Identity: Why Sex Is Too Important to Define Who We Are*. Downers Grove, IL: IVP Books, 2011.

About the Author

Ty Mansfield is a marriage and family therapist currently living in Provo, Utah, with his wife and their three kids. He chronicled his own spiritual journey with same-sex attraction as coauthor of *In Quiet Desperation* (Salt Lake City: Deseret Book, 2004) and later compiled *Voices of Hope: Latter-day Saint Perspectives on Same-Gender Attraction—An Anthology of Gospel Teachings and Personal Essays* (Salt Lake City: Deseret Book, 2011). He also codirects the Voices of Hope Project, a website extension of the book, and has been featured in the May/June 2012 issue of *LDS Living* magazine and on the Church website "Mormons and Gays." Ty is a cofounder of the nonprofit organization North Star, a faith-affirming support organization for LDS individuals and families addressing issues of sexual or gender identity who desire to live within the framework of the doctrines and teachings of The Church of Jesus Christ of Latter-day Saints.

Notes

1. Brad Wilcox, "Seeing the Big Picture," in *Voices of Hope: Latter-day Saint Perspectives on Same Gender Attraction—An Anthology of Gospel Teachings and Personal Essays*, ed. Ty Mansfield (Salt Lake City: Deseret Book, 2011), 33.

2. Screenshot of Young Men General Presidency, 179th annual general conference, Saturday afternoon session, April 4, 2009, at 4:33, https://www.lds.org/general-conference/2009/04/the-sustaining-of-church-officers.

3. Alma 38:12.

4. Ritch Savin-Williams, "Who's Gay? Does It Matter?" *Current Directions in Psychological Science* 15, no. 1 (February 2006): 40; Warren Throckmorton and Mark Yarhouse, Sexual Identity Therapy (SIT) Framework, which was referenced favorably throughout the APA's 2009 report on "Appropriate Therapeutic Responses to Sexual Orientation," https://www.apa.org/pi/lgbt/resources/therapeutic-response.pdf.

5. Subhana Barzaghi, quoted by M. Catherine Thomas, "A Gift of Love: Perspectives for Parents," *Voices of Hope: Latter-day Saint Perspectives on Same-Gender Attraction* (Salt Lake City: Deseret Book, 2011), 107.

6. Sam Keen, *Fire in the Belly: On Being a Man* (New York: Bantam Books, 1992), 174.

7. Sonja Lyubomirsky, "New Love: A Short Shelf Life," *New York Times*, December 1, 2012, http://www.nytimes.com/2012/12/02/opinion/sunday/new-love-a-short-shelf-life.html?pagewanted=all&_r=0.

8. American Psychological Association, "Answers to Your Questions for a Better Understanding of Sexual Orientation & Homosexuality," http://www.apa.org/topics/lgbt/orientation.pdf.

9. Lisa M. Diamond, "Just How Different Are Female and Male Sexual Orientation?" lecture given on October 17, 2013, as part of the Human Development Outreach and Extension Program, http://www.cornell.edu/video/lisa-diamond-on-sexual-fluidity-of-men-and-women.

10. Lisa M. Diamond, "What Does Sexual Orientation Orient? A Biobehavioral Model Distinguishing Romantic Love and Sexual Desire," *Psychological Review* 110, no. 1 (January 2003): 173–92.

11. Dallin H. Oaks, "Same-Gender Attraction," *Ensign*, October 1995, 9.

12. M. Scott Peck, *The Road Less Traveled: A New Psychology of Love, Traditional Values and Spiritual Growth* (New York: Touchstone, 1988), 52–53.

13. John Taylor, *The Gospel Kingdom: Selections from the Writings and Discourses of John Taylor, Third President of the Church of Jesus Christ of Latter-day Saints*, collector's edition (Salt Lake City: Bookcraft, 1987), 61.

14. N. T. Wright, *Simply Christian: Why Christianity Makes Sense* (Grand Rapids, MI: Zondervan, 2010), 219.

15. Abraham 3:21–22.

16. *The Incredibles*, directed by Brad Bird (Los Angeles: Disney/Pixar, 2004), DVD.

17. See Daniel 2:31–45.

18. Hugh Nibley, "The Prophets and the Open Mind," in *The World and the Prophets* (Provo, UT: FARMS; Salt Lake City: Deseret Book, 1987), 134.

19. Elizabeth Kubler-Ross, *Death: The Final Stage of Growth* (New York: Simon & Schuster, 1975), 96.

20. Cited in Spencer W. Kimball, *Faith Precedes the Miracle* (1972; repr. Salt Lake City: Deseret Book, 2001), 98.

21. D&C 103:4.

22. D&C 105:4.

23. D&C 105:3.

24. Suzanne Evertsen Lundquist, "Chastity and the Environment," unpublished manuscript, 2, emphasis in original; copy in author's possession.

25. Matthew 19:16–22.

26. Jeffrey R. Holland, "The Will of the Father" (Brigham Young University devotional, January 17, 1989), 3, https://speeches.byu.edu/?act=viewitem&id=729.

27. Neal A. Maxwell, "Spiritual Ecology," *New Era*, February 1975, 36.

28. The First Presidency and Council of the Twelve Apostles of The Church of Jesus Christ of Latter-day Saints, "The Family: A Proclamation to the World," September 23, 1995, https://www.lds.org/toics/family-proclamation.

29. Jeffrey R. Holland, "The Cost—and Blessings—of Discipleship," *Ensign*, May 2014, 8.

30. Jeffrey R. Holland, "Helping Those Who Struggle with Same-Gender Attraction," *Ensign*, October 2007, 42.

31. Brad Wilcox, "His Grace Is Sufficient," Brigham Young University devotional address, July 12, 2011, https://speeches.byu.edu/talks/brad-wilcox_his-grace-is-sufficient/.

32. Proverbs 29:18, New English Translation.

17

SCIENCE AND RELIGION: FRIENDS OR FOES?

David H. Bailey

Some Latter-day Saints and others presume that science and religion are mortal enemies. However, they have much in common. What's more, in Latter-day Saint discourse there is no such thing as a miracle completely beyond natural law, so there is no need for "war" between science and religion. Still, many are troubled by scientific studies regarding the origin of the earth and its inhabitants that appear to differ from scriptural accounts. But upon careful examination of the relevant issues in areas such as biblical scholarship, the origin and evolution of life, and Big Bang cosmology, it is clear there is no need for conflict.

We often read that science and religion are enemies, pitched in a life-or-death battle for the minds and hearts of the public. There is some truth to this. Some scientists and secular scholars are outspoken opponents of modern religion, arguing that religion is fundamentally irrational and even harmful. Some religious writers perceive science as a mortal threat to religion and believe it their solemn duty to oppose science at every turn in the public arena.

Yet, from a fundamental point of view, surely there cannot be any war between the two disciplines. Both are part of a fundamental quest for truth. Both espouse the "idea of progress," which American sociologist Robert Nisbet defined as the notion that "mankind has advanced in the past, is now advancing, and may be expected to continue advancing in the future,"[1] a definition remarkably similar to the ninth article of faith. Both scientists and religious persons can stand in awe at the natural world and the universe we inhabit, which is now known to be far more vast and more magnificent than we realized, based on discoveries just in the past two or three decades.

Science Defined

Much of the perceived conflict derives from confusion over what science is and what it is not. Perhaps the most succinct definition of science is the one given by the National Academy of Science: "*The use of evidence to construct testable explanations and predictions of natural phenomena, as well as the knowledge generated through this process.*"[2] The academy elaborated on this definition, noting: "In science, explanations must be based on naturally occurring phenomena. Natural causes are, in principle, reproducible and therefore can be checked independently by others. If explanations are based on purported forces that are outside of nature, scientists have no way of either confirming or disproving those explanations."[3] Thus science, properly defined, cannot possibly conflict with religion, since it can say nothing one way or the other about the existence or nature of a supreme being.

It is widely presumed that miracles are contraventions of natural law. But Church authorities have rejected this notion. Brigham Young declared, "Yet I will say with regard to miracles, there is no such thing save to the ignorant—that is, there never was a result wrought out by God or by any of His creatures without there being a cause for it. There may be results, the causes of which we do not see or understand, and what we call miracles are no more than this—they are the results or effects of causes hidden from our understandings."[4] James E. Talmage, who later became an Apostle, was even more explicit: "Miracles are commonly regarded as occurrences in opposition to the laws of nature. Such a conception is plainly erroneous, for the laws of nature are inviolable. However, as human understanding of these laws is at best but imperfect, events strictly in accordance with natural law may appear contrary thereto. The entire constitution of nature is founded on system and order."[5]

In short, scientists and Latter-day Saint authorities reject the fundamental basis for a conflict between science and religion. Nonetheless, many young people and adults alike often ask questions about how science and religion interact. While definitive answers are often not attainable, direct and honest information should be provided whenever possible, and truth should be embraced no matter its source.

Biblical Inerrancy

Many common misunderstandings in the science-religion arena are rooted in the idea of *biblical inerrancy*, the notion that the Bible is an *infallible* and *complete* repository of God's word, so it must be read as a scientific and historical treatise as well as a religious text. Biblical inerrantists typically insist that Genesis should be read very literally as the creation of the earth (or the entire universe) *in toto* (completely) and *ex nihilo* (out of nothing) over a six-day period, approximately six thousand years ago.

But this view of the Bible goes well beyond the view taught by the leaders of the Church. Indeed, the term *biblical inerrancy*, and the relatively inflexible philosophy it represents, are absent in Latter-day Saint discourse. Joseph Smith, in his history of the First Vision as recorded in the Pearl of Great Price, recalled his great frustration at the numerous contending preachers in his area who all quoted the Bible to advance their particular interpretations.[6] He ultimately concluded that many of the issues he was concerned about could not be resolved solely by literal readings of biblical scripture—additional revelation was needed. In a similar vein, the Book of Mormon, which was published a few years after his first vision, noted that many "plain and precious things" had been deleted through the years from the biblical text.[7]

Joseph Smith's successor Brigham Young was rather explicit in acknowledging that the Bible should not be read as a scientific textbook in matters of the Creation: "As for the Bible account of the creation we may say that the Lord gave it to Moses, or rather Moses obtained the history and traditions of the fathers, and from these picked out what he considered necessary, and that account has been handed down from age to age, and we have got it, no matter whether it is correct or not, and whether the Lord found the earth empty and void, whether he made it out of nothing or out of the rude elements; or whether he made it in six days or in as many millions of years, is and will remain a matter of speculation in the minds of men unless he give revelation on the subject."[8]

President Joseph Fielding Smith, while frequently emphasizing the truth and accuracy of the scriptures, still acknowledged that limits must be placed on highly literal readings:

> Even the most devout and sincere believers in the Bible realize that it is, like most any other book, filled with metaphor, simile, allegory, and parable, which no intelligent person could be compelled to accept in a literal sense....
>
> The Lord has not taken from those who believe in his word the power of reason. He expects every man who takes his "yoke" upon him to have common sense enough to accept a figure of speech in its proper setting, and to understand that the holy scriptures are replete with allegorical stories, faith-building parables, and artistic speech....
>
> Where is there a writing intended to be taken in all its parts literally? Such a writing would be insipid and hence lack natural appeal. To expect a believer in the Bible to strike an attitude of this kind and believe all that is written to be a literal rendition is a stupid

thought. No person with the natural use of his faculties looks upon the Bible in such a light.⁹

Some may be surprised at these passages, but they all are consistent with the Church's long-standing approach that while the scriptures must be read carefully and taken seriously (more so than taught by some other faiths), the Bible in particular has faults, and the biblical inerrancy doctrines often taught by denominations that contend with science and that presume science and religion to be at war are definitely rejected. With the more flexible Latter-day Saint view of scripture in mind, most issues in the science-religion arena fade into relative insignificance.

While the scriptures in general are devoid of specifics regarding scientific issues, a few biblical passages have some relevance to science. There are a few references to astronomy, including, interestingly enough, mention of specific stars and constellations. Other passages reflect the ancient cosmology, where the sun, moon, and stars revolve around the earth, which is presumed to be immovable.[10] Many have ridiculed the Bible for such passages, but a more honest reading of these passages reveals they always appear in a poetic context, praising God for the wonders of Creation, and were never intended to be read as scientifically precise declarations of literal fact.

Not a single passage of the Bible or any other scripture is written in the precise, quantitative, testable style of a modern scientific research work. So those who read the Bible or other scriptures as scientific textbooks are mistaken. As Apostle James E. Talmage noted, "the beginning chapters of Genesis, and scriptures related thereto, were never intended as a textbook of geology, archaeology, earth-science, or man-science."[11]

Biblical Chronology

Scholars through the centuries, including the medieval Jewish scholar Maimonides and the seventeenth-century mathematician-physicist Isaac Newton have attempted to develop a comprehensive chronology for the Bible. Some success has been obtained for the period from the reign of King David, roughly 1050 BC, to the Babylonian captivity in 586 BC. Dating earlier than this time is quite problematic, due to numerous historical gaps and discrepancies in the biblical record.[12] Partly for this reason, the Bible Chronology in the latest edition of the Bible published by the Church provides no specific dates for events from the Creation to the start of Saul's reign, roughly 1095 BC.[13]

Similarly, there is no solid archaeological evidence relating to the Old Testament before the Merneptah Stele, dated to 1207 BC, which contains the first mention of Israel in ancient archaeology.[14] This certainly does not mean that earlier biblical figures or biblical events are fictitious, as some have argued, but only that there is no solid scientific evidence to confirm them. After all, science can say nothing one way or the other about specific persons who, like almost all figures in biblical history, were relatively obscure on the world stage during their lifetimes, nor can it say anything one way or the other about events that are presumed to be beyond the realm of what can be studied by scientific experimentation.

In any event, the message for discussions of science and religion is clear: any attempt to specify an exact date for an early event such as the Creation, based solely on the biblical text, is an exercise in futility. Some may be disappointed in this conclusion, but surely the Bible was never intended to be read primarily as a historical treatise any more than a scientific treatise. Questions such as whether Adam lived 6,000; 60,000; or 600,000 years ago or whether the Exodus occurred in the sixteenth century BC or in the thirteenth century BC are relatively unimportant to the grand themes of religion in general and the scriptures in particular, which are identifying the purpose of human existence, obtaining salvation from sin, developing a code of moral conduct, and serving the poor and downtrodden.

According to the Gospel of Matthew, when Jesus was asked whether Jews should pay taxes to Rome, he replied, "Render therefore unto Caesar the things which are Caesar's; and unto God the things that are God's."[15] Similar advice could be helpful in this discussion: Render unto science the things which are scientific and unto religion the things that are religious.

The Age of the Earth

What does science say about the age of the earth? The oldest mineral ever found, a zircon specimen found in the Jack Hills region of Western Australia, has been measured to be 4.4 billion years old.[16] The oldest meteorites, which were formed at roughly the same time as the earth, are 4.56 billion years old, so this figure is generally taken to be the age of the earth.

The various epochs of the earth's existence have similarly been dated by geologists. For example, the Cambrian explosion, when many skeletal organisms arose, has been dated as a period spanning 20 million years, starting 541 million years ago. Similarly, the last of the dinosaurs perished, evidently from a meteoritic impact, 66 million years ago. A listing of the currently understood geologic time scale can be found in any recent geology reference.[17]

The figures mentioned above are all based on measurements of the levels of certain radioactive nuclear isotopes in mineral samples. The phenomenon of radioactivity is well understood through the use of quantum mechanics, so the formulas used in these calculations are on very solid ground. It is also worth noting that when astronomers view a supernova exploding in a distant galaxy, say 100 million light-years away, that explosion actually occurred 100 million years ago. Yet, from all evidence, the processes of radioactive decay and other phenomena seen in these supernovas are indistinguishable from the results of experiments in earth-based laboratories today. Thus a telescope is a time machine of sorts, permitting scientists to see in considerable detail the laws of physics and radioactivity in operation long ago and to verify that these laws have not significantly changed over the eons.

Like any scientific procedure, radiometric dating measurements are subject to errors and uncertainties. But decades of study have led to a thorough understanding of these pitfalls and specific ways to avoid them. Thus scientists today have considerable confidence in radiometric dating when used in accordance with well-established procedures. Tens of thousands of rigorously peer-reviewed radiometric dating measurements have been published in scientific journals, and thousands more are added each year.[18]

Radiocarbon dating, also known as Carbon-14 dating, is based on the fact that when a plant or animal organism dies, it stops ingesting Carbon-14, and the amount of Carbon-14 gradually decreases, with a half-life of 5,730 years. Because of this relatively short half-life, Carbon-14 measurements are useful for dating artifacts of a relatively recent vintage, as far back as roughly 50,000 years ago. But radiocarbon dating and its potential errors have no bearing one way or the other on the age of the earth or the ages of any of the major geologic eras, since these epochs are all much more ancient than 50,000 years old.

The Church's Position on the Age of the Earth

Some past Church authorities, mostly in the nineteenth and early twentieth centuries, taught that the earth was just a few thousand years old, but others espoused a more expansive view. Brigham Young taught there was no specific revelation on the topic.[19]

Elder Bruce R. McConkie once taught that the Creation lasted 6,000 years,[20] but he later wrote that each day was "an age, an eon, a division of eternity."[21] More recently, Elder Russell M. Nelson declared: "In Genesis and Moses, those periods are called days. But in the Book of Abraham, each period is referred to as a time. Whether termed a day, a time, or an age, each phase was a period between two identifiable events—a division of eternity."[22]

In short, the Church does not officially state the age of the earth, nor by what specific means it was created. As the article "Earth" in the *Encyclopedia of Mormonism* explains, "The scriptures do not say how old the earth is, and the Church has taken no official stand on this question.... Nor does the Church consider it to be a central issue for salvation."[23]

Evolution

Merriam-Webster's Collegiate Dictionary lists several definitions for the word "theory," including (a) "a plausible or scientifically acceptable general principle or body of principles offered to explain phenomena, e.g., the wave theory of light" and (b) "a hypothesis assumed for the sake of argument or investigation; an unproved assumption."[24] In most scientific discourse, scientists use definition (a), while in popular public discourse, definition (b) is more widely assumed. This distinction is the root of the widespread misunderstanding of the phrase "theory of evolution."

Evolution is certainly not a theory in the sense of a sketchy conjecture that has never been seriously tested. On the contrary, evolution has passed more than a full century of rigorous empirical tests covering every aspect. It is termed a theory in the same sense that one refers to *atomic theory* or the *theory of relativity*, namely because it is a general principle with substantial explanatory power and falsifiability that has withstood rigorous scrutiny.

On the other hand, most scientists are content with the double meaning of "theory" as a form of self-imposed humility and resistance against taking any theory as unchangeable truth. The tentative nature of scientific theories was impressed on scientists most vividly in the early twentieth century when Newton's classical laws of motion and gravitation, which had dominated scientific research for more than three centuries, were displaced by Einstein's relativity for objects traveling at very high speeds and by quantum mechanics for very small objects, such as atoms and subatomic particles. Thus, even well-established theories are often modified and refined as more experimental evidence is accumulated. This could be the case with evolution as well.

So what exactly is the theory of evolution? It is the theory that differences between organisms have developed over eons of time because of processes such as mutation and natural selection, ultimately resulting in different species; in particular, species today on earth are descended from common ancestors over millions of years. The principal lines of evidence supporting evolution can be briefly summarized as follows:

1. **Geological evidence:** Various geological eras, as identified by the fossils they contain, nearly always appear in the same order worldwide and yield the same geological dates when measured by radiometric dating techniques.
2. **Fossil evidence:** The partial record of prehistoric species that have populated the earth over eons of geological time is preserved in stone.
3. **Morphological evidence:** Similarities between the physical structure and function of existing biological species are evidence of common ancestry, and the degree of similarity can be used to organize species into a family tree.
4. **DNA evidence:** Direct analyses of DNA sequences or protein chains, analyses that are made possible by the recent dramatic advances in DNA sequencing technology, provide a clearer picture of the interrelationship of species and diversification over time.

Evidence is not always bulletproof, but as scientists have continued to collect more data and develop new technologies, uncertainties have been minimized or eliminated. For example, even today gaps exist in the fossil record. But almost all biological organisms that have ever lived were either eaten by predators or otherwise destroyed soon after death, leaving no trace. Most that persisted in some form, through preserved skeletons, were later destroyed by chemical effects or were part of a geological layer that subsequently disappeared into the earth's molten mantle. Almost all fossils that have survived these and numerous other perils lie far beneath the earth's surface and will never be seen by humans. Consequently, the fossil record will never be complete—all we can expect is to capture glimpses of the earth's flora and fauna over its multi-billion-year history.[25]

Even so, numerous gaps that were once thought to exist in the fossil record have been filled. For example, scientists once despaired of ever finding transitional fossils linking ancient land mammals and marine mammals such as orcas, whales, and dolphins. But within the last two or three decades, at least thirty intermediate fossil species for these groups have been found, with exactly the expected combination of terrestrial and aquatic features.[26] Also, in 2004 researchers discovered the Tiktaalik fossil in a remote area of Ellesmere Island, above the Arctic Circle in Canada. It spans the transition between ancient fish and the earliest four-legged creatures.[27] Many, many other examples could be listed.

In the past few years, modern genome sequencing and computer technology have placed an enormous volume of DNA data only a mouse-click away from researchers worldwide. The first draft of the human genome was completed in 2000 after a ten-year effort that cost hundreds of millions of dollars. Fortunately, now all genomes can be sequenced much more inexpensively—at a cost of roughly one thousand dollars.[28] Among other things, DNA analysis provides a new means, independent of studies of comparative anatomy and other methods used in the past, of quantitatively measuring the evolutionary distance between species and, hence, can be used to convincingly and objectively arrange species in an evolutionary family tree.

For instance, DNA studies have shown that the DNA sequence for human beta globin, a component of blood, is identical to that in chimpanzees and differs in only one amino acid location from that of gorillas, but it is increasingly different from the similar sequence in other animals. Similarly, the gene that when mutated results in cystic fibrosis in humans is nearly identical to the corresponding gene in chimpanzees but is progressively less similar to the corresponding gene in orangutans, baboons, marmosets, lemurs, mice, chickens, and puffer fish.[29]

Another interesting example is the "GULO" gene, which is an essential part of the biochemical machinery that makes Vitamin C in animals. Humans and some primates lack a functioning copy of this gene—it is mutated; scurvy results when these species don't get enough Vitamin C in their diet. But even though the human GULO gene is mutated and completely useless, humans and chimpanzees have very similar copies of it (98 percent identical). Evidently, a common ancestor of humans and chimps adopted a diet rich in fruits and vegetables. Thus a chance mutation that disabled Vitamin C production was not damaging and was passed on to posterity to both branches of the family tree.[30]

Transposons, or "jumping genes," are mutations where sections of DNA have been copied from one part of an organism's genome and pasted in another. Most of the time, these inserted genes do no damage because they land in relatively unimportant sections of DNA. They do, however, provide an excellent means to classify species into their family tree relationship. This is because it is exceedingly unlikely that the same random insertion of an entire gene would occur at the same spot in the genomes of two or more different species—unless, of course, each inherited this curious feature from a common ancestor.

The diagram below illustrates how transposon data can be used to determine the family tree relationship of various primates. The columns labeled ABCDE denote five known blocks of transposons, and x and o respectively denote that the block is present or absent. It is clear from this data that our closest relatives are bonobos and chimpanzees.[31]

Transposon Blocks

Species	A	B	C	D	E
Human	o	x	x	x	x
Bonobo	x	x	x	x	x
Chimp	x	x	x	x	x
Gorilla	o	o	x	x	x
Orangutan	o	o	o	x	x
Gibbon	o	o	o	o	o

From evidence such as the above, nearly all scientists are convinced that evolution is the best scientific explanation for the observed data. Species have evolved over millions of years, are still evolving, and are descended from common ancestors.

DO SCIENTISTS UNDERSTAND THE ORIGIN OF LIFE?

Not all questions can be answered through evolutionary biology. For example, scientists do not yet fully understand the origin of life. In particular, the origin of the first self-reproducing biomolecules, on which evolutionary processes could operate to produce more complicated systems, remains unknown. However, recent research has yielded tantalizing clues. For example, in December 2014 scientists produced the four bases of RNA, a relative of DNA, in a laboratory experiment simulating the meteorite bombardments of the early earth.[32] But researchers are still far from fully understanding the origin process. Some scientists even speculate that the first living microbes came from outside the earth, possibly on a meteorite from Mars, although this does not solve the origin mystery.

There are also numerous unanswered questions on the path from the origin of life leading up to multicellular organisms. Unlike bony structures that leave fossil records, the early stages of biological evolution on the planet very likely have been completely erased, so we may never know for sure the full details of what transpired.

In addition, some questions remain as to the driving forces for evolutionary change and speciation. The current hypothesis is that the principal forces behind evolution are largely *random* mutations combined with largely *nonrandom* forces of natural selection. But even here, there have been changes in the prevailing theories. For example, the appearance of transposons, mentioned above, has challenged earlier notions that mutations are *local* events in DNA. It is also known that epigenetic effects, namely effects not connected to changes in DNA, can be passed on to posterity. For example, a father's smoking history may affect the health of his sons and grandsons, even though his DNA sequence is not involved and even if no secondhand smoke is involved.[33]

But in any event, questions such as how life started, whether mutations and natural selection suffice to account for evolutionary changes, or whether the pace of natural evolution is sufficiently rapid are all quite irrelevant to the basic issue of whether or not evolution has occurred. The evidence that evolution has occurred and continues to occur is overwhelming and universally accepted by the scientific community.

Is the Biological World "Designed"?

Some have argued that there is design in the natural world that suggests direct, hands-on creation by God. Surely there are many beautiful and wondrous features in the natural world. But as with many issues in the science-religion arena, caution should be taken before embracing this concept.

After all, looking for design in nature is a two-edged sword, since design fails by itself to explain the pain, violence, and suffering apparent in the natural world. For example, scurvy, that scourge of British sailors on the high seas and Mormon pioneers at Winter Quarters, occurs in humans when they do not get enough Vitamin C. Although almost all other mammals generate their own Vitamin C, this machinery doesn't work in humans because mutations have inactivated a key process, as previously noted.[34] Numerous other examples could be cited.

So did God meticulously and deliberately design humans with these specific defects and vulnerabilities, or did he, at a much higher level, create the world and a system of elegant laws that are conducive to the formation of living creatures, including us? And is it not our sacred duty to utilize the scientific method to understand these problems, and, where possible, to counter their effects and mitigate the suffering that results from them?[35] At the least, available evidence suggests that design should be seen in a high-level sense, perhaps even in the laws governing the earth and the universe, rather than in specific, low-level mechanics of individual organs and species.

THE CHURCH'S POSITION ON EVOLUTION

In 1909, the First Presidency released a statement entitled "The Origin of Man." It included the following passage: "It is held by some that Adam was not the first man upon this earth, and that the original human being was a development from lower orders of the animal creation. These, however, are the theories of men."[36] However, a few months later, an editorial by the First Presidency in the *Improvement Era* addressed the following question: "In just what manner did the mortal bodies of Adam and Eve come into existence on this earth?" The editorial responded: "Whether the mortal bodies of man evolved in natural processes to present perfection, through the direction and power of God; whether the first parents of our generations, Adam and Eve, were transplanted from another sphere, with immortal tabernacles, which became corrupted through sin and the partaking of natural foods, in the process of time; whether they were born here in mortality, as other mortals have been, are questions not fully answered in the revealed word of God."[37]

In 1925, the First Presidency released a statement titled "Mormon View of Evolution." This statement was essentially a shortened and edited version of the 1909 statement. But it did not include the passage discussing whether humans developed from earlier species.[38]

In 1930, Elders Joseph Fielding Smith, Brigham H. Roberts, and James E. Talmage were debating the issue of whether there were humans or other creatures before the Fall of Adam. Elder Smith argued against the possibility of pre-Adamites, or, in a larger sense, of any evolution, a view that he later expanded in his book *Man: His Origin and Destiny*.[39] Elder Roberts countered that we should pay attention to findings of scientific research, a view that he elaborated on in his 1931 manuscript *The Truth, the Way, the Life*: "To limit and insist upon the whole of life and death to this side of Adam's advent to the earth, some six or eight thousand years ago, as proposed by some, is to fly in the face of the facts so indisputably brought to light by the researcher of science in modern times."[40] Elder Talmage's view is indicated by the following statement, from a 1931 talk: "Geologists say that these very simple forms of plant and animal bodies were succeeded by others more complicated; and in the indestructible record of the rocks they read the story of advancing life from the simple to the more complex, from the single-celled protozoan to the highest animals, from the marine algae to the advanced types of flowering plant—to the apple-tree, the rose, and the oak.... What a fascinating story is inscribed upon the stony pages of the earth's crust!"[41]

In 1931, after some period of discussion between these authorities, the First Presidency sent a letter to all Church leaders that concluded: "Upon the fundamental doctrines of the Church we are all agreed. Our mission is to bear the message of the restored gospel to the people of the world. Leave Geology, Biology, Archaeology and Anthropology, no one of which has to do with the salvation of the souls of mankind, to scientific research, while we magnify our calling in the realm of the Church."[42]

In 1992, the Brigham Young University Board of Trustees and the First Presidency approved a packet of materials on "Evolution and the Origin of Man." It includes the 1909 First Presidency statement, a 1910 First Presidency comment, the 1925 statement, and the 1992 *Encyclopedia of Mormonism* article on evolution. The *Encyclopedia of Mormonism* article on evolution, which was prepared under the direction of President Gordon B. Hinckley, includes the passage from the 1931 First Presidency letter previously quoted.

It is quite apparent that in regards to evolution, as with the age of the earth, Church leaders are not interested in engaging in technical debates that are well outside the scope of the Church's central mission. Instead, they have stated that such matters should be left to scientific research.

Along this line, Brigham Young University and BYU–Idaho offer robust areas of study in modern science, including astronomy, botany, zoology, geology, physics, chemistry, computer science, and mathematics. Evolution and old-earth geology, in particular, have been taught at the university for decades with full approval from Church leadership, with several of the BYU and BYU–Idaho faculty making notable contributions to these fields.

Big Bang Cosmology and the "Cosmic Coincidences"

The Big Bang is the name given by scientists for the origin of our visible universe, which has been dated to 13.8 billion years ago. The Big Bang cosmology theory arose in the 1920s, when American astronomer Edwin Hubble showed that the distances to far galaxies were roughly proportional to their outward velocities. This implied that the entire universe is expanding, and there must have been a time when the universe was much denser than it is today. The Big Bang cosmology received additional support in 1964, when two radio astronomers showed that low-level noise in an antenna was the echo of the universe itself from 300,000 years after the Big Bang.[43]

At about the same time, theoretical calculations by researchers concluded that the Big Bang would have produced a universe that is roughly 75 percent hydrogen and 25 percent helium, with traces of other elements, which matches observed figures in impressive detail.[44] More recently, measurements of the cosmic microwave background using satellites, beginning in 1993, show spectacular agreement with the theory.[45] Some questions remain concerning the *inflation* scenario, wherein the universe underwent a spectacular expansion in the first tiny fraction of a second after the Big Bang, but the basic notion that the universe we see originated in an event 13.8 billion years ago is based on solid scientific data.[46]

With regards to physics and the Big Bang cosmology, recent research has revealed some truly intriguing features, often termed the "cosmic coincidences," which suggest our particular universe and its laws seem astonishingly fine-tuned for the rise of intelligent life. For example, if gravitation had been only slightly stronger in the early universe, the expansion would have stopped and even reversed long ago, ending the universe long before any intelligent creatures would have arisen. On the other hand, if gravitation had been ever so slightly weaker, stars and galaxies might not have formed until matter was too dispersed, leaving the universe a cold and lifeless place.

Numerous other coincidences have been noted in scientific literature, for example:

a. **Carbon resonance and the strong force:** The Big Bang theory is remarkably successful in explaining the abundances of hydrogen, helium, and lithium. The synthesis of heavier elements, beginning with carbon, remained a mystery until 1951 when astronomer Fred Hoyle hypothesized and then discovered a nuclear *resonance* that is just energetic enough to permit carbon to form. The energy at which this resonance occurs depends sensitively on the interplay between the strong nuclear force and the weak nuclear force. If the strong force were slightly stronger or slightly weaker (by just 1 percent in either direction), there would be no carbon or any heavier elements anywhere in the universe and thus no carbon-based life forms like us.[47]

b. **The electromagnetic-gravitational strength ratio:** In 1974, Brandon Carter noted that if gravity were slightly stronger, all stars would be radiative rather than convective, and planets might not form. But if gravity were somewhat weaker (so that the ratio was higher), then all stars would be convective and supernovas might not happen. Since all elements on the periodic chart from carbon on up are synthesized in supernova explosions, there would be no carbon-based life.[48]

c. **The proton-to-electron mass ratio:** The ratio of the mass of the neutron to the mass of the proton is approximately 1.0013784. In other words, the neutron's mass is slightly more than the combined mass of a proton, an electron, and a neutrino. As a result, free neutrons, or those neutrons that are not tied up in the nucleus of an atom, spontaneously decay with a half-life of about ten minutes. If the neutron were slightly less massive, then it could not decay without energy input. If its mass were lower by 1 percent, then isolated protons would decay instead of neutrons, and very few atoms heavier than lithium could form.[49]

d. **The cosmological constant:** This paradox derives from the fact that when one calculates, based on known principles of quantum mechanics, the "vacuum energy density" of the universe, focusing on the electromagnetic force, one obtains the absurd result that empty space should "weigh" 10^{93} grams per cc, whereas the actual average mass density of the universe is 10^{-28} grams per cc. This is a discrepancy factor of 10^{120}, which is the number 1 followed by 120 zeroes![50] Physicists who have fretted over this huge discrepancy for decades have noted that calculations such as the above involve only the electromagnetic force, so perhaps when the contributions of the other known forces are included, all terms will cancel out to exactly zero as a consequence of some currently unknown principle of physics.

These hopes were shattered with the 1998 discovery that the expansion of the universe is accelerating, which implies that the cosmological constant, which is tied to the vacuum energy density through Einstein's general relativity, must be slightly positive. But this means that physicists are left to explain the startling fact that the positive and negative contributions to the cosmological constant cancel to 120-digit accuracy yet fail to cancel beginning at the 121st digit. Curiously, this observation is in accord with a prediction made by physicist Steven Weinberg in 1987, who argued from basic principles that the cosmological constant must be zero to within one part in roughly 10^{120}. If not, the universe either would have dispersed too fast for stars and galaxies to have formed or else would have recollapsed long ago.[51]

In short, numerous features of our universe seem fine-tuned, often astoundingly so, for the existence of intelligent life. As British astronomer Fred Hoyle said, "A commonsense interpretation of the facts suggests that a super-intellect has monkeyed with physics, as well as the chemistry and biology, and that there are no blind forces worth speaking about in nature. The numbers one calculates from the facts seem to me so overwhelming as to put this conclusion almost beyond question."[52]

Some scientists have invoked the "anthropic principle" to explain such phenomena. In other words, they postulate that our universe is merely one of an enormous (possibly infinite) multitude of universes, and the reason we find ourselves in a universe with such an extremely fine-tuned set of parameters conducive to intelligent life is that if our universe were not like this, we would not be here to ask the question. But other researchers find such "anthropic" reasoning most unsatisfying.[53]

God of the Gaps

Many argue that apparent design in the biological world or the cosmic coincidences of the universe constitute *proof* that our universe was designed by a supreme being. But caution is in order since experience has taught us that claims that one can prove God based on inexplicable phenomena in the natural world often disappoint in the long run. Such reasoning even has a name: the "God of the Gaps" approach to science and religion. It has, in most cases, left a legacy of disappointment as science advances.

To begin with, there is no fundamental reason, scientific or theological, why God should only be found in the gaps of scientific knowledge. To the contrary, as noted biologist and author Kenneth Miller, a Roman Catholic, observed: "[God of the gaps proponents] inevitably look for God in what science has not explained or in what they claim science cannot explain. Most scientists who are religious look for God in what science does understand and has explained."[54]

Furthermore, invoking a Creator or a Designer every time unexplained phenomena arise is a "thinking stopper," burying the grand questions of science and religion in the inaccessible mind of God while lessening our motivation to discover the principles underlying these phenomena on our own. So while the earth and the universe are indeed magnificent beyond description, let's not think that we can *prove* God with technical reasoning. Faith is still necessary.

Embracing Science and Religion in One's Quest for Truth

This is an exciting time to be alive. The fields of science and technology are surging ahead with remarkable discoveries on many fronts: artificial intelligence, DNA sequencing, biomedical technology, commercial space travel, discovery of numerous planets orbiting other stars in the habitable zone, and a never-ending stream of amazing advances in computer technology. President Gordon B. Hinckley summarized these developments when he declared:

> But in a larger sense [the twentieth century] has been the best of all centuries. In the long history of the earth there has been nothing like it. The life expectancy of man has been extended by more than 25 years. Think of it. It is a miracle. The fruits of science have been manifest everywhere. By and large, we live longer, we live better. This

is an age of greater understanding and knowledge. We live in a world of great diversity. As we learn more of one another, our appreciation grows. This has been an age of enlightenment. The miracles of modern medicine, of travel, of communication are almost beyond belief. All of this has opened new opportunities for us which we must grasp and use for the advancement of the Lord's work.[55]

What's more, it is inarguably true that everyone, of both scientific and religious backgrounds, can stand in awe at the majesty of the universe. Albert Einstein understood this principle well, even though he personally had difficulties with traditional notions of God. He once wrote: "On the other hand, I maintain that the cosmic religious feeling is the strongest and noblest motive for scientific research. . . . Those whose acquaintance with scientific research is derived chiefly from its practical results easily develop a completely false notion of the mentality of the men who, surrounded by a skeptical world, have shown the way to kindred spirits scattered wide through the world and through the centuries. Only one who has devoted his life to similar ends can have a vivid realization of what has inspired these men and given them the strength to remain true to their purpose in spite of countless failures. It is cosmic religious feeling that gives a man such strength."[56]

But while discussions of evolution, astronomy, physics, and cosmology may be engaging and even inspiring, it is not clear that they relate in a substantive way to what most religious people experience. Was Mother Teresa inspired by the "cosmic coincidences" to devote her life to India's poor? Did Johann Sebastian Bach have the "God of the Big Bang" in mind when he composed over a thousand pieces of sacred music? Are millions of contemporary persons, of Latter-day Saint and other religious traditions, inspired by discovery of the Higgs boson when they devote their lives to religious service? Probably not. As Holmes Rolston observed, "The religion that is married to science today will be a widow tomorrow. . . . Religion that has too thoroughly accommodated to any science will soon be obsolete."[57]

So in the end, religious beliefs cannot be either proven or disproven by science. Individuals are still more likely to find God on their knees, in the soup kitchen, and in living a righteous, productive, and charitable life than in the scientific laboratory.

Additional Resources

Bailey, David H. "Science vs. Religion: Can This Marriage Be Saved?" In *Science and Mormonism 1: Cosmos, Earth and Man*, edited by David H. Bailey, Jeffrey M. Bradshaw, John H. Lewis, Gregory L. Smith, and Michael R. Stark, 13–39. Orem, UT: The Interpreter Foundation; Salt Lake City: Eborn Books, 2016.

Bailey, David H. "Twenty Questions about Science and Religion." In *Science and Mormonism 1: Cosmos, Earth and Man*, 41–72.

Aczel, Amir. *Why Science Does Not Disprove God*. New York: William Morrow, 2014.

Fairbanks, Daniel J. *Relics of Eden: The Powerful Evidence of Evolution in Human DNA*. New York: Prometheus Books, 2007.

Miller, Kenneth R. *Finding Darwin's God: A Scientist's Search for Common Ground between God and Evolution*. New York: Cliff Street Books, 1999.

National Academy of Sciences. Institute of Medicine. *Science, Evolution, and Creationism*. Washington, DC: National Academies Press, 2008.

See other articles on science and religion by D. H. Bailey at http://www.sciencemeetsreligion.org.

About the Author

David H. Bailey is a mathematician/computer scientist, recently retired from Lawrence Berkeley National Laboratory and is also affiliated with the University of California, Davis. He is the author of six books and over two hundred technical articles in the area of high-performance scientific computing, computational mathematics, mathematical finance, and computational biology. He has received the Sidney Fernbach Award from the IEEE Computer Society, the Gordon Bell Prize from the Association for Computing Machinery, and the Chauvenet Prize and Merten Hesse Prize from the Mathematical Association of America. In addition, he operates the website Science Meets Religion, with over eighty articles on science and religion and a blog. He and his wife, Linda, live in Alamo, California. They are the parents of four children and have seven grandchildren. They serve in the Alamo First Ward of the Danville California Stake.

Notes

1. Robert Nisbet, *History of the Idea of Progress* (1980; repr., Piscataway, NJ: Transaction Publishers, 1993), 4–5.

2. National Academy of Sciences, Institute of Medicine, *Science, Evolution, and Creationism* (Washington, DC: National Academies Press, 2008), 10; emphasis added.

3. National Academy of Sciences, *Science, Evolution, and Creationism*, 10.

4. Brigham Young, in *Journal of Discourses* (London: Latter-day Saints' Book Depot, 1854–86), 12:141 (July 11, 1869).

5. James E. Talmage, *The Articles of Faith* (1899; repr., Salt Lake City: Deseret Book, 1966), 220 (from a 1931 address).

6. Joseph Smith–History 1:5–10.

7. 1 Nephi 13:28–40.

8. Brigham Young, in *Journal of Discourses*, 14:116 (May 14, 1871).

9. Joseph Fielding Smith, *Doctrines of Salvation*, 3 vols. (Salt Lake City: Bookcraft, 1956), 3:188.

10. See, for example, Job 38:31–33; 1 Samuel 2:8; 1 Chronicles 16:30; Psalm 93:1; 104:5; Ecclesiastes 1:5.

11. James E. Talmage, "The Earth and Man," *Instructor*, January 1966, 9–15.

12. J. Philip Hyatt, *The Heritage of Biblical Faith* (St. Louis: Bethany Press, 1964), 33–44.

13. *The Holy Bible, Containing the Old and New Testaments* (repr.; Salt Lake City: The Church of Jesus Christ of Latter-day Saints, 2013).

14. Eric H. Cline, *Biblical Archaeology: A Very Short Introduction* (New York: Oxford University Press, 2009), 23.

15. Matthew 22:21.

16. Simon A. Wilde, John W. Valley, William H. Peck, and Colin M. Graham, "Evidence from Detrital Zircons for the Existence of Continental Crust and Oceans on the Earth 4.4 Gyr Ago," *Nature 409* (January 2001): 175–78, http://www.geology.wisc.edu/%7Evalley/zircons/Wilde2001Nature.pdf.

17. Wikipedia, s.v. "Geologic Time Scale," http://en.wikipedia.org/wiki/Geologic_time_scale.

18. G. Brent Dalrymple, *Ancient Earth, Ancient Skies: The Age of Earth and Its Cosmic Surroundings* (Stanford, CA: Stanford University Press, 2004).

19. Brigham Young, in *Journal of Discourses*, 14:116 (May 14, 1871).

20. Bruce R. McConkie, *Mormon Doctrine* (1958; repr., Salt Lake City: Deseret Book, 1966), 130, 184.

21. Bruce R. McConkie, "Christ and the Creation," *Ensign*, June 1982, https://www.lds.org/ensign/1982/06/christ-and-the-creation.

22. Russell M. Nelson, "The Creation," *Ensign*, May 2000, https://www.lds.org/ensign/2000/05/the-creation.

23. Morris Petersen, "Earth," in *The Encyclopedia of Mormonism*, ed. Daniel H. Ludlow, 5 vols. (New York: Macmillan, 1992), 2:431.

24. *Merriam-Webster Collegiate Dictionary*, 11th ed., s.v. "theory."

25. For a further discussion of this issue, see David H. Bailey, "Do Gaps in the Fossil Record Present Serious Difficulties for the Theory of Evolution?," Science Meets Religion, accessed December 18, 2013, available at http://www.sciencemeetsreligion.org/evolution/fossils.php.

26. Carl Zimmer, *Evolution: The Triumph of an Idea* (New York: HarperCollins, 2001), 138.

27. Donald R. Prothero, *Evolution: What the Fossils Say and Why It Matters* (New York: Columbia University Press, 2007), 228–29.

28. Ashlee Vance, "Illumina's DNA Supercomputer Ushers in the $1,000 Human Genome," *Business Week*, January 14, 2014, accessed January 20, 2014, http://www.businessweek.com/articles/2014-01-14/illuminas-dna-supercomputer-ushers-in-the-1-000-human-genome.

29. National Academy of Sciences, *Science, Evolution, and Creationism*, 30.

30. Daniel J. Fairbanks, *Relics of Eden: The Powerful Evidence of Evolution in Human DNA* (New York: Prometheus Books, 2007), 53–55.

31. Alan R. Rogers, *The Evidence for Evolution* (Chicago: University of Chicago Press, 2011), 89.

32. Colin Barras, "Formation of Life's Building Blocks Recreated in Lab," *New Scientist*, accessed December 8, 2014, http://www.newscientist.com/article/dn26672-formation-of-lifes-building-blocks-recreated-in-lab.html.

33. Rowan Hooper, "Men Inherit Hidden Cost of Dad's Vices," *New Scientist*, January 6, 2006, accessed December 8, 2014, http://www.newscientist.com/article/mg18925334.000-men-inherit-hidden-cost-of-dads-vices.html.

34. Fairbanks, *Relics of Eden*, 85.

35. Francisco J. Ayala, *Darwin's Gift to Science and Religion* (Washington, DC: Joseph Henry Press, 2007).

36. "Evolution and the Origin of Man," packet of statements compiled by Brigham Young University (Provo, UT: Brigham Young University, 1992), http://biology.byu.edu/DepartmentInfo/EvolutionandtheOriginofMan.aspx (hereafter referred to as "BYU Packet").

37. BYU Packet.

38. BYU Packet.

39. Joseph Fielding Smith, *Man: His Origin and Destiny* (Salt Lake City: Deseret Book, 1952).

40. B. H. Roberts, *The Truth, the Way, the Life* (1931; repr., Salt Lake City: Smith Research Associates, 1994), 364.

41. James E. Talmage, "The Earth and Man," *The Instructor* 100, no. 12 (December 1965): 474–77.

42. William E. Evenson, "Evolution," in *Encyclopedia of Mormonism*, ed. Daniel H. Ludlow (New York: Macmillan, 1992), 478.

43. Alan H. Guth, *The Inflationary Universe* (New York: Helix Books, 1997), 57–83.

44. Guth, *The Inflationary Universe*, 101–3.

45. Max Tegmark, *Our Mathematical Universe: My Quest for the Ultimate Nature of Reality* (New York: Knopf, 2014), ch. 5.

46. Amanda Gefter, "What Kind of Bang Was the Big Bang?," *New Scientist*, July 2, 2012, accessed January 6, 2014, available at http://www.newscientist.com/article/mg21428710.100-what-kind-of-bang-was-the-big-bang.html.

47. Paul Davies, *Cosmic Jackpot: Why Our Universe Is Just Right for Life* (New York: Houghton-Mifflin, 2007), 133–38.

48. Davies, *Cosmic Jackpot*, 144.

49. Davies, *Cosmic Jackpot*, 145.

50. Leonard Susskind, *The Cosmic Landscape: String Theory and the Illusion of Intelligent Design* (New York: Little, Brown and Company, 2005), 70–78.

51. Susskind, *The Cosmic Landscape*, 80–82. For more examples of cosmic coincidences, see David H. Bailey, "What are the Cosmic Coincidences, and What Do They Mean?," *Science Meets Religion*, http://www.sciencemeetsreligion.org/physics/cosmic.php.

52. Fred Hoyle, "The Universe: Past and Present Reflections," *Engineering and Science* 45, no. 2 (November 1981): 8–12.

53. Natalie Wolchover, "Is Nature Unnatural?," *Quanta Magazine*, May 24, 2013, https://www.simonsfoundation.org/quanta/20130524-is-nature-unnatural.

54. National Academy of Sciences, *Science, Evolution, and Creationism*, 15.

55. Gordon B. Hinckley, "Thanks to the Lord for His Blessings," in Conference Report, April 1999, http://lds.org/conference/talk/display/0,5232,23-1-19-35,00.html.

56. Albert Einstein, *Ideas and Opinions* (New York: Crown Publishers, 1954), 36–40.

57. Holmes Rolston III, *Science and Religion: A Critical Survey* (1987; repr., Philadelphia: Temple University Press, 2006), ix.

Index

A
Aaronic Priesthood, 60, 61–62
Abdy, Edward Strutt, 162
Abel, Elijah, 164, 168–69
Abraham, 119. *See also* Book of Abraham
Adam and Eve, 231
adieu, 36
adultery, 132
agency, 209
Alger, Fanny, 131
anachronisms, in Book of Mormon, 33–41
angels, 60, 61–62, 121, 130–31
animals, naming unknown, 37
anthropic principle, 235
archaeology, 104
associative retrieval, 13–14
astronomy, 224
attraction, 204–5, 206–8
axle, 35

B
baptism, 60, 62
Barstow, George, 9
Beaman, Louisa, 122, 134
Benjamin, 22

Bible
  anachronisms in, 35–36
  Joseph Smith Translation, 70, 83, 101
  King James Version, 35–36, 70–71
  language of KJV in Book of Mormon, 70–71
  science and biblical inerrancy, 222–24
  science and chronology of, 224–25
Big Bang, 232–35
blackness, curse of, 160, 166–67
blind faith, 173
boating, xi–xii
Book of Abraham, 79–80
  Egyptian and Jewish representations in, 87–88
  further study of, 88
  and Grammar and Alphabet of the Egyptian Language, 84–85
  history of papyri, 80–81
  Joseph Smith interpretations compared to modern discoveries, 85–87

Book of Abraham (*continued*)
  and priesthood restriction, 160
  translation of papyri, 81–84, 101–2
Book of Breathings, 86
Book of Mormon. *See also* Book of Mormon people; Book of Mormon translation; Book of Mormon witnesses
  anachronisms in, 33–41
  authors of, 29
  changes to, 27–29
  Isaiah in, 69–76
  lost manuscript pages of, 171–72
  universal salvation declared in, 166
Book of Mormon people, 179–80
  and ancestry of Native Americans, 183–85
  currently unanswerable questions regarding, 189–90
  and DNA as genealogical tool, 182–83
  and empty continent theory, 180–82
  intermingling among, 187–88
  lack of DNA evidence regarding, 188–89
  and Middle Eastern DNA in Native Americans, 186–87
Book of Mormon translation, 21–22
  and anachronisms in Book of Mormon, 35–41
  artistic renderings of, 25–27
  versus authorship, 29
  and Book of Mormon witnesses, 46–47
  faith and seer stone in, 22–24
  and Isaiah in Book of Mormon, 70–71

Book of Mormon translation
  process of, 24, 83
  seer stone and Urim and Thummim in, 24–25
Book of Mormon witnesses, 45–46
  additional, 51–52
  Eight Witnesses, 49–51
  secular explanations regarding, 52–55
  significance of testimonies of, 55
  Three Witnesses, 46–49
Brodie, Fawn M., 53
Brown, Hugh B., 170
Bryan, William Jennings, 163
Burgess, Dean R., 205

C
Cain, 160, 166–68
candles, 35–36, 40
Carbon-14 dating, 34, 226
carbon resonance, 233
celestial glory, 121
chariots, 34, 35, 36–37, 38–40
Charnay, Désiré, 36–37
chastening, 213–14
chastity, 212–15
children
  polygamy and birth of, 118–19
  teaching sensitive topics to, xii
choice, 209
chromosomes, 182–83
Church of Jesus Christ of Latter-day Saints, The
  changing perception of role of women in, 198–200
  equality in, 195–96
  gender roles and division of labor in, 194–95

Church of Jesus Christ of Latter-day Saints, The (*continued*)
   position of, on age of earth, 226
   position of, on evolution, 231–32
Clayton, William, 97–99, 107
Coe, Truman, 26
Cole, Abner, 1
Combs, Abel, 81
commandments, 209
companionate love, 207
consecration, 212–15
cosmic coincidences, 233–34
cosmological constant, 234
Cowdery, Oliver
   and 1832 account of First Vision, 11
   as Book of Mormon witness, 46–49, 50, 51, 53, 54, 55
   and Isaiah in Book of Mormon, 70
   and polygamy, 131
   and restoration of priesthood, 60, 61–64, 65–66
cup, of Joseph of Egypt, 22

D

Dahlquist, Charles W. II, 205
damnation, 122
deer, 37
degrees of glory, 121
desire, 206–8
divorce, 134
DNA
   and ancestry of Native Americans, 183–85
   currently unanswerable questions regarding Book of Mormon people and, 189–90

DNA (*continued*)
   as evidence for evolution, 228–29, 230
   as genealogical tool, 182–83
   and genetic drift, 187–88
   lack of, evidence, 188–89
   Middle Eastern, in Native Americans, 186–87

E

earth
   age of, 225–26
   creation of, 232–35
   as designed, 230–31
   multiplying and replenishing, 118–19
Egyptian Alphabet, 84–85, 101–2, 106–9
Egyptian antiquities, 80. *See also* papyri
Egyptian language, 84–85, 101–2, 106–9
Eight Witnesses, 49–51, 52, 53, 55
Einstein, Albert, 236
electromagnetic-gravitational strength ratio, 233–34
Elias, 64–65, 120
Elijah, 64–65, 120
empty continent theory, 180–82
endowment, 149–54, 197. *See also* temple ordinances
equality, 195–96
eternal marriage, 120–21, 133
Ether, plates of, 23–24
evolution, 227–29, 231–32

F

Facsimile 1, 81–82, 85, 86–87
Facsimile 2, 87
Facsimile 3, 87

faith, and Book of Mormon translation, 22–24
First Vision
  associative retrieval and 1835 account of, 13–14
  and making memory, 9–10
  and memory consolidation, 10–11
  primary accounts of, 8–9
  and rearrangement of memory, 16
  rejection of 1832 account of, 11–13
  retrieval of 1835 and 1838–39 accounts, 14–16
  significance of accounts of, 7
folklore, 31n21
folk magic, 3–4, 22–23
fossils, 227, 228
Freemasonry
  endowment and rituals of, 149–54
  Heber C. Kimball and, 143–44, 146–47
  history of, 145–46
  in Nauvoo, 148–49
Fugate, Wilbur, 95, 96, 97

G
gender roles, 194–95, 196–98
genes, 229. *See also* DNA
genetic drift, 187–88
glass looking, 2, 3
glory, degrees of, 121
Godhood, 210–11
God of the Gaps, 235
gold plates, 24, 94. *See also* Book of Mormon translation; Book of Mormon witnesses
Gordon, Sam, 193–94
Grammar and Alphabet of the Egyptian Language, 84–85, 101–2, 106–9

gravitation, 233–34
Greek, 104
GULO gene, 229

H
"Ha e oop hah," 107, 108–9
Hagar, 119
Halliwell Manuscript, 145
Hancock, Levi, 131
Harris, Martin
  as Book of Mormon witness, 46–49, 50, 51, 53, 54, 55
  and lost Book of Mormon manuscript pages, 171–72
Harris, W. P., 95, 96
harrow up, 38
Haven, Charlotte, 104–5, 112n7
Hebrew, 102–4, 106
Hinkle, George, 99
Hiram of Tyre, 144
Holmes, William Henry, 36–37
homosexuality. *See* same-sex attraction
horses, 34–35, 37, 38–40
Hurlbut, Philastus, 2–3

I
Iceland, 183–85
identity, 211–12
interracial marriage, 165, 168
intimacy, 204–5, 206–7
Isaiah, 69–70
  authorship of, 71–73
  and King James language in Book of Mormon, 70–71
  and prophetic vision, 75–76
  scriptural perspective of, 73–74

J
jaguar palanquins, 40
James, Jane Manning, 169
Jaredites, 179–80
John the Baptist, 61–63

Jonas, Abraham, 148, 150
Joseph of Egypt, 22
Joseph Smith Translation, 70, 83, 101
Josephus, 36
jumping genes, 229, 230

K
Kimball, Heber C., 143–44, 146–48, 149, 152, 153–54
Kimball, Helen Mar, 136–37
Kimball, Spencer W., 170
Kimball, Stanley B., 97, 98, 99, 100
Kimball, Vilate, 147, 152
Kinderhook plates, 93–95
    as forgeries, 95–100
    lesson from, 110
    and traditional translation, 104
    and translation by revelation, 104–5
    translation of, 100, 105–9
King James Version
    anachronisms in, 35–36
    language of, in Book of Mormon, 70–71
kings, Maya, 40
Kirtland Safety Society Anti-Banking Institution, 172
Kirtland Temple, 64–65, 66, 120, 147

L
Lamanites, 181–82, 187
Lehites, 179–80, 186–87, 188
Lewis, Q. Walker, 165
life, origin of, 230
lifestyle, 209
litters, 40

M
magic, 3–4, 22–23
marriage
    eternal, 120–21, 133
    interracial, 165, 168

married women, Joseph Smith's sealing to, 131–34
Masonry. *See* Freemasonry
McConkie, Bruce R., 170
McCrary, William Warner, 164–65
McKay, David O., 170
Melchizedek Priesthood, 62–63
memory/memories, 9–11, 16
men, intimacy between, 205, 207
metal plates, 42n20. *See also* gold plates; Kinderhook plates
Methodism, 14
miracles, 222
mitochondria, 182
money digging, 1–4
Moore, George, 94, 104–5, 112n7
Morgan, William, 144
Mormon, 21, 29, 182
Mormons
    inclusiveness of, 161–62, 165
    racialization of, 162–64
Moroni, 21, 29, 60
Moses, 64–65, 120
Mosiah, 23–24
mtDNA, 182, 183–85
Mulekites, 179–80
multiplying and replenishing earth, 118–19
mutations, 230

N
Native Americans
    ancestry of, 180–85
    Middle Eastern DNA in, 186–87
    population decline of, 188–89
"natural" feelings and impulses, 209–10
Nauvoo, Illinois, 147–49, 168
Neider, Michael A., 205
Nephi, 69–70
Nephites, 187, 189
New York Herald, 106–7
nuclear DNA, 182

O

oil lamps, 35–36, 40
origin of life, 230

P

Page, Hiram, 49–51, 55
palanquins, 40
Palmer, Grant, 53
papyri. *See also* Book of Abraham
    and Grammar and Alphabet of the Egyptian Language, 84–85
    history of, 80–81
    Joseph Smith interpretations compared to modern discoveries, 85–87
    translation of, 81–84, 101–2
Partridge, Eliza, 123
passionate love, 207
peep stone, 2. *See also* seer stone
persecution
    Joseph Smith's memory of, 15–16
    and racialization of Mormons, 162
plural marriage. *See* polygamy
polyandry, 132
polygamy, 117–18
    among early Saints, 122–23
    challenges of, 130
    as commandment, 122
    and commandment to multiply, 118–19
    customized trials of, 119–20
    Emma Smith and, 134–36
    end of, 124
    and Fanny Alger, 131
    and imperfection of Joseph Smith, 137–38
    Joseph Smith's practice of, 129–30

polygamy (*continued*)
    and Joseph Smith's young wives, 136–37
    as part of "restitution of all things," 120–21
    and racialization of Mormons, 162–63
    and sealings to legally married women, 131–34
popular religion, 3–4, 22–23
Pratt, Parley P., 98–99
premortal existence, 167
priesthood
    beginning of restriction on, 164–70
    gender roles and, 196–98
    given to black men, 160
    understanding ban on, 170–73
priesthood, restoration of, 59–60
    Aaronic Priesthood, 61–62
    lack of documentation regarding, 65–66
    Melchizedek Priesthood, 62–63
    restoration of keys, 64–65, 120
    and unfolding of restored gospel, 60–61
prophecy, 75–76
proton-to-electron mass ratio, 234

R

race
    beginning of priesthood and temple restrictions, 164–70
    racialization of Mormons, 161–64
    restrictions based on, in early Church, 159–60

race (*continued*)
    understanding priesthood and temple bans, 170–73
    whiteness in American history and culture, 160–61
racism, 173
radioactivity and radiometric dating, 225–26
Regius Manuscript, 145
relationships
    chastity and, 214–15
    and complexity of sexuality, 204–5
    sexual behavior and, 209–11
Relief Society, 150–51, 194, 198
religion
    in quest for truth, 235–36
    science and, 221–22
"restitution of all things," 120–21
Religion and the Decline of Magic (Thomas), 3
Restoration, 60–61, 66, 120, 194–95. *See also* priesthood, restoration of
revelation, 65–66, 75–76, 173
Riley, I. Woodbridge, 52
Royal Arch Masonry, 146, 150, 156n29, 156n30
royal litters, 40
Rupp, Israel Daniel, 9

S

sacred experiences, 65–66
same-sex attraction, 208. *See also* sexuality
    and chastity, consecration, and spirituality, 212–15
    and complexity of sexuality, 204–5
    shift in conversation regarding, 215–16
Samuel principle, 171

Sarah, 119
science
    and age of earth, 225–26
    and biblical chronology, 224–25
    and biblical inerrancy, 222–24
    Big Bang, 232–35
    and biological world as designed, 230–31
    defined, 222
    evolution, 227–29
    in quest for truth, 235–36
    religion and, 221–22
    and understanding of origin of life, 230
scurvy, 229, 231
sealing, 120–21, 131–34
seer stone, 22–25, 27. *See also* peep stone
self-discipline, 210
selfhood, 212–13
sexuality. *See also* same-sex attraction
    complexity of human, 203–5
    understanding, 204–12
sexual orientation, 208. *See also* same-sex attraction
skin of blackness, curse of, 160, 166–67
Skousen, Royal, 28
Smith, Bathsheba B., 130
Smith, Emma, 52, 131, 134–36
Smith, Hyrum, 49–51
Smith, Joseph F., 164, 169
Smith, Joseph, Jr. *See also* Book of Mormon translation; First Vision
    and biblical inerrancy, 223
    and Book of Abraham, 85–87
    and Book of Mormon witnesses, 46–50, 52–55

Smith, Joseph, Jr. (*continued*)
   and changes to Book of
      Mormon, 27, 28
   education of, 21–22, 30n2
   and Freemasonry and endow-
      ment, 148–53
   as imperfect, 137–38
   and Isaiah in Book of Mormon,
      70–71
   and Kinderhook plates, 93,
      94, 97–100, 105–10
   and money digging, 1–4
   and polygamy, 117–18, 122,
      129–38
   religious background of, 59–60
   and restoration of priesthood,
      60–66
   and traditional translation,
      101–4
   and translation by revelation,
      100–101, 104–5
   and translation of papyri,
      80–84
   trials of faith and, 171–72
Smith, Joseph, Sr., 49–51, 52, 59
Smith, Katherine, 52
Smith, Lucy Mack, 52, 59, 81
Smith, Samuel, 49–51
Smith, William, 52
Snow, Eliza R., 131
Snow, Lorenzo, 123
spirits, unborn, 118
spiritual progress, 171, 210–11
Stowell, Josiah, 1, 2, 4

T
Taylor, John, 94–95, 130, 168
temple ordinances. *See also* en-
    dowment
   beginning of restriction on,
      164–70
   and Freemasonry, 151–52

temple ordinances (*continued*)
   understanding ban on,
      170–73
testimony, compared to boat,
   xi–xii
theory, 227
Thomas, Keith, 3
Three Witnesses, 46–49, 52, 53,
   54–55
transfiguration, 53–54
transposons, 229, 230
treasure seeking, 1–4
trials
   blessings of, 213
   of polygamy, 119–20, 123,
      130
   priesthood and temple bans
      as, 171–72

U
Urim and Thummim
   and Book of Mormon trans-
      lation, 24–25, 27
   and translation of papyri, 83

V
Vitamin C, 229, 231
Vogel, Dan, 53

W
Walker, Lucy, 123
Walters, Wesley P., 3
War in Heaven, 167
Wentworth, John, 9
wheel and axle, 35
Whiston, William, 36
whiteness
   in American history and
      culture, 160–61
   Mormons move toward, 164
Whitmer, Christian, 49–51
Whitmer, David, 46–49, 50, 51,
   53, 54, 55

Whitmer, Jacob, 49–51, 55
Whitmer, John, 11, 49–51, 55
Whitmer, Mary, 51
Whitmer, Peter, Jr., 49–51
Wiley, Robert, 93–94, 95, 97
Winchester, Nancy M., 136
witnesses. *See* Book of Mormon
      witnesses
women
    changing perception of role
      of, 198–200
    equality and, 195–96
    gender roles and, 194–95
    and priesthood, 196–98
Woodruff, Wilford, 94–95, 124

Y
Y chromosomes, 182–83
Young, Brigham
    and changes to Book of
      Mormon, 28
    and polygamy, 130, 137
    and priesthood restriction,
      160, 164–68
    and racialization of Mormons,
      163
young brides, 136–37

Z
Zion, 213–14